THE FIRST TEACHER OF DREW
THE REV. JOHN McCLINTOCK, D.D.
President and Professor of Practical Theology,
1867-1870

THE TEACHERS OF DREW
1867-1942

A COMMEMORATIVE VOLUME

issued

on the occasion of

The 75th Anniversary of the Founding of

DREW THEOLOGICAL SEMINARY

October 15, 1942

Edited by

JAMES RICHARD JOY

DREW UNIVERSITY, *Madison, N. J.,* 1942

Minutes of the

TRUSTEES' COMMITTEE ON THE 75TH ANNIVERSARY OF DREW
THEOLOGICAL SEMINARY, MADISON, N. J., OCTOBER 16, 1941

On motion of Dean Hough it was voted "To approve
the publication of a volume of biographies of the Seminary Faculty, and to authorize the Anniversary Committee to proceed with arrangements for its publication
under the editorship of Dr. James R. Joy."

F. Taylor Jones,
Secretary

Minutes of the

TRUSTEES' COMMITTEE, NOVEMBER 19, 1941

"The chairman appointed a sub-committee to have
direction of the Commemorative Volume as follows:
Lynn Harold Hough, James R. Joy, F. Taylor Jones."

F. Taylor Jones,
Secretary

192247, cop. 5

TABLE OF CONTENTS

LIST OF ILLUSTRATIONS

vii

INTRODUCTION

This volume is undertaken as a formal part of the celebration of the seventy-fifth anniversary of the founding of Drew Theological Seminary. The general history of its origin and development has already been admirably set forth. Those who desire the story will find it in the half-century volume issued by President Tipple in 1917 with the cooperation of members of the Faculty, Drew Theological Seminary, 1867-1917, *and in Professor Charles F. Sitterly's* The Building of Drew University, *which covers the whole period, including the recent expansion of the university by the opening of Brothers College. This Commemorative Volume in no way displaces these books. They will long continue to serve as reservoirs of information regarding the inception of the school, the critical struggles of the first years, when the endowment failed utterly and the faculty were removed by death or by the call of the General Conference, and the long period of healthy growth in equipment, personnel, curriculum and endowment. But in both these histories the emphasis has been on other phases than teaching. Therefore this supplemental volume has been projected in order to record and preserve for those who come after the personality and work of the faculty, the figures of the past as well as their successors of the present day, who are the essential Drew. For it is not grounds or buildings or funds that make a seminary a real seed-bed, as the name implies. It is the men—and the women—who have taught here and infused their spirit into the young men who have resorted hither from the beginning until the day we celebrate. The committee offers this modest volume to the alumni on this occasion as a cooperative product of many sympathetic contributors.*

Lynn Harold Hough,
James R. Joy,
F. Taylor Jones,
Arlo Ayres Brown, Ex-officio,
Committee

Madison, N. J.
August 15, 1942.

EDITORIAL NOTE

THE TEACHERS OF DREW includes in its purview all those who have given instruction in the Seminary. It is not concerned with that fine group who are making Brothers College a worthy associate of the Seminary. We find them classified as professors, visiting professors, associate professors, assistant professors, and adjunct professors; after these come instructors, visiting instructors, assistants and teaching fellows; followed by lecturers, visiting and special lecturers. The total number in these groups is about 150. The first catalog, 1868, listed but five, McClintock, Nadal, Strong, Buttz and Worman. The Seminary catalog for 1942 names a teaching body of 23, not counting five who are rated as "retired."

The editorial plan provides for individual biographical sketches or appreciations of those who have held professorships. In each case a summary "Who's Who" statement is appended, giving in tabloid form the bare facts of degrees, ministerial or educational service, and titles of publications. Similar information is given for each instructor and lecturer, although no attempt has been made, except in special instances, to print sketches of these short-term incumbents, many of whom have been scholars of distinction either before or after their service here.

The editor has found it necessary to impose rather strict limitations on the length of the biographical contributions. Otherwise some of the sketches might have filled a volume without exhausting their subject.

From its inception this volume has been a cooperative enterprise. In inviting writers to participate in its production, the committee has sought to assign the subjects in such a way as to assure not only competent but sympathetic treatment. Each contribution is signed with the initials of the contributor. Unsigned articles are editorial. In case the initials do not suggest the name of the author, we list the writers alphabetically; President Arlo Ayres Brown, Professor J. Newton Davies, Dr. Mark A. Dawber, Dr. Ralph E. Diffendorfer, Professor Edwin L. Earp, Dean Lynn Harold Hough, Professor F. Taylor Jones, Professor Edwin Lewis, Professor Ernest F. Scott of Union Seminary, Professor Harry Jason Smith, Dr. Edmund D. Soper, Dr. William J. Thompson, Dr. Ralph B. Urmy and Bishop Herbert Welch.

It is a pleasure to report that in no case did any contributor decline his assignment. Indeed, in most cases the task has been accepted with expressions of gratitude for being asked to render this service to Alma Mater.

The editor acknowledges his heavy obligation to the registrar of the university, Professor F. Taylor Jones, under whose direction the list of teachers was assembled and the biographical details compiled from authentic sources. Frank Ditmars Dennis, B.D. 1941, of his staff, was especially helpful in this work. The registrar also deserves the credit for assembling the illustrative material, and in general for the typographical excellence of the publication.

The editor may perhaps be allowed a personal word. Though a layman, and neither an alumnus nor a teacher of Drew, he has known with varying degrees of intimacy five of the six presidents of the Seminary—all except the first. He has been acquainted with a majority of the professors, several of whom have admitted him to their inner circle of friends. Most of the pastors of the church of which he has been a member for half a century, have had their training here. Moreover, he has had such familiarity with the affairs and personnel of the institution as is afforded by membership for 27 years in the Board of Trustees. To have been selected to edit this Commemorative Volume was a surprise to him, though not unwelcome. He sincerely hopes that his performance of the task may have justified the committee's choice, and that *The Teachers of Drew* may merit the approval of the taught.

St. John's Colony,
New York City,
July 15, 1942.   JAMES RICHARD JOY

Three-Quarters of a Century

As Drew Theological Seminary was a comparatively late comer upon the American educational scene, it seems advisable to introduce this Commemorative Volume, which deals chiefly with the teaching and teachers of this institution, with a sketch of the origin and development of formal ministerial training in the Protestantism of this continent.

MEAD HALL IN THE "HORSE AND BUGGY" SIXTIES

The mansion of Williams Gibbons, Esq., of "The Forest," erected 1833-6. Named "Mead Hall" after the maiden name of Mrs. Daniel Drew. For forty years it housed all the activities of the Seminary and is still the administrative center.

1867

I

THE TRAINING OF AMERICAN PREACHERS

The first colonists brought their ministers with them. Whether Puritans and Independents, as in New England, or Scotch Presbyterian, Dutch Reformed, German Lutheran or Moravian, or Huguenot, as in the Middle and South Atlantic Colonies, or Anglican missionaries of the London Society for the Propagation of the Gospel, they cherished the tradition of an educated ministry. Although they were slow to improvise their own training schools, they saw to it that the early colonial colleges, Harvard, William and Mary, and Yale, made provision for instruction in at least some of the subjects which were considered essential to an educated ministry. Harvard inscribed her seal with the words *Christo et Ecclesiae,* "For Christ and the Church." Yale was founded by ten Congregational ministers of Connecticut, who brought books from their own shelves as the nucleus of the college that was to be. The regular course in the New England colleges until well into the 19th

century included Hebrew, the Greek New Testament
and Evidences of Christianity—if not the Westminster
Catechism.   They all existed for the purpose expressly
stated in Yale's charter to train young men "for service
in the Church and Civil State."   No more impressive
wording of the educational purpose of the New England
colonists could be given than that which is still to be read
on the main gateway to the Harvard Yard:[1]

AFTER GOD HAD CARRIED VS SAFE TO NEW ENGLAND
& WEE HAD BVILDED OVR HOVSES PROVIDED NECESSARIES
FOR OVR LIVELIHOOD REARED CONVENIENT PLACES FOR
GODS WORSHIP AND SETTLED THE CIVILL GOVERNMENT ONE
OF THE NEXT THINGS WEE LONGED FOR AND LOOKED AFTER
WAS TO ADVANCE LEARNING AND PERPETVATE IT TO POSTER-
ITY DREADING TO LEAVE AN ILLITERATE MINISTRY TO THE
CHVRCHES WHEN OVR PRESENT MINISTERS SHALL LIE IN
THE DVST.

So thoroughly was this purpose interwoven with the
educational program of Harvard for the first century
and more, that it was a common practice for a graduate
to proceed immediately to the pastorate of a church.
Another practice, in favor of which much might be said
even in these days, made it by no means unusual for a
ministerial candidate to serve a species of apprenticeship with a veteran pastor in active service.   The
younger man would live in the manse, pursue directed
studies under the eye of his senior, observe and sometimes participate to a reasonable extent in the activities
of the parish.   It is told of certain divines, who had an
aptitude for this type of tutorship, that in the course
of a long—sometimes lifelong—pastorate they would

---

[1] New England's First Fruits.   London, 1643.

have a hand in the making of as many as threescore future ministers. The process resembles somewhat that of early American Methodism, when a "junior preacher" was teamed up with a veteran by the bishop's appointment, an exceptionally desirable arrangement for "traveling preachers" on immense circuits.

The Dutch Reformed Church is credited with the establishment of the first separate theological seminary, which was located in Flatbush, L. I., N. Y., in 1774. Ten years later the United Presbyterians founded the school in Ohio, which now survives as Xenia Seminary in St. Louis, Mo. In 1810 the Reformed Presbyterians opened a school in Pittsburgh, and two years later the Presbyterians organized their first school for ministers in Princeton, N. J., close by but organically distinct from Princeton College. Meanwhile things had been changing in New England. New England Orthodoxy, so called, had become suspicious of certain liberalizing tendencies in Harvard's theological teaching, where the Divinity professor espoused the Unitarian creed, and accordingly had set up a fully equipped school of its own on Andover Hill. This was in 1807. Harvard's move was to establish a Divinity School (1819) with four professors, (Unitarian). Yale, in 1822, established its Divinity School, (Trinitarian). Before the 19th century was one third over, most of the leading denominations had supplied themselves with training schools for their young ministers, strategically located throughout the country. Their motives were in part a laudable desire to furnish their congregations with shepherds who were capable of feeding their flock. Quite as certainly the movement was designed to perpetuate the tenets of the conservative group, who were alarmed at the progress of the newer ideas. Still another weighty consideration was that ambitious young men, desiring the best preparation for the ministry to which they felt called were liable to seek their training in the seminary of another denomination, if their own church opened no school doors to them.

II

METHODISM MOVES SLOWLY

The Methodist Episcopal Church was organized in 1784-5. At that time, with the exception of Bishop Thomas Coke, who had an Oxford degree, it is doubtful whether any Methodist preacher in the New World had seen the inside of a college, though it is equally true that not a few of these unschooled young men, as even Bishop Asbury himself, their great field marshal, were conscious of their deficiencies and were eagerly studying the Biblical languages and striving to avail themselves of the means of self-culture which Wesley had provided for his followers. The British Conference, not without a disturbing opposition, largely personal, which resulted in the secession of a small group of the disaffected, had set up a Theological Institution in 1833, before the American Methodists had launched their first school. But the idea encountered deep-rooted opposition here. During the first half century of Methodism in this country there were no Methodist colleges, saving the short-lived Cokesbury in Maryland. The pioneer preachers, recruited from the common people, and delivering their message to hearers of the same sort, did not feel the need of book-learning, except the One Book. Indeed, in the older settlements, they had found themselves bitterly opposed by the college-bred clergy of the established churches, the "standing order," and so came to feel that education and Methodism were mutually antagonistic. That even Bishop Asbury may have had his doubts about higher education is suggested by the fact that the text of a sermon which he preached at the inauguration of the president of Cokesbury, the first Methodist college, was from 2 Kings iv. 40, "O thou, man of God, there is death in the pot." When Dr. Nathan Bangs first proposed a required course of study for preachers, his motion was promptly tabled. But John Dempster, whose father was trained in Edinburgh University, could not rest until the Methodists should open some opportunity for their ambitious young men. Through his efforts, supported by a few progressive New Englanders, a Biblical Institute was set up in Newbury, Vt., about 1841, in connection with the Methodist academy there. The name of "theological seminary" was cautiously avoided, as that title would set all the horned cattle of Bashan in a roar. This school itinerated to Concord, N. H., in 1847, where it operated under Dempster's leadership, taking the name of Methodist General Biblical Institute. Thence in 1867 it removed to Boston, as Boston Theological Seminary. And, when President Warren's Boston University came into being in 1871, it promptly took the fledgling under its wing, as Boston University School of Theology. Meanwhile a wealthy Chicago woman, Mrs. Eliza Garrett, was taking counsel as to the greatest service which her fortune could perform for Methodism. John Dempster and Dr. John McClintock, a scholarly New York minister, were taken into consultation, and the outcome in 1855 was Garrett Biblical Institute, at Evanston, Ill., of which Dempster was the worthy head.

New York felt the stirrings of the new movement. In *The Christian Advocate* (N.Y.), of December 22, 1853, appeared a long article signed by one James Strong, of Flushing, L. I., a layman, presenting a powerful array of arguments in favor of establishing a Methodist theological seminary in the vicinity of New York City. The editor, Dr. Bond, though opposed to the idea, timorously admitted the article in the interest of fair play. He stirred up a hornets' nest. The angry insects—not honey bees!—buzzed about his head, until he printed their stinging articles. They ridiculed the notion of a "Central Salvation Seminary," where there would be "Professorships of Plenty of Religion." Methodism with its unschooled preachers had far outstripped the churches whose clergy wore academic or Genevan gowns and who tacked cabalistic initials to their names. (A few years earlier a General Conference had been bombarded with protests against the growing practice of conferring the honorary degree of Doctor of Divinity on our ministers. The petitioners averred that "none of the Apostles had a D.D." They wished to prohibit a preacher from accepting such a doubtful honor, and demanded that the church should withdraw its support from any college offering to confer it.)

III

THE BIRTH OF DREW SEMINARY

Circumstances soon altered the case. Agitation in favor of a denomination-wide celebration of the Centenary of American Methodism led to the decision of the General Conference of 1864 to hold such a commemoration in 1866. A small committee was charged with planning the financial objectives of the celebration—for in Methodism it has always been assumed that all anniversaries are *ipso facto* occasions for taking a collection! The committee, by chance if not by Divine Providence, was weighted with men who were the declared advocates of education. A Central Committee, which was charged with organizing the work of Centenary benevolence, consisted of three ministers,— John McClintock, chairman, Daniel Curry, and George R. Crooks—and three laymen,—James Bishop, Oliver Hoyt, and C. C. North. It is significant to observe that all these men were to become either teachers or trustees of Drew!

A great meeting sponsored by this committee was held in St. Paul's Church, New York, Jan. 25, 1866, at which Dr. McClintock made an eloquent plea for Methodist ministerial education. This was Daniel Drew's Church, and the speaker had been his pastor and intimate friend, as had John Dempster, and Dr. Randolph S. Foster, who had discussed the project of a seminary with Mr. Drew. The Centenary celebration crystallized an idea that had long been in Mr. Drew's mind. He had been a liberal giver to Dr. Dempster's Concord school. He now determined to devote a portion of his large fortune to the establishment of a school for the training of ministers. His intention was to locate it in Carmel, Putnam County, N. Y., his native village. A charter was procured from the New York Legislature, April 16, 1866, "for the establishment, maintenance and support, within the county of Putnam . . . of a theological seminary, and theological instruction and education therein in promotion of the doctrine, tenets and discipline of the Methodist Episcopal Church, under the

direction and supervision of the General Conference."
The Board of Trustees organized on March 13, 1867,
at a meeting held in Mr. Drew's house, on the S.W.
corner of Broadway and 17th Street, New York. Dr.
McClintock was elected president of the faculty, and it
was decided to "put the school into practical operation
the next autumn,"—this even before property had been
purchased or a faculty appointed and a course of study
adopted! Something happened which led to the aban-
donment of the Carmel site. In May the trustees were
hopefully considering the offer of the grounds and buildings of the Eaglewood School in Perth Amboy, N. J., but
on June 27, *The Christian Advocate* announced: "The
site of the Drew Theological Seminary is finally settled
by the purchase of the magnificant estate called 'The
Forest' at Madison, N. J., late the residence of W. Gibbons, Esq., constituting a noble park. The buildings
are large, elegant and commodious, and will readily be
adapted to all the purposes of the institution. The
necessary changes will be begun at once, so that the seminary may be opened in the autumn." On Feb. 12,
1868 a new charter was granted by the State of New
Jersey, and on July 23, 1868, Mr. Drew and Roxana
Mead, his wife, conveyed the property to the trustees.

President McClintock lost no time in putting the
institution in running order. An agent in Europe,
Mr. Lane, was instructed to buy books for the library
and $10,000 was set aside for that purpose. On May 3,
1867, a second member of the faculty was elected, the
Rev. Bernard H. Nadal, who was assigned to the chair
of Historical Theology. John Wesley Lindsay, of
Genesee Wesleyan Seminary, Lima, N. Y., was elected
to the chair of Exegetical Theology, though, for some
unexplained reason, he did not occupy it and subse-

quently served for many years on the faculty of Boston
University School of Theology. When the school
opened, Nov. 6, 1867, the faculty consisted of the
President, Professor Nadal, and Mr. J. H. Worman,
librarian and tutor.

IV

THE STANDARD CURRICULUM

The theological curriculm of 1867 differed very little
from the formula of all the early seminaries. The four
accepted divisions of theological study were (1) Exegetical (2) Historical (3) Systematic and (4) Practical
Theology. Their respective content has been given
thus:

" (1) *Exegetical Theology* consisted of selected portions
of Scripture read by the class, the theological
and practical significance of which was explained
by the professor. Much time was given to the
study of Hebrew and Greek, as the original
languages in which the Scriptures were composed.

" (2) *Historical Theology,* occupying relatively little
time, consisted of a brief survey of the history of
the Church with special reference to the branch
to which the institution belonged.

" (3) *Systematic Theology,* the center of the curriculum, consisted of an elaborate statement of the
doctrinal position of the church or denomination in question, with its defense against opposing
views. Natural theology taught what could be
known of God by reason; revealed theology
dealt with the doctrine made known by supernatural revelation.

" (4) *Practical Theology* had to do with the practical training for the pastoral office: (a) in the liturgical churches, the liturgy and prayer-book; (b) in the non-liturgical churches, the preparation and delivery of sermons."

President McClintock, in his initial announcement, set forth the following:

REGULAR COURSE OF STUDY

Junior Year

Exegetical Theology—Hebrew Grammar; Hebrew Bible, begun; Greek Gospels; Introduction to Old and New Testaments; (Geography, Archaeology).

Historical Theology—History of the Old Covenant; Life of Jesus; Apostolical Age.

Systematic Theology—Mental Philosophy; Outline and Method of Theological Science; Doctrinal Theology, begun.

Practical Theology—Exercises in Writing and Speaking.

Middle Year

Exegetical Theology—Hebrew Bible, continued; Greek Testament, (Acts, Romans); Introduction to Old and New Testaments; (Canon, Interpretation, Versions).

Historical Theology—Church History to the Reformation; History of Doctrines; Christian Archaeology.

Systematic Theology—Doctrinal Theology, continued; Moral Science and Christian Ethics.

Practical Theology—Catechetics; Homiletics, begun; Exercises in Writing and Speaking.

Senior Year

Exegetical Theology—Hebrew Bible and Exegesis (Prophetical Books); New Testament Exegesis

(Epistles); Inspiration and Interpretation; with reference to recent Controversies.

Historical Theology—Church History (Reformation to
present Time); Comparative Symbolics; History of
Doctrines; History of Missions; Statistics.

Systematic Theology—Doctrinal Theology, continued;
Apologetics; Polemics; Comparison of Heathen and
Christian Religions.

Practical Theology—Homiletics; Pastoral Care; Church
Polity and Discipline; Sunday Schools; Missions;
Worship.

"This," the announcement ran, "is the regular course
of study, requiring three years for its completion. It is
arranged with reference to the attainments and studies
of college graduates. It is earnestly desired that all
students whose circumstances will allow them to obtain
a college education, will do so before coming to the
Seminary. Students whose age or want of preparatory
education will not allow them to pursue the regular
course, may pursue a partial course of study, requiring
two years for its completion. Students who complete
the partial course, and pass a satisfactory examination,
will receive the diploma of the Seminary."

There soon became evident a demand for a combination course of theology and liberal arts, designed to
meet the requirements of those who could not offer
the college degree requisite for admission to the regular
course. The catalog of 1870 offered a five-year course,
"for those who can not possibly go through college."
This provided "two years' careful instruction in the
classics and in science," together with "three years'
regular scientific study of theology, including the full
course, in which Hebrew, Greek and, to some extent,

Latin are in constant use." In recommendation of
the five-years course the catalog went on to say, "Such
a course faithfully gone through must result in a degree
of culture but little inferior to that of the regular college
curriculum, while for the minister of the Gospel it has
the double advantage of being secured in contact with
the great problems of theology and of embracing the
knowledge essential to his sacred calling." The next
catalog, 1871-72, issued under the administration of
President Foster, further expands the course, naming the
two preparatory years, freshman and sophomore. Their
schedule of required work was as follows:

FRESHMAN YEAR

First term—Algebra, Livy, Greek Grammar, History
of Greece, Selections from Greek Historians.

Second term—Geometry, Trigonometry, Horace, Latin
Prose Composition, Homer's Iliad, Greek Prose Com-
position, History of Rome, Rhetorical Exercises in
Elocution and English Composition.

SOPHOMORE YEAR

First term—Analytical Geometry, Cicero De Officiis,
Terence or Juvenal, Latin Prose, Aeschines and
Demosthenes, Greek Prose and Rhetoric.

Second term—Mechanics, Plautus, Latin Prose, Plato's
Phaedo, Aeschylus, Prometheus, Greek Prose, Logic,
Natural Philosophy, Rhetorical Exercises, Essays and
Declamations throughout the year.

This preparatory department lasted but a few years.
President Hurst, with his high academic standards
evidently considered such elementary work to be beneath
the dignity of the seminary. The catalog ceased in 1873

to advertise the preparatory work, and in 1875, the courses were dropped and the instructors in the classics and sciences appeared no longer. The liberal arts had to wait outside the Drew portal, until the founding of Brothers College in 1928 admitted them again.

V

FACULTY—THE FIRST FLIGHT

It was not an easy matter to select the faculty for the new theological seminary. The obvious selection for president was Dr. McClintock, even if Mr. Drew had not nominated him—his pastor—for this vital position. It was generally agreed by those acquainted with the facts that no other Methodist minister of his generation was so well fitted for the task of organizing the school, and setting its standards. It is true that he had never entered a theological seminary. Neither had any other Methodists, except the limited number of young men who had attended the Biblical Institutes in New England and Evanston. Up to that time few Americans, almost certainly no Methodists, had enjoyed the superior advantages afforded by the Scottish and German universities. Even graduate study for the degree of Doctor of Philosophy was practically unknown here. The president, himself, was an alumnus of the University of Pennsylvania. By incessant study to the extent of undermining his health he had amassed an extraordinary store of learning in the theological field and had achieved the substance if not the symbols of scholarship. Doubtless as the time drew near for the realization of his dream of a theological school, he must have foreseen

that he would be responsible for choosing its first
teachers. In May 1867 the second member of the
faculty was selected. It was the Rev. Bernard Harrison
Nadal. Here, again, was a man of large and varied
intellectual gifts, mostly self-trained. He had had
but two years in college, but had given a good account
of himself as a college teacher in Indiana Asbury (now
DePauw). Most important was the fact that Dr.
McClintock had long known him personally, and
admired his broad literary culture, his good sense and
his sterling character. Historical Theology was to be
his chair—later to be known as Church History. Exegetical Theology presented a more difficult field. The first
choice was Prof. John Wesley Lindsay, of Genesee
Wesleyan Seminary, Lima, N. Y., who was listed in the
preliminary announcement as professor-elect. Just
why he never came to Madison does not appear. The
second choice for this place was a surprise. James Strong,
the layman who had been one of the earliest advocates
of the establishment of such a school, and who had
shifted his interests from business to Oriental studies,
found himself installed as professor of Exegetical Theology, his task to teach young ministers the languages of
Holy Writ and the precious truths contained in them.
Not many lay teachers have been confronted with such
a task, and few have been more successful in its performance. Shortly before Professor Strong's election in
1868, appeared the first of the group who ruled the
lecture-rooms of Drew for a quarter of a century, and
who became known and revered by successive generations of students as "the Big Five"—Buttz, Strong, Miley,
Crooks, and Upham. In 1868 the Rev. Henry A. Buttz
was the young pastor of a neighboring Methodist church.
A graduate of Princeton College, he had attended

lectures in the Dutch Reformed seminary in New Brunswick, and Dr. McClintock, swiftly taking his measure, brought him over from Morristown for part-time instruction in New Testament Greek. This soon developed into a full professorship for which the estate of an admiring parishioner, Col. George T. Cobb, furnished the endowment. Other scholarly Newark Conference pastors, Jonathan K. Burr, Wesleyan '45, and Jonathan T. Crane, Princeton '43 (father of the novelist Stephen Crane), helped out for brief periods with instruction in Hebrew and Greek. The librarian was a gifted young German, James H. Worman. During the early years of the preparatory department the seminary had the services of the Rev. Charles R. Barnes, the Rev. Stephen L. Baldwin, the Rev. John T. Gracey, the Rev. Henry C. Whiting and others, including such accomplished instructors in elocution as Mark Bailey of Yale and Robert McLean Cumnock, later of Garrett and Northwestern.

The fourth full professorial chair, that of Systematic Theology, was vacant until 1869, when it was filled by the Rev. Randolph S. Foster, then pastor of Washington Square Church, New York City, and previously a pastor of Daniel Drew, in whose favor he was reputed to stand high. In fact Dr. Foster thought that he was Mr. Drew's first choice for the presidency, which he declined in favor of Dr. McClintock. He was another self-educated man of conspicuous pulpit talents and a taste for theology and philosophy, who was elevated to the episcopacy before he had full opportunity to display his teaching quality.

Such was the first flight of the teachers of Drew— McClintock, ceaselessly planning for the upbuilding of the Seminary; Nadal learned and cultured in the literature of the Old World; Strong, versatile, eager scholar; Foster, thoughtful, imaginative and oratorical; and young Buttz, tall, slender, dark-haired, somewhat in the background for the present, but destined to remain longest on the scene and eventually to take the center of the stage.

VI

"THE BIG FIVE"

No Methodist theological school had started under fairer omens. Its physical accommodations at Madison were incomparable. Its financial position seemed secure. It was without debt for land, buildings, library or equipment, and for endowment it held the note of an individual whose credit rated AA1, yielding 7 per cent, sufficient to meet all bills for salaries and upkeep. The oldest professor was but 55, the youngest 33. Yet within 8 years three of the faculty were removed, two of them by death, and every dollar of the endowment was swept away in a financial typhoon, which at the same time paralyzed the nation's business.

President McClintock, never in rugged health, broke down and died March 4, 1870, aged 55, before he had completed three full years in office. His trusted colleague, Professor Nadal, made acting president, fell dead three months later at the age of 58. President Foster continued in office only until the General Conference of 1872, which elected him to the episcopacy. Only Dr. James Strong, the layman, and the young Greek professor, Henry A. Buttz, remained to carry on. In the emergency the trustees turned to Professor John

"THE BIG FIVE"

Samuel F. Upham   Henry A. Buttz   George R. Crooks
James Strong   John Miley

F. Hurst, aged 38, who had recently been brought from Germany by Dr. Nadal after the death of Dr. McClintock and installed in the chair of Historical Theology. This promising young American scholar was elected president. He had not been in office three years when Mr. Drew notified him that he was without funds to meet either interest or principal on his endowment note. This was catastrophic news! The panicky trustees would have mortgaged the property to meet the expenses, but the young president faced them down. Leave it to him. He would appeal to the Methodist friends of ministerial education throughout the nation to make good the fund which Wall Street had engulfed. Though young and practically unknown, he went from Conference to Conference, and from layman to layman, telling the tragic story and letting the facts make their appeal. The country was financially prostrate. Prophets of pessimism said it was a waste of railroad fares to permit this man to pursue a forlorn hope all over the land at a time when individual Methodists and societies had enough to do to care for their local interests and obligations. The task was rendered the more difficult by the fact that the Seminary was rather widely regarded as the private creation of one Wall Street millionaire and not really a child of the church. But Dr. Hurst had courage, persistency, faith in his cause and in the Methodist people. He won the victory. Within three years the endowment was more than made good, by thousands of gifts, large and small—and incidentally, there was not a Conference in America—indeed scarcely a Methodist fireside—in which the Drew disaster was not common knowledge, and the achievement of this new man Hurst a thing to be praised. It is easy to trace a connection between this accomplishment

and Dr. Hurst's election to the episcopacy at the next
General Conference. But before that he had much to
do. There was the faculty to be rebuilt, around the
fine nucleus of Strong and Buttz. Professor Daniel P.
Kidder had already been brought from Evanston by
President Foster to succeed Dr. McClintock in the chair
of Practical Theology (1871). Dr. John Miley came
from the pastorate of Washington Square Church, New
York City, (1873) as professor of Systematic Theology,—
the third member of the "Big Five." In 1880 Dr. George
R. Crooks, whom McClintock had been unable to lure
away from his fighting post on *The Methodist,* having
won his battle for lay representation, accepted the chair
of Historical Theology, making the fourth of the five
stars in the Drew constellation. The next year, 1881,
saw the first New Englander, Samuel F. Upham of
New England Southern Conference, seated in the chair
of Practical Theology, which was to be his throne for
nearly a quarter of a century (1881-1904). Thus the
pedagogical pentagon was made perfect. In 1880
President Hurst had gone on to his great career as bishop
and university chancellor, and Dr. Buttz, once the
junior member of the original faculty, had become
President Buttz, the head of the five corners.

The individual sketches of the several members of
that famous faculty that held the fort for an entire
generation, take their place in chronological order in
the following pages, and need not be anticipated here.
It would be difficult to describe the collective impression
which they made upon the young men who studied here.
But that they did make a collective impression both on
and off the campus can not be gainsaid. Except for
Dr. Buttz, who spanned the gap between the founders
and the modern age, they represented much the same

type of theological thinking. Together they had
come through the same periods of stress and strain
regarding Biblical criticism, natural science, evolution
and the like, and had not dragged their anchors. For
that reason there were those who tended to regard Drew
in those years as a fortress of conservatism, as perhaps
it was, though never a center of militant "fundamen-
talism." Men like Crooks and Buttz were too broad in
their culture and too clear-eyed in their mental vision to
be absolutely fettered by the past, however reluctant
they may have been to admit that there might be a
modicum of truth in the new views. Probably in the
later years of their reign the faculty which was the
pride and boast of Drew was rated in some quarters as
"the Five Old Men," even as there have been those
who have allowed themselves to disparage the venerable
Justices of the Supreme Court. But the young men on
the Drew Campus looked up to their teachers with
honor, reverence and even awe. Personality, character,
flavor, all ripened by long years of acquaintance with
men and books, gave these men a prestige such as few
members of any faculty have ever enjoyed. Men came
away from Drew with their minds stretched by reason of
"Uncle John" Miley's arguments. They spiced their
sermons with "Uncle Sammy" Upham's witty comments
on human foibles; they worked harder on their sermons
because they had seen what prodigies of learning a
worker like James Strong could acquire and put to use;
Dr. Crooks touched every subject in a dull curriculum
with lfe; and Dr. Buttz—well, he was just Henry Anson
Buttz, for whom the title of "Saint John" did not seem
an exaggeration. They felt, as a rule, that association
with this remarkable cluster of men was a tonic for their
souls and minds.

VII

THE ERA OF EXPANSION

When James Strong retired and Robert W. Rogers was elected in his stead a new element entered the Drew faculty. This man had not been a pastor, though educated for the ministry. He had never been a General Conference delegate; never edited a church paper. Indeed his education had been gained mostly outside of denominational schools. Johns Hopkins, Leipzig, Oxford were the words written on his heart. Drew had had scholarly men on its teaching force, but most of them had come by their learning by the hard way—self-education. Rogers was a school man. He sought the best and found the means of achieving it. As the fruits of his scholarship became known through his books on ancient oriental history Drew gained recognition in the older centers of learning. Harvard and Princeton invited him to lecture. Dublin and Oxford welcomed him, adopted him. His type was a distinct addition to the teachers of Drew. It is not likely to become extinct.

As one turns the following pages, in which an attempt has been made to present in outline the characteristics of the professors, the reader will observe that the list includes more than one type. The "Ph.D. fetish" has never dominated Drew. Good men have been found to be good teachers, even if their academic gowns were not quite *en regle*. He will observe also, since the arrangement is chronological, that the chairs of instruction begin to bear new names. The hard and fast theological categories: Exegetical, Historical, Systematic and Practical, begin to subdivide or to be qualified. New and unfamiliar titles appear, indicating that the scope of church activity has widened, bringing new subjects into the curriculum. Dr. Earp's chair, "Christian Sociology" (1909) was new not only at Drew but everywhere. Dr. W. J. Thompson's (1911) "Religious Psychology and Pedagogy" would have puzzled Daniel Drew, and might have flustered "The Five." Three years later, (1914) Dr. Soper was commissioned to teach "Missions and Comparative Religions." From 1920 to 1925 an ex-officer of the British Indian Army taught oriental languages—not the Rabbi Rogers' "Oriental" of Mesopotamia, but Captain Shellabear's "Oriental" of Singapore! "Home Missions" was recognized in the election of Dr. W. M. Gilbert in 1923. Dr. George W. Briggs in 1925 began to teach Sanskrit. Another expansion brought Dr. James V. Thompson to teach "Administration of Religious Education." "Practical Theology and Applied Christianity" as taught by Dr. Diefendorf, registered the enlarged content of the original chair of similar title. And since 1931 we have had "Rural Sociology." "Homiletics" was once a part of Practical Theology, as Dr. Upham taught it. With Dr. MacMullen's arrival it became a separate chair, and Dean Hough has added the suggestive words "And the Christian Criticism of Life."

The last twenty years have witnessed radical changes in the organization of the institution. From 1867 to 1928 there was only one legal entity, and one faculty, though their names were sometimes printed more than once and under different headings in the same catalog. In 1928 the name of the institution was legally changed to Drew University, and the work of instruction was divided clearly between two faculties, viz.: Drew Theo-

logical Seminary and Brothers College. Other names
which were employed in what may now be called the
period of transition—such as the College of Missions,
the College of Theology, the Graduate School, the
Graduate School of Theology, the College of Religious
Education and Missions, whether before or after 1928,
were descriptions of aspects of the work of Drew
Theological Seminary, and meant very little as to
separate organizations.

The work of the Seminary has fallen into three main
categories: (a) the professional divinity course for
which the institution was founded and which has
remained its fundamental task; (b) pre-theological
experiments; and (c) graduate work beyond the B.D.
degree.

The basic course has been given continuously since
1867, leading to the B.D. degree for those who had had
previous college training or, until 1931, to a diploma for
those who had not. There was a two-year "English
course" on the diploma level from 1894-'95 to 1898-'99.
Degree and diploma students were instructed together
until 1927-'28, when a few separate diploma courses
were set up under the "College of Missions" heading.
The last "diploma student" was graduated in 1931, but
there were undergraduates in the B.D. courses until
the end of the College of Religious Education and
Missions in the spring of 1934. Since then there have
been none with the exception of special students and
"auditors" and an occasional Brothers College upper-
classman.

Pre-theological work has never been important at
Drew. There were first year and second year "introductory" courses from 1869-'70 to 1872-'73, "freshman"
and "sophomore" courses partly overlapping these from

1871-'72 to 1875-'76, and, on a different basis but with a similar aim, a "College of Religious Education and Missions" from 1930-'31 to 1933-'34 which admitted senior college and special students and through which were awarded 19 B.A. degrees. The "College of Missions" was a curriculum through which the Seminary faculty offered, from 1920-'21 to 1929-'30, a three-year diploma to high school graduates and an M.A. degree to college graduates preparing for home or foreign missionary service. Beginning with the commencement of 1929 all degrees at whatever level have been conferred in the name of Drew University.

In 1934 a new era was marked by the creation of the office of Dean with administrative responsibility for the life of the Seminary and Dr. Lynn Harold Hough, Drew '05, Professor of Homiletics and the Christian Criticism of Life, was elected to this office. Dean Hough has infused the school with his own high educational ideals and has given particular attention to graduate work, taking the chairmanship of the Committee on Graduate Work.

The opening of Brothers College on the Drew Campus in the fall of 1928 led to a reorganization of the University. After the initial experiments with "introductory" and five-year courses to care for the men who lacked adequate preparation the Seminary settled down to a regular three-year course, granting the bachelor degree to graduates who had completed their A.B. work, and giving a "diploma" to those who lacked the bachelor degree. Beginning with the class of 1915 students receiving advanced degrees (e.g. Th.D.) were classified as of the Graduate School; B.D. and diploma courses were as of the "College of Theology." In 1921 a

"College of Missions" was added. In 1930 the entire organization of the university was changed. In place of the College of Missions a senior College of Religious Education and Missions was set up, leading to the B.A. degree. The present arrangement, adopted in 1934, provides for a simpler organization of the university, by which the Drew Theological Seminary offers courses leading to the degrees of B.D., M.A., and Ph.D., and Brothers College of Liberal Arts offers a program leading to the A.B. degree.

The Centenary Celebration in Methodism, 1919-1920 had its repercussions in the educational set-up at Drew and other Methodist institutions. The prospect of sharing generously in the enlarged giving of the churches, which was the immediate result of the Centenary cultivation, together with the necessity of providing the means of training for the young workers who were to man the enlarged missionary and other benevolent activities of the church, prompted the reorganization of 1920 as outlined above. For a few years the theological seminaries did receive substantial subsidies which were expended on enlarged faculties and new courses of study. This will appear to any reader of this book, who goes to the trouble of noting the number of instructors added in these years and their subjects. The brevity of their term of service is no reflection upon their ability; but rather follows the descending curve of Centenary receipts and appropriations to theological education. Thus Drew, which largely owed its origin to one Methodist Centenary (1866) suffered severely from the fever and ague of another (1920). That period is now an unhappy memory. The Baldwin gifts to Brothers College, the rich Wendell-Swope legacies, and the bequests

ROSE MEMORIAL LIBRARY (left) AND MEAD HALL

of Lenox S. Rose and Mrs. E. S. Tipple, have stabilized
the university's finances on the best footing they have
ever known. They are administered with rare prudence
and skill in the difficult conditions of these times by the
treasurer, Noel E. Bensinger. While pressing need still
exists for several additional buildings, for library maintenance and other special requirements, the university,
and notably the Seminary, enters the last quarter of its
first century under propitious circumstances.

VIII

THE TEACHERS' TOOL-CHEST

At the celebration of the 25th anniversary of the
founding of Drew Seminary in 1892, Dr. Crooks said
of the library: "The work of the living teacher at the
desk must be supplemented by the labors of the dead
teachers whose thoughts have been gathered into books,
and are there preserved for the use of their successors.
If the living teacher is of any worth, dead men will
speak through him."

From the first the teachers of Drew have been lovers
of books, as well as writers of books. Their own productions, if collected, would form a substantial library
of themselves and would touch a wide range of subjects.
Before Dr. McClintock had selected his first faculty,
he had commissioned Mr. Harvey B. Lane in Europe
to purchase the indispensable volumes which must be
the nucleus for a theological seminary. The library,
according to his theory and practice was a species of
"teachers' tool-chest." The $10,000—some say $25,000—
which Mr. Drew placed in his hands for this purpose was

not frittered away. The standard reference works in English, French and German were the first choice. The editor of McClintock & Strong's *Cyclopedia* did not need to consult any expert bibliographer in this field. He knew them at first hand and by intimate use.

This then formed the sound core of the library, which was lodged in Mead Hall upstairs, as indeed was everything, chapel, lecture and recitation rooms, in fact all except the residences of the faculty, and the dormitories, which were adapted from the spacious carriage-house and granary of the Gibbons mansion and became the Asbury and Embury Halls known to generations of students, who ate and studied and slept—and dreamed!—there before Hoyt-Bowne and the refectory were erected.

For the first three years the librarian was James H. Worman, a young German who was educated in Europe and versed in the primitive library science of the time. After him the responsibility was carried in turn by several professors, usually with a junior assistant. Thus Dr. Buttz (1870-1872), Dr. Kidder, (1872-1880), Dr. Upham, (1881-1895). During the closing years of Dr. Upham's tenure he associated with himself a young alumnus, Samuel Gardner Ayres (assistant 1889-1896; librarian 1896-1911) who displayed such aptitude that he was eventually given full sway. Almost immediately the library entered upon an era of growth such as few libraries have ever known. In 1895 he issued his first printed report. The collection then numbered 32,139 volumes and 17,415 pamphlets, and it had doubled since 1888. Seven years later he reported 71,922 volumes and 57,578 pamphlets—doubled again! Another septennium carried it past the 100,000 mark and rated it among the first four theological libraries in America. It now has 191,500 volumes and ranks third. Many of the accessions were gifts or bequests; and some were of unique interest and value. The Osborne Collection of British Methodistica, the private collections of McClintock, Strong, and Foster, the choice David Creamer collection of Hymnology, the Luke Tyerman collection of 2500 English pamphlets relating to the Wesleyan Movement, the Hartzell Collection on Africa and Slavery, many books from the libraries of Bishops Newman, and Neely, Professor Faulkner, Professor Rogers, Robert Crook (Ireland), Dr. J. M. Freeman, Dr. J. M. Buckley, and numerous others. A department which grew rapidly was that of Methodist History. To it came the Abel Stevens papers, the Robert Emory papers, the Freeborn Garrettson papers, the diaries of George Coles, and similar source materials. In later years by the will of Mrs. Edna White Tipple the rarities of Wesleyana in book, tract, MS., print, paint, and Staffordshire, collected at large expense and with a sportsman's ardor by President Tipple, came to the new Rose Memorial Library, for which a Treasure Room was set apart. Thus the Drew collections of autograph letters of Wesley, Asbury and other Methodist leaders were enormously enriched. Through the persistent efforts of Mr. Ayres and his successors up to the present time Drew has become the richest depository in America of source-material for the study of every phase of Methodism. Mr. Ayres' magic wand touched perennial springs of annual reports, conference journals, minutes, etc., which are still flowing. The library was long recognized by the General Conference of the Methodist Episcopal Church as the depository of all General Conference archives. Its files of this material run back as far as 1800, and include the handwritten journals of General Conference from that date to 1840.

Not all of this acquisitive achievement is directly due to Dr. Ayres, though he set the pace and enjoyed special and unique opportunities, as when Joseph C. Thomas, of the New York Methodist Historical Society, left him more than 6000 volumes, and 14,000 pamphlets, and Dr. Homer Eaton, publishing agent of the Methodist Book Concern at New York, gave him a free hand with the "Editor's Library," which had been built up to thousands of volumes in the course of a century, and for which there was no longer space in the Book Concern Building. Among several thousand items from this source Mr. Ayres took over several hundred bound volumes of religious periodicals, British and American, raising the Drew collection in this field to the top rank in the United States, if not in the world.

Librarian Ayres was called away to practise his magic in Garrett Biblical Institute in 1912. His successors and emulators were C. W. Smiley (1911-1912), Robert E. Harned (1912-1919), Charles Burgess Ketcham (1919-1920), and Elizabeth Louisa Foote (1920-1922), the latter an exemplar and teacher of modern library science, Josephine M. Stultz (1922-1928), and Harry J. Smith (1928-1930), a brilliant teacher of church history and theology who was given this temporary responsibility in addition to a heavy classroom schedule. By this time the Cornell Library, erected in 1888, for 40,000 volumes was stuffed with books, pamphlets and MSS. from basement to tower, to a degree of repletion that baffled the most scientific practitioner.

In 1930 the Rev. O. Gerald Lawson was installed as librarian. He was Canadian born, educated at Victoria University and Boston, and had served on the staff of the New York University Library. He was wrestling manfully with the impossible task of operating the library under the suffocating conditions (150,000 volumes in a building planned for 40,000!) when out of a clear sky came the news that the late Lenox S. Rose of Madison had left $600,000 for the erection of a memorial building, which the trustees promptly designated for a library. The Rose Memorial Library is the monument to him and his wife. To Mr. Lawson fell the responsibility of cooperating with the architects to produce such an edifice as should serve the Seminary for a century at least. He had the more onerous and less pleasing task of planning and executing the removal of the contents of the old library, which was in process of demolition, to the new stacks. The work was carried out without delay and with admirable precision, the activities of the library being but slightly interrupted. The scant professional staff, headed by Miss Ruth Mary Gray, and ably supported, until he was called for military service this July, by Dr. Niels Henry Sonne, a graduate of Union Seminary and Columbia, have brought order out of chaos to a remarkable degree, though thousands of pamphlets remain to be cataloged. Book funds and endowment for maintenance are sorely needed.

At the close of his second report, June 1, 1896, Mr. Ayers, then librarian-in-charge, wrote "We desire everything illustrating the history of Methodism that we can procure. Also all literature representing forms of aggressive Christianity, as well as books for every department of our regular work. We desire to make our library such that it will be the resort of specialists, and also the means of satisfying inquiry in the broadest lines of literature and education. In fact to use it as a means to the development of broad-minded men. We desire to make the library of such importance that it will not only serve the seminary, but all Methodism."

Anyone who is familiar with the results of the intelligent and devoted labors of the wise men who preceded
him and the highly trained personnel who carry on in
our own day, will be prompt to testify that the great
library of Drew University wonderfully fulfills the
dreams of its projectors and the builders who have
brought their plans to fruition.

IX

THE DREW OF 1942

And so we come to the close of the seventy-five year
period which we celebrate. It may be profitable to survey briefly what has grown from the educational acorn
that was dropped under the oaks of Drew Forest in
1867. Twenty-five years hence, when the Centennial
volume is written, this sketch of Drew Seminary in 1942
may serve the future historian as a milestone along the
road.

The 1942 catalog lists a faculty of 23, including 11
professors, a visiting professor, two associate professors,
and one assistant professor, besides instructors, lecturers
and teaching fellows.

The objectives of the Seminary are declared to be:
"To prepare men and women for various kinds of
Christian service. These include the ministry of preaching, missionary work at home and abroad, the ministry
of education, the teaching of religion and allied subjects
in secondary schools and colleges, and such other forms
of religious work as require specialized technique."

The Seminary courses of study lead to several degrees:
(1) Bachelor of Divinity, a three years course for stu-

dents who can offer the equivalent of a bachelor's degree
in a college of repute; (2) Master of Arts, for graduates
who devote not less than one year of resident study in
one special field; and (3) Doctor of Philosophy, for the
small group of students who are justified in undergoing
more prolonged intellectual discipline.

The library, always an outstanding feature, and now
enjoying the superb facilities of the Rose Memorial
Library Building, numbers over 191,000 volumes and
about as many pamphlets. In some fields, such as Methodist history, it is not surpassed anywhere. But it is
not narrowly denominational, or even theological in its
content. From the beginning it has sought to include
the whole range of intellectual interest, and has succeeded to a remarkable degree. The fields of missionary effort are well covered. Everything essential to
Biblical research is here. Thanks to generous gifts, the
working library is supplemented by substantial holdings
of New Testament MSS., incunabula, ancient, curious
and rare editions and versions of the Bible, and extensive collections of hymnolgy and bibliography. As has
already been said in this volume, no American library
owns a more exhaustive store of religious periodicals.
The reading room receives and keeps on file all the
leading religious periodicals, American and British,
numbering over three hundred.

The physical equipment of Drew compares favorably
with that of any seminary in the country. The campus
occupies a wooded park of 120 acres, developed a century ago as the manorial residence of William Gibbons,
whose mansion, Mead Hall, now the administration
building, is said to have been in its day, the finest
domestic establishment north of the Potomac, except
the White House, which its architecture somewhat

resembles, and which struck a classical note which the architect has happily repeated in the Rose Library building, which is connected with it by a colonnade. Dormitories, a recitation hall, refectory and gymnasium, with swimming pool, tennis courts and athletic fields serve their purpose admirably. Residences are provided for the President, Dean and several of the professors. Another dormitory, a chapel and a student union figure in the president's list of "wants." The campus is being developed on a studied plan for drives, walks and the location of future buildings. Notable features are the Gothic Bowne Memorial Gateway and the Lukeman equestrian statue of Francis Asbury, the Prophet of the Long Road, which was the gift of Mr. William S. Pilling in memory of his brother, the Rev. Edward Stellwagon Pilling of the Class of 1885. Brothers College, an integral part of Drew University, founded in 1928 by two friends of Drew, the brothers, Leonard D. and Arthur J. Baldwin, as a college of liberal arts, occupies a beatiful building of Colonial design, which is the first of a group which eventually will include dormitories and laboratories. One can never cease to praise the judgment of the founding fathers, who turned away from Mr. Drew's original choice of location and from the later selection of the Eaglewood site at Perth Amboy, N. J., to decide upon "The Forest" as the proper soil in which to plant their acorn, whose growth into a "tall oak" we celebrate with just pride.

From funds provided by the Rose estate, the Tipple bequest, Mr. William S. Pilling and others, a considerable number of scholarships and fellowships, ranging in annual value from $100 to $1000 are available for both undergraduates and graduates. Other endowments provide prizes for special excellence. The Christian Biography Lectures established by Dr. and Mrs. Tipple bring distinguished speakers before the Drew audience from time to time, as do the Haddon-Colt lectureship which "deals positively and affirmatively with some phase of the general problem of the relations of the natural and the supernatural." It is also the custom of the Seminary to extend its hospitality to the eminent religious leaders who visit New York from this and other lands, and to have them address the student body. The proximity of Madison to the metropolis greatly facilitates such opportunities.

As we have already printed the course of study announced by President McClintock seventy-five years ago, it may be of interest, in showing the development of theological training, to present the bachelor of divinity curriculum as announced in the Drew Theological Seminary 1942 Catalog. It is reproduced in full, with the foot-notes:

	First semester	Second semester
Junior (first) year:		
The Christian Criticism of Life (course 400)..	1 unit	
New Testament Greek [1]	1 unit	1 unit
Required basic courses [2]	3 units	3 units
Elective [3]	1 unit	2 units
Physical education (course 930)	....	....
Speech [4] (unless excused after audition)	½ unit	½ unit
	6½ units	6½ units
Middle (second) year:		
The Preacher's Use of his Materials (course 416)	1 unit	......
The Interpretation of Life and Religion in the English-speaking World (course 401)	......	1 unit
Remaining departmental requirements	2 units	2 units
Elective courses [3] and major	3 units	3 units
	6 units	6 units
Senior (third) year:		
Elective courses and major [3]	6 units	6 units

Notes:

[1] Only the second semester of Greek (course 171) is actually required, but those who have not had Greek in college need the first semester's work in preparation. Students have the option of substituting a more advanced Greek course for course 171.

[2] The following courses, or alternatives in the same field approved by the professor in charge, must be taken before the end of the second year. The student may choose which ones to take in either year but should note that each one is given in a particular semester: 120-B, The Old Testament and Its Background; 160-B, New Testament and Its Background; 200-B, Christianity Through the Ages; 303-B, Sociology and Social Progress; 500-B, Introduction to the History of Religions; 501-B, The World Outlook of the Christian Churches; 600-B, The Church and Religious Education; 700-B, Christian Ideals and Beliefs; 841-B, Public Worship; 800-B, Missionary Fields in the United States.

[3] Parish supervision (course 870) is required of students who are employed by churches. Juniors who have churches may take 870 in either the first or second year.

Not more than two units may be credited in the B.D. course through private study of "reading" courses.

A major of seven units, including the required basic course in the field selected, is required. The student declares his choice of a major field after the completion of all the departmental required courses, but not before he has completed 18 units of work.

A candidate for the B.D. degree may offer a maximum of four units in seminar courses in his major field, plus two units outside his major field, unless the Credits Committee in special cases requires more. B.D. candidates may take seminars in their major field as middlers and as seniors; in fields outside the major only as senior.

Students who have not had or are not taking Course 870, Parish Supervision, are required to take Course 871, The Work of the Minister, in the senior year.

[4] The speech requirement is determined individually after an audition. Juniors are usually required to take Course 860, followed by whatever other training is necessary to enable them to meet a standard established by the instructor.

The following tabulations, furnished by the registrar, Professor F. Taylor Jones, present from various points of view the "output of the plant" from the beginning in

1867 to June 1942, when the latest finished product came off the assembly line.

I

Drew Theological Seminary and Drew University enrolments, by five year periods

	1867	1870 1871	1880 1881	1890 1891	1900 1901	1910 1911	1920 1921	1930 1931	1940 1941	1941 1942
B.D. candidates	10	42	74	109	166	131	116	112	140	152
Other degree candidates ...				4	15	11	16	88	93	96
Non-degree students	8	40	10	15	13	24	29	80	27	38
Total Seminary enrolment	18	82	84	128	194	166	161	280	260	286
Brothers College.								69	200	213
Total University registration								349	460	499

II

Occupations of Drew Theological Seminary Alumni, 1869-1942
From the First Class to May, 1942

No one is counted twice. Each category includes some who might also be counted in a later division, but are not: i.e., college presidents are counted only as such.

	Living Alumni May 1942	Deceased	No. Present Record	Total
Bishops	12	6	0	18
College Presidents	32	29	3	64
Deans	7	4	0	11
Secretaries and directors of connectional boards	45	33	4	82
College professors	114	45	7	166
Missionaries*	139	52	20	211*
Pastors	1724	883	122	2729
Women not classified elsewhere	112	11	49	172
Laymen	94	117	83	294
Occupation unknown	7	77	103	187
Totals	2286	1257	391	3934

*Plus 38 counted elsewhere, making a total of 249 missionaries.

III

Denominational Distribution of Drew Alumni in the Pastorate

	Living Alumni May 1942	Deceased	No. Present Record	Total
Methodist	1592	798	76	2466
Presbyterian	42	20	13	75
Congregational	35	22	6	63
Episcopal	23	32	13	68
Baptist	10	3	4	17
Reformed	8	3	1	12
Evangelical	5	3	2	10
Unitarian	3	—	1	4
Brethren	3	—	1	4
Christian	1	—	—	1
Lutheran	1	—	2	1
Jewish	1	—	—	1
Universalist	—	1	—	4
Catholic	—	1	1	2
Pentecostal	—	—	1	1
Nazarene	—	—	1	1
Totals	1724	883	122	2729

One of the pioneers of ministerial training in American Methodism gave this considered statement of the distinctive aims of a seminary like ours. He said:

"The purpose of the theological school is to use the truth of Christ in the spirit of Christ, for the largest possible service to mankind."

It would be difficult to express more concisely or more comprehensively the purpose which animated and guided the pioneers of ministerial education in American Methodism—or, indeed, in any of the denominations of evangelical Protestantism in this country. In so far as bare figures can show, these tabulations testify to the fidelity of Drew Theological Seminary to this threefold aim. Its 4000 graduates have been pastors,

missionaries, educators, executives, and bishops of the
church. They have given a good account of their
ministry and have honored the Seminary and its teachers, whose character and work this volume attempts to
set forth.

1942

The Teachers

PLATE I—PRESIDENTS AND DEAN

RANDOLPH S. FOSTER, 1870-1872   JOHN F. HURST, 1873-1880
HENRY A. BUTTZ, 1880-1912   EZRA S. TIPPLE, 1912-1929
ARLO AYRES BROWN, 1929—   LYNN HAROLD HOUGH, 1934—

The Rev. JOHN McCLINTOCK

A.B., A.M., D.D., LL.D.

President and Professor of Practical Theology, 1867-1870.

THE REV. JOHN McCLINTOCK was but 53 years old when Daniel Drew named him for the presidency of the seminary. Yet he was very near his end. For twenty years he had scarcely known a well day. Ill health had forced him to leave Wesleyan University early in freshman year, never to return. A tremendous worker, he accomplished four years work in three at the University of Pennsylvania, in his native Philadelphia. He began preaching, but a bad throat choked that effort, and he took to teaching at Dickinson, mathematics at first, later the classics. Still toiling, it is said that the light in his window burned later than that in any student's room. The inspiring Durbin was president of the college. His fellow-townsman George R. Crooks was a professor, and then or soon after, a slight flaxen-haired youth from the Eastern Shore of Maryland named John Hurst would matriculate—a lad o' pairts! All four of these Dickinsonians were destined to shine on the roll of the teachers of Drew. When President Olin of Wesleyan died, the chair was offered to McClintock, but he preferred the call to the editorship of *The Methodist Review,* a post which he held with distinction for eight years. It was then that he embarked on the ambitious project, hitherto attempted by no one outside of Germany, to compile a *Cyclopedia of Biblical,*

Theological and Ecclesiastical Literature. For this task he discovered and called to his aid one James Strong, another name for the future Drew to conjure by. When in 1852 he became pastor of St. Paul's Church, at 22d St. and Fourth Ave., New York, he found among the pewholders a well-to-do family of Wendels and a certain rugged and adventurous Wall Street operator named Daniel Drew. You see what was preparing! His next move was to Paris, where he could work on his Cyclopedia in the Biblioteque Nationale, while serving the American Chapel as pastor. The Civil War broke, and the liberty-loving pastor rallied the American Colony for the Union cause, while by visitation and by correspondence with leading Wesleyans across the Channel, he helped to counteract the Tory propaganda of *The Times.* Always over-working to the point of collapse, we find him writing to America in 1863, "When we return it must be to the quiet of a retired place, where I may be allowed to do some service to the Church with my pen." But when he returned it was to resume the pulpit of St. Paul's. And so to Drew! For in the Methodist Centenary Celebration of 1866, of whose Central Committee he was the leading member, one of the main financial objectives was made the strengthening of institutions for the training of young men for the ministry. Mr. Drew came forward promptly with his offer to build, equip and endow a theological seminary in the vicinity of New York City. One fundamental stipulation he laid down was that his pastor should be president. From that day until his death three years later, Dr. McClintock had but one object in life, to build the school sure and strong on this foundation. Himself a thorough scholar, he laid out courses of study wisely designed to meet the special requirements of the Meth-

odist ministry. He surrounded himself on the faculty
with men whose character and attainments were personally known to him. His purchasing agent in
Europe was furnished with lists of books which should
form the nucleus of the library. One who visited
Madison at that time brought back word that he found
the president looking after every detail, from the examination of candidates for admission to the purchase of
potatoes for the dining hall. "He was like a great
general, who allows no detail of fort, field or camp-life
to escape his vigilance." With amazing versatility and
with an expenditure of energy that would have done
credit to a stronger man, he toiled unceasingly. The
faculty of four was so limited that the president had to
carry his full teaching load. We hear that his lectures,
which dealt with such matters as sermon making and
pastoral care, were interesting and instructive, though
as a teacher he had the not uncommon fault of "failing
to sympathize sufficiently with the tardy movements of
the slower minds." Whether his classroom contacts
were stimulating or not, the very aspect and bearing of
the teacher were an inspiration. He had a massive head,
on a short and unimpressive body. Incessant labor had
stored that brain with learning in many fields, learning
which his powerful and orderly mind was constantly
turning to useful ends. He was no recluse. Outside
his study he was friendly, sympathetic and genial in his
intercourse with professors, students and others, a
lovable companion. Yet one did not have to know him
intimately to discover that all he had and was, he had
consecrated to the service of his fellows. He could
conceive of no greater service to the Christian Church
than the training of ministers of the Gospel of his Lord.
And such was the force of his personality and example

that he impressed their stamp indelibly upon the school. His successors in the presidency for half a century, Nadal, Foster, Hurst, Buttz, were his personal friends. Some had been his pupils, others were his appointees. One and all they held his name in veneration and labored to carry forward the enterprise which he had so wisely planned. Thus a leadership which, measured by the calendar, lasted but three years, in fact has never ceased.

JOHN MCCLINTOCK: b. Philadelphia, Pa., Oct. 27, 1814; Wesleyan Univ.; A.B., Univ. of Pennsylvania, 1835; A.M., 1835; D.D., 1848 LL.D., Dickinson Coll., 1859; LL.D., Rutgers Coll., 1866; m. (1) Caroline Wakeman, 1836; m. (2) Catherine Wilkins Emory, 1857; entered Philadelphia Conf., 1835; pastor, Jersey City, N. J., 1835-36; ass't. professor, mathematics, Dickinson Coll., 1836-37; professor, mathematics, 1837-40; professor, ancient classics, 1840-48; editor, *Methodist Review*, 1848-56; New York Conf., 1857; pastor, St. Paul's, New York, N. Y., 1857-60; American Chapel, Paris, France, 1860-64; chairman, Centenary Comm. of American Methodism, 1866-67; president and professor, Practical Theology, Drew, 1867-70; del., Gen. Conf., 1856, 1860, 1868; del., Evangelical Alliance, Berlin, 1856; fraternal del., Wesleyan Methodist Conf. of England, and the Irish, French, and German Confs., 1856; elected president, Wesleyan Univ., but declined; president-elect, Troy Univ., 1857-58; pub., *A Second Book in Greek*, 1848; *A Second Book in Latin*, 1853; *Sketches of Eminent Methodist Ministers*, 1854; editor, *History of the Council of Trent*, 1855; *The Temporal Power of the Pope*, 1855; coauthor, *A First Book in Latin*, 1846; *A First Book in Greek*, 1848; *Cyclopedia of Biblical, Theological, and Ecclesiastical Literature*, 1867-82; *Living Words*, 1871; *Lectures on the Theological Encyclopedia and Methodology*, edited by John T. Short, 1873; translated from the German with C. E. Blumenthal, *The Life of Christ in its Historical Connection and Historical Development*, 1848; contr., relig. periodicals; d. March 4, 1870.

The Rev. RANDOLPH SINKS FOSTER

D.D., LL.D.

Professor of Systematic Theology, 1869-1873; President, 1870-1873.

DR. FOSTER was the third of that first flight of Drew teachers—McClintock and Nadal were the others—

whose connection with the school was brief but notable. He came out of a very different background—was in fact a Westerner, born in an Ohio county jail, of which his father was the keeper. His grandfather, adventuring into Kentucky from Virginia, had been killed by the Indians in that "dark and bloody ground." Young Foster gleaned such schooling as he could in Ohio and entered Augusta College, in Kentucky, the earliest Methodist college west of the mountains, where a little faculty, headed by the versatile Martin Ruter, and numbering such future leaders as John P. Durbin and Henry B. Bascom, was trying to light a torch for the sons of the pioneers. Tall and lithe, with a piercing eye, and a vein of poetry in his soul, this youth of 17 found more satisfaction in preaching up and down the countryside than in listening to lectures on theology or Greek literature and mathematics. Unwise friends advised him that he was called to preach, and should set about it without delay. So he dropped his books and went to the session of Ohio Conference in 1837 seeking admission on trial. His sponsor recommended him as "A splendid young man." This brought the old stager, David Young, to his feet. "Mr. Bishop," he said, "You are new to the West and do not know our ways. Out here we call a potato splendid!" But Randolph Sinks Foster was no small potato. He began riding circuits in the Ohio Valley as a junior preacher, and soon realized that he had made a mistake in leaving college. But he had the sense to perceive that by intense application to the means of self-culture that came within his reach he might in some degree make up his deficiencies. Before he was thirty he had an opportunity to exhibit the unusual quality of his mind. The struggle between Calvinism and Arminianism was at its height in that section, and a Presbyterian minister brought out a book which dealt with the doctrine of Election and Free Grace in a challenging way. It was not easy to answer, but it had to be answered. Young Foster took it upon himself to make the reply, in the form of a series of letters to the *Western Christian Advocate,* of which Matthew Simpson was editor. The pebble from his sling smote Goliath between the eyes. He was hailed far and wide as the champion of the Wesleyan faith. His stature loomed so high that he had invitations from Atlantic seaboard churches, and was soon preaching to the principal congregations of New York, and associating on equal terms with the leaders of Methodism. Northwestern University at Evanston, Ill., was just struggling to its feet, and, needing a strong man for president, turned to Dr. Foster. He remained there only three years—long enough to win the affection and esteem of the student body and the admiration of the public, and quite long enough to convince himself, and probably others, that educational administration was not his forte. He resigned and returned to the pastorate and the pulpit where he reigned. He had been Mr. Drew's pastor in Mulberry Street and enjoyed many opportunities of discussing the ways in which wealth might be applied to the service of the church. He was one—though by no means the only one—who claimed to have brought the founder's mind to its decision to build and endow a theological seminary near New York. Perhaps he might have been its president,—he thought so!—but, with the Evanston experience still fresh in his mind, he waived the offer in favor of McClintock. However this may be, he was named as first occupant of the chair of Systematic Theology, which he held from 1869 until his election as bishop in 1872.

Meanwhile death had vacated the presidential office, and because of his close relations with Mr. Drew and his supposed influence with him, Professor Foster was considered the most available man for president, and was accordingly elected. It is evident that these conditions were unfavorable to a man who was addressing himself for the first time to the teaching profession, and we do not find much evidence that he impressed himself greatly as an instructor upon the few classes over which he presided. Had conditions been otherwise, he would have probably been a marked success. For Systematic Theology was a world in which he was at home. He had studied it with delight for years. He had made himself familiar with its literature, and, when release from episcopal duties left him free to follow his bent, he devoted the rest of his life to the writing of his *Studies in Theology,* though he lived to complete only six of the projected eleven volumes. This undertaking was to have been his *magnum opus.* But he had unfortunately delayed too long. While occupied with many official duties here and there around the world, he had failed to keep in touch with the theological thought and literature of a new generation. He had worked diligently and meditated deeply. But most of what he now had to say no longer had an appeal to the public to which it was offered. Yet he should not be judged by this ill-advised adventure. His fame will abide as that of one of the most powerful and compelling preachers who ever graced the Methodist pulpit. To look upon him at such times was an inspiration. For in face and form he presented a magnificent appearance. He was tall, erect, strong of physique, with piercing eyes, and abundant hair and beard, which in his later years were snow-white. Never light or trifling

in speech or manner, he always maintained a becoming
dignity without stiffness.

RANDOLPH SINKS FOSTER: b. Williams-
burg, O., Feb. 22, 1820; Augusta Coll.,
1835-37; D.D., Ohio Wesleyan Univ.,
1853; LL.D., 1858; m. Sarah Miley;
entered Ohio Conf., 1837; ass't. pastor,
Charlestown, O., 1837-38; West
Chester, O., 1838-39; West Union, O.,
1839-40; Hillsboro, O., 1840-41; pastor,
Portsmouth, O., 1841-42; Hillsboro,
O., 1842-43; Cincinnati, O., Ninth
St., 1843-44; Lancaster, O., 1844-46;
Springfield, O., 1846-48; Wesley
Chapel, Cincinnati, O., 1848-50; New
York Conf., 1850; Mulberry St., New
York, N. Y., 1850-52; Greene St., New
York, N. Y., 1852-54; New York
East Conf., 1854; Pacific St., Brooklyn,
N. Y., 1854-56; New York Conf.,
1856; Trinity, New York, N. Y.,
1856-57; president, Northwestern Univ.,
1857-60; Washington Square, New
York, N. Y., 1860-62; Sing Sing,
N. Y., 1862-64; Eighteenth St., New
York, N. Y., 1864-67; Washington
Square, New York, N. Y., 1867-68;
professor, Systematic Theology, Drew,
1868-73; president, Drew, 1870-73;
bishop, Methodist Episcopal Church,
1872-1903; del., Gen. Conf., 1864,
1868, 1872; fraternal del., British
Wesleyan Conf., 1868; del., Methodist Ecumenical Conf., 1891; del.,
Methodist Centennial Conf., 1884;
pub., *Objections to Calvinism,* 1848;
Christian Purity, 1851; *The Ministry
Needed for the Times,* 1852; *Theism,*
1872; *Beyond the Grave,* 1879; *Centenary Thoughts for the Pew and
Pulpit of Methodism,* 1884; *Studies
in Theology: Prolegomena,* 1889; *The
Supernatural Book,* 1889; *Theism,* 1889;
Philosophy of Christian Experience,
1890; *The Union of Episcopal Meth-
odisms,* 1892; *Creation,* 1895; *God:
Nature and Attributes,* 1897; *Sin,*
1899; d. May 1, 1903.

The Rev. JOHN FLETCHER HURST
A.B., A.M., D.D., LL.D.

Professor of Historical Theology, 1871-1880;
President, 1873-1880.

JOHN FLETCHER HURST (1834-1903) occupied the chair
of Historical Theology in Drew from 1871 until his
elevation to the episcopacy in 1880. His genius as an
executive under challenging conditions must not be
allowed to obscure his unusual gifts as a teacher. A
bookish youth, he had gone from Dickinson College
to Hedding Literary Institute, Ashland, N. Y. to teach
belles lettres; where John Burroughs was a pupil and

Catherine LaMonte, whom he married afterward, was a faculty mate. Advised by Dr. McClintock, he spent two years in German universities and European travel, preparing himself for a professorship. He had been a pastor seven years in Newark Conference, when in 1866 he was called back to Germany as theological tutor in the Methodist Mission Institute in Bremen, (later Frankfort). His *History of Rationalism,* published in New York and London, had already marked him as a scholar of exceptional promise. His accurate learning, his strong faith and his ardent sympathy with his students gave him a powerful influence over the young Swiss and German preachers in the school. He was ready for Drew, and Drew for him. President McClintock, founder and mighty man of letters died in 1870. His confidential friend and colleague, Dr. Nadal, acting president, summoned the young American from Germany to join the shaken teaching corps. Dr. Nadal died within a few months, and his successor, Randolph S. Foster, soon vacated the presidency for the episcopal bench (1872). The trustees turned to Prof. Hurst, one of the youngest on the faculty, not yet 40 years old, to take the leadership of the infant institution. He had already commended himself to the students by the richness of his erudition, the breadth of his culture, his devotion to the church, and his cordial sympathy with "the boys" and their many problems. They listened with attention to his illuminating lectures, and enjoyed even more keenly his excursions outside the subject, when he would discourse to them of his travels abroad and of the great personalities he had known in the German theological world. A tireless walker, he was a familiar figure on all the quiet roads and byways of Morris County, and he loved nothing better than to

fall in step with some like-minded student on these
jaunts—an experience which a few survivors cherish to
this day. In the classroom and out of it, he exalted
learning and thorough scholarship, as a basic requirement of the Christian minister. Five years of this
congenial occupation had passed, when Daniel Drew's
fortune was swept away in a Wall Street cyclone, and
the school was left without endowment. The panicky
trustees proposed to secure funds to pay salaries by
mortgaging Drew Forest. But President Hurst interposed his veto. He wrote his wife: "Mine is to be the
immortality, if any, of making good the money that
Wall Street has swallowed up." The modest scholar
was transformed into a master of finance. His plan
of campaign won the support of key laymen; he was his
own campaign director and traveled at large through
the connection, addressing the several Annual Conferences, and drawing the picture in such appealing
colors as to compel hearty cooperation. A few large
gifts and many small ones within three years brought
in $311,000 of new endowment had and more than
replaced the $250,000 lost by the founder's collapse.
Through it all, the indomitable president had carried
on his classroom work almost uninterruptedly. His
high educational ideals are reflected in the changes
which were introduced in the curriculum of the seminary. The liberal arts courses, originally intended to
meet the requirements of students who were inadequately prepared to take up the regular theological
studies, were dropped, and the theological curriculum
expanded. Probably it was President Hurst's success
in saving Drew, that advertised to the denomination that
in him it possessed, not only a scholar of distinction,
but a leader of rare wisdom and force, the kind of man

"who brings things to pass," to use a Methodist phrase. He was "a coming man." His Conference showed its appreciation by electing him repeatedly to the General Conference at the head of its delegation. The General Conference of 1880 at Cincinnati elected him bishop on the first ballot. And so farewell to Drew! But Drew men never lost interest in the little giant who was their second founder. They observed with pride his constructive work as Bishop resident, in Des Moines, Buffalo, and Washington; his founding of the Malaya Mission by appointing W. F. Oldham to Singapore; the stream of scholarly volumes broad and deep that came from his pen and from others which he directed and inspired; and finally his ambitious plan for a graduate school in Washington, D. C., an American University, which should fulfill a dream of George Washington's. Drew men, too, read with surprise and delight the report of the sale of the "Hurst Collection," which brought under the hammer the extraordinary library which he had assembled, item by item, in the lifelong search which gave him his most exquisite pleasure, and yielded some $60,000 to his estate. Manuscripts of Irving and Poe, incunabula, association books, works in the American Indian languages, autographed volumes from Washington's library, New England Primers, Benjamin Franklin imprints, etc., bear witness to his catholic taste and his prowess as "a Nimrod among book hunters" as he was called by Albert Osborn, Drew '77, whose *John Fletcher Hurst—A Biography* is a painstaking record of a remarkable life—in nothing more remarkable than in the nine years spent in Drew Forest.

As a youth John Hurst is described as below medium height, slender, flaxen-haired, with blue eyes which were notably large. His mouth was large and expressive.

In middle life he wore a goatee which became sandy-white, like his rather thin hair, which someone has said, "looked as if he was in the habit of running his hands through it." His chief recreation, save book-hunting, was walking and mountain-climbing. With one or two boon-companions, who could talk as well as hike, he loved to take long pedestrian tours among the hills, in the Old World and in the New.

JOHN FLETCHER HURST: b. Dorchester Co., Md., Aug. 17, 1834; A.B., Dickinson Coll., 1854; A.M., 1858; D.D., 1866; LL.D., 1877; Univs. of Halle and Heidelberg, Germany, 1856-57; LL.D., Indiana Asbury Univ. (DePauw), 1877; D.D., Princeton Univ., 1896; m. (1) Catherine E. LaMonte, Apr. 28, 1859, m. (2) Ella Agnes Root, Sept. 5, 1892; ord. dea., 1860; ord. eld., 1862; entered Newark Conf., 1858; teacher, Greensboro, Md., 1854; teacher, Hedding Literary Inst., Ashland, N. Y., 1854-56; pastor, Irvington, N. J., 1858-59; Passaic, N. J., 1895-61; Fulton St., Elizabeth, N. J., 1861-63; Water St., Elizabeth, N. J., 1863-65; Trinity, Staten Island, N. Y., 1865-66; professor, Theology, Martin Mission Inst., Bremen, (later Frankfort-am-Main), 1866-71; professor, Historical Theology, Drew, 1871-80; president, Drew, 1873-80; bishop, M. E. Ch., 1880-1903; chancellor, American Univ., 1891-1902; del., Gen. Conf., 1876, 1880; del., Methodist Ecumenical Conf., 1891, 1901; mem., Centennial Meth. Conf., 1884; pres., American Soc. of Ch. History; founder, American Univ.; pub., *Why Americans Love Shakespeare*, 1856; *History of Rationalism*, 1865; *Martyrs to the Tract Cause*, 1872; *Outline of Bible History*, 1872; *Life and Literature in the Fatherland*, 1875; *Outline of Church History*, 1875; *Our Theological Century*, 1876; *Elementos de la Historia de la Iglesia*, Mexico, 1878;

Christian Union Necessary for Religious Progress and Defense, 1880; *Bibliotheca Theologica*, a Bibliography of Theology, and General Literature, 1883; *The Gospel a Combative Force*, 1884; *Short History of the Reformation*, 1884; *The Success of the Gospel and the Failure of the New Theologies*, 1886; *Short History of the Early Church*, 1886; *Short History of the Mediaeval Church*, 1887; *The Theology of the Twentieth Century*, 1887; *Short History of the Modern Church in Europe*, 1888; *The Wedding Day*, 1889; *Short History of the Church in the United States*, 1890; *Parochial Libraries in the Colonial Period*, 1890; *Indika: The Country and People of India and Ceylon*, 1891; *Short History of the Christian Church*, 1893; *Literature of Theology*, 1896; *Journal of Captain William Pote, Jr.*, 1896; *History of the Christian Church* (2 vols.), 1897-1900; *Upon the Sun-Road*, 1901; *The New Hearthstone*, 1901; *The History of Methodism* (7 vols.), 1902-04; translated, Hagenbach's *History of the Christian Church in the Eighteenth and Nineteenth Centuries*, (2 vols.) 1869; Van Oosterzee's *Apologetical Lectures on John's Gospel*, 1869; Lange's *Commentary on Paul's Epistle to the Romans*, 1869; co-editor, Seneca's *Moral Essays*, 1877; *The Biblical and Theological Library* (9 vols.), 1878-1900; *Theological Encyclopedia and Methodology*, 1884; *American Church*

History Series (13 vols.) 1892-95; *pedia* (8 vols.), 1892-95; d., May 4, assoc. ed., Johnson's *Universal Cyclo-* 1903.

The Rev. HENRY ANSON BUTTZ

A.B., A.M., D.D., LL.D.

Adjunct-Professor of Greek, 1868-1871; Librarian, 1870-1872; Professor of Greek and New Testament Exegesis, 1871-1918; President, 1880-1912; President Emeritus, 1912-1920.

In the winter of 1897-8, at the annual meeting of the Drew Alumni of New York, reference was made to the vote for bishop which Dr. Buttz had received at the preceding General Conference. One of his devoted former students suggested that the making of men was of greater importance than the making of appointments, and pictured the president as saying in substance as to the allurements of the episcopal office, "I am doing a great work, I cannot come down." The cynical response of a prominent ecclesiastic who was present was, "The only trouble was, Buttz did not receive enough votes."

But there was more to the case than that. If the theological president had desired, no doubt his many admirers, who would have been only too happy to serve under his administration, might have given him enough votes. If he had been elected, he probably would have obeyed the mandate of the church, but he had no desire for such elevation, no desire to leave the work so close to his heart. From the start of the balloting he had an impressive vote, which steadily increased until on the fifth ballot he led the list, receiving an actual majority. On the sixth and seventh ballots, still leading, he was within fifty votes of the necessary two-thirds. After the eighth ballot, his vote fell off rather sharply, and he is reported to have said to Mrs. Buttz, "It is going our way now." And on his return home, he remarked, "I never was happier in my life than I was when my vote for the episcopacy began to go down."

This was not the forced and reluctant utterance of a disappointed man, but the simple outbreathing of one who believed in divine oversight and divine guidance, who had surrendered himself utterly to the will of God and yet was praying in simple sincerity, "Let this cup pass from me." To him a removal from the place of service which he filled so amply and so happily would have been, not a promotion but a sacrifice. He may be compared to that other eminent and modest servant of God, Dr. Albert S. Hunt, when he was being thrust forward, not by his own will but by the wish of loving friends, as an episcopal possibility. In his private journal, Dr. Hunt wrote in 1884: "The hearts of all men are in the hands of God, and I pray that He will do with me what He pleases, not permitting either friend or opponent to bring anything to pass which is not in harmony with His plan for me and for the church. Thy will be done, O God." Such men live above the clouds, their heads always in God's sunshine.

It is not amiss to dwell upon this single incident in the long life of Dr. Buttz, for it gives the key to the whole. This man was never seeking for personal advancement or advantage. He said more than once, "No one is so poorly cared for as he who starts out in the ministry to care for himself," and he lived out his own theories. In this he was an example to his students, and saved many from that common curse of the ministry, the craving for official recognition, for promotion in "grade" and in salary, and from regarding the Christian ministry as a profession rather than a calling. He taught and exemplified the steady, faithful, unself-seeking service of men and Christ and the church, which alone is worthy to be called a Christian ministry. He put character above talent. "If I believe in a man," he was accustomed to say, "he cannot preach a poor sermon to me; if I do not believe in him, he cannot preach a good one."

Such was the man who for more than five decades taught at Drew and for more than three decades presided over its faculty and students. He had had a pastoral experience of nine years in half a dozen charges before his connection with the Seminary, and it was while he was preaching at the church in Morristown that this young man, one of the rare ministerial college graduates of that day who had enjoyed in addition some theological training, attracted the favorable notice of the alert McClintock and began his long academic career. He had been present at the formal opening of the Seminary on November 6, 1867, and within a few months found himself a part of the small instructing force.

As a teacher he reveled in his work. At times he taught first year Hebrew, of which language he had acquired a working knowledge, but his passion was always the New Testament and its Greek. He did not undertake the wide range of modern Bible study; there was no bird's-eye view of that early Christian literature as a whole. And, at least in some stages of his experience, he gave no courses in the Gospels. Many students of half a century ago left Drew without ever having heard of the "Synoptic Problem." Dr. Buttz was a devotee of Paul, and besides Hebrews, chose Romans and Galatians as the major subjects for the three years' work in his department.

To these he gave an almost microsopic study. The Greek particles were a delight to his meticulous scholarship. He led his students to accuracy, rather than to broad, superficial conclusions. They may have missed the sweep of the forest, but at least they learned something at close range about the trees! As Dr. Tipple wrote, in his admirable review of Dr. Buttz' life,[1] "No one could question the amplitude or accuracy of the scholarship, the richness of his spiritual insight and knowledge, the purity and strength of his love for the Book."

But any man, looking back to Drew and its outstanding president, would agree that his classroom work was the least of his contributions to the Seminary and its students. For thirty-two years he carried the heavy burdens of administration. The Seminary was poor, ill-endowed. A deficit of from $5,000 to $20,000 a year in its running expenses had to be found somewhere. As a young professor Mr. Buttz had had some experience in seeking financial help in the strenuous days of President Hurst; but now the whole responsibility was his, and the taxing business of personal solicitation had to be repeated year by year. He faced the demands with quiet courage and patience. Current bills were met, five new buildings were erected, endowment was increased, faculty enlarged. He did not quite find Drew in brick and leave it in marble; the more striking and luxurious improvements were left for a later day. But Dr. Buttz, refusing other and seductive calls, had the satisfaction of seeing "the little one become a thousand." Indeed, three thousand students

---

[1] *The Methodist Review*, March, 1921.

passed under his care and went out bearing upon them some imprint of his personality.

For he gave tone to the whole institution. He was on the ground from the beginning, and he remained when all his elders had passed on. There were in the old days few departments; the "Big Five' made up the teaching staff. They were men competent in their departments, but not especially marked by breadth of interest or comprehensive contacts. "Uncle John," they would be called, or "Uncle Sammy" or "Uncle Henry." There was a family rather than an institutional atmosphere surrounding the spot. Easily first among his peers in influence, as in stature, President Buttz made his unconscious impress on the lives and ideals of the youth by whom he was surrounded. By a kind of spiritual osmosis he infiltrated them with his own gentle yet virile spirit. He was utterly kind to them all. He was never a harsh or sarcastic instructor, satisfying a sense of superiority at the expense of a luckless student.

That quaint pursing of the lips and lifting of the brows, that inquiring expression, had about it something naive, almost elfish. But if any supposed that his winsomeness and simplicity were tokens of weakness, they still had something to learn. Dr. Buttz won friends and funds for his school because people believed in him and loved him. But he was also an adept in the art of approach, and sincerity did not preclude skill and shrewdness. He may have been called the "St. John of Methodism" with good reason because of his purity and devoutness, but he was a practical James as well as a mystic John. And for the noble example of a spotless and selfless life, dedicated to God and to men, his students rise up and call him blessed.

H. W.

Henry Anson Buttz: b. Middle Smithfield, Pa., April 18, 1835; Union Coll.; A.B., Princeton Univ., 1858; A.M. 1861; D.D. 1875; A.M., Wesleyan Univ. 1866; D.D. 1903; LL.D., Dickinson Coll., 1885; Theol. Sem. of the Reformed Church, New Brunswick; m. Emily Hoagland, April 11, 1860; Ord. dea. 1860; Ord. eld. 1862; entered Newark Conf., 1858; pastor, Millstone, N. J., 1858-59; Irvington, N. J., 1859-60; Woodbridge, N. J., 1860-62; Mariners' Harbor, N. Y., 1862-64; Paterson, N. J., Prospect St., 1864-67; Morristown, N. J., 1867-69; adjunct professor Greek, Drew, 1868-71; librarian, Drew, 1870-72; professor Greek and New Testament Exegesis, Drew, 1871-1918; president, Drew, 1880-1912; president emeritus, Drew, 1912-20; del. Gen. Conf., 1884, 1888, 1892, 1896, 1900, 1904, 1908, 1912; del., Ecumenical Conf. 1891, 1911; del. Methodist Centennial Conf., 1884; mem. Board of Missions, Methodist Episcopal Church; mem., Comm. on Versions, American Bible Soc.; trustee, Methodist Episcopal Hospital, Brooklyn; American Exegetical Soc.; American Philological Ass'n; pub., *Epistle to the Romans in Greek;* editor, *The New Life Dawning,* by B. H. Nadal; *The Student's Commentary—The Book of Psalms,* by Dr. James Strong, 1896; contr., relig. periodicals; d. Oct. 6, 1920.

The Rev. EZRA SQUIER TIPPLE
A.B., A.M., Ph.D., D.D., LL.D.

Professor of Practical Theology, 1905-1929; President, 1912-1929.

Ezra Squier Tipple had something of the mien and manner of a country squire, (which, it may be said, was the way his intimates pronounced his middle name). It came to him together with certain life-trends, from his maternal grandsire, "itinerant preacher, and gentleman of the old school, the Rev. Ezra S. Squier," who was a minister of the old Black River Conference. After working his way through Syracuse University, this ambitious youth entered Drew—and from that hour Drew entered and possessed him. The "Big Five"— Buttz, Crooks, Strong, Upham, Miley—were the faculty, and what a faculty! He left school to become a preacher of the Gospel, with a marked gift for managing men and institutions. It did not take many years of pastoral service in New York City for him to win the confidence of the remarkable group of great-hearted laymen who were then influential in Conference affairs. They recognized executive gifts, even in the garb of a parson. They set him heavy tasks of organization and finance— and backed him. When he succeeded they opened to hm fresh opportunities. Thus in 1905 he came back to Drew Forest as professor of Practical Theology, the chair of the sage McClintock, the suave Kidder and the salty Upham. Though not a pedagogue by training or by choice, his experience among men as pastor and as fellow-worker in large Christian enterprises had put his own theology to practice, and supplied him with first-hand teaching material. He loved young men and was determined to help them. Seven years later, when President Buttz retired, his mantle fell on Professor Tipple, who had meanwhile broadened his outlook by extensive foreign travel, and whose pen had produced a number of valuable books, such as *The Heart of Asbury's Journal, The Life of Francis Asbury* and *Some Country Parishes*. Although he continued to give the courses in his department, the development of the Seminary increasingly absorbed his attention, and relegated classroom work to a secondary place. As an executive and builder he was at his best. Although his eye was centered on the main objective, the training of ministers, he recognized that classroom and library were not the whole of it. A lover of art and a firm believer in the cultural value of beauty in all its expressions, he set about the making of Drew Forest the lovely place for which it was adapted by nature and art. The trees, flowers and paths received his special care. The Bowne Memorial Gateway dignified the main entrance,

and, facing the portal and "the long road," Mr. Pilling
erected the equestrian statue of the Bishop Asbury,
the field-marshal of the circuit-riders. The friends who
had stood by him in his New York days, and who had
shared in the prosperity of the time, were drawn into
the Drew circle and new buildings and new endowments began to give fresh evidence of their liberal
cooperation in the president's plans. The faculty was
expanded, new schools were added, and representative
men were brought from far and near to lecture on subjects outside the curriculum, but closely related to a
modern ministry which must understand and influence
all sorts and conditions of men.

His friendship, long continued and closely knit, with
three of the finest and foremost Methodist ministers of
his generation, Bishop William Fraser McDowell, Dr.
Frank Mason North, and Dr. William Ingraham Haven,
was a rich resource both for him and for the Seminary.
As the older teachers retired he filled their places with
men of rare gifts and graces, who gave themselves with
enthusiasm to the carrying out of the president's program. When two former parishioners, the Baldwin
brothers, broached their design for a liberal arts college
on the Drew campus, the president adopted it eagerly
and threw the great weight of his personality in its favor.
So Brothers College started on its promising career,
and Drew began to bear the title of University, to which
it had always been entitled by the terms of its charter.
It is impossible to think or write about Dr. Tipple's
administration without recalling the part which Mrs.
Tipple played in it all. She was as charming a hostess
as ever graced a presidential mansion. No one could
enter her door without becoming her admirer. What
this Christian woman's influence must have contributed

to some of her husband's greatest successes can not be set down in cold type. When the rich Wendel-Swope legacies were announced, they were variously accounted for, and doubtless many factors contributed to produce their munificence. But not the least was the assiduous and welcome attention which the president and the first lady of Drew Forest gave to the maintenance of the cordial relations between Drew and the Wendels, which had existed from the time when Dr. McClintock and Dr. Foster had been their pastors, and when Dr. Buttz was one of the few privileged visitors at "the house of mystery" at the corner of Fifth Avenue and 39th Street. And the Rose benefactions, the Rose Memorial Library and the scholarship foundation which is helping so many deserving young men to gain an education in the Seminary and in the College are directly traceable to the friendly relations which existed so long between Mr. and Mrs. Lenox Rose and their friends and neighbors in the presidential manse. It has been well said that President Tipple gave, not merely his best, but his all to Drew. His wife no less. He did not over estimate her value to him, when he dedicated one of his books

> "To Her
> whose brightness shortens every journey
> whose enthusiasm glorifies every scene,
> whose comradeship makes the whole
> world beautiful."

She joined with him in large gifts in his lifetime, including the endowment of the Biographical Lectureship, and by her will her large estate, passed to the university, together with her husband's uniquely valuable collection of Wesleyana—books, prints, letters, manuscripts and Staffordshire figures—which is deposited in the Treasure Room of the university library which will be known henceforth as the Tipple Room.

EZRA SQUIER TIPPLE: b. Camden, N. Y., Jan. 23, 1861; A.B., Syracuse Univ., 1884; A.M., 1885; Ph.D., 1886; D.D., 1899; LL.D., 1913; B.D., Drew, 1887; L.H.D., Allegheny Coll., 1933; m. Edna E. White, June 24, 1897; ord. dea., 1887; ord. eld., 1890; entered New York Conf., 1887; pastor, St. Luke's, New York, N. Y., 1887-92; Grace, New York, N. Y., 1892-97; St. James, New York, N. Y., 1897-1901; exec. sec., Metropolitan Thank-Offering Comm., 1901-04; Grace, New York, N. Y., 1904-05; professor, Practical Theology, Drew, 1905-29; president, 1912-29; honorary president, 1929-33; president emeritus, 1933-36; del., Gen. Conf., 1904, 1908, 1912, 1916, 1920, 1924, 1928, 1932, 1936; del., Methodist Ecumenical Conf., 1901, 1921; trustee, Syracuse Univ., 1898-1930; trustee, Drew, 1904-06; trustee, Drew Sem. for Young Women; Bd. of Mgrs., Missionary Soc., 1895-1906; Bd. of Mgrs., Bd. of Foreign Missions, 1907-36; trustee, Bd. of Edn., 1904-28; rec. sec., 1904-24; sec., Methodist Book Comm.; exec. comm., Methodist Book Com., N. Y.; com. on Versions, Am. Bible Soc.; admin. comm. and comm. on internat. justice and good will, Federal Council of Churches of Christ in America; president, Methodist Historical Soc., N. Y.; special speaker, YMCA, France and England, 1918; Relig. Edn. Ass'n.; Am. Soc. of Church History; Phi Beta Kappa; Quill Club, (pres., 1904-05); advisory council, St. Christopher's Home for Children; comm. on unification, M. E. Church; National Geographical Soc.; Nat'l. Edn. Ass'n; pub., *Heart of Asbury's Journal*, 1905; *The Minister of God*, 1906; (ed) Drew Sermons, first series, 1906, second series, 1907; Drew Sermons on the Golden Texts, 1908, 1909, 1910; *Life of Freeborn Garrettson*, 1910; *Some Famous Country Parishes*, 1911; *Life of Francis Asbury*, 1916; (ed) *Drew Theological Seminary, 1867-1917*, 1917; *The Wendels*, 1936; art., *The Beginnings of American Methodism*, in A New History of Methodism, London, 1909; contr., relig. periodicals; d. Oct. 17, 1936.

The Rev. ARLO AYRES BROWN

A.B., B.D., Litt.D., L.H.D., D.D., LL.D.

President, 1929—.

IN 1929, WHEN ARLO AYRES BROWN became president of Drew University, he was in his forty-sixth year and already had behind him a rich and varied experience of life and many significant achievements.

He was the son of the Rev. Robert Ayres and Lucy Emma (Sanders) Brown and grew up in a Methodist parsonage. The broad plains of Illinois furnished the background of his boyhood.

When the time for college came he entered Northwestern University from which he was graduated in 1903 receiving the degree A.B. and achieving the honorary fraternity Phi Beta Kappa. Thirty-five years later his Alma Mater conferred upon him the degree Doctor of Laws. This degree he had already received from Syracuse University in 1927. Cornell College had made him a Doctor of Divinity in 1921. The University of Chattanooga admitted him to the Doctorate in Literature in 1929. On the occasion of the one hundredth anniversary of Boston University he received the degree Doctor of Humane Letters. Dr. Brown's professional theological training was received at Drew Theological Seminary from which he received the degree B.D. in 1907. He took part-time graduate work at Union Theological Seminary during the years 1908 to 1911 and at the graduate school of Northwestern University during the years 1919 to 1921.

During his active life he has been a minister of the Methodist (formerly Methodist Episcopal) Church. He was ordained deacon in 1907 and elder in 1909. He was a member of the New York Conference from 1907 to 1921, of the Holston Conference from 1921 to 1929 and has been a member of the Newark Conference since 1929. In the year of his graduation from Drew Theological Seminary Dr. Brown became associate pastor of the Madison Avenue Church of New York City. Here he worked with Dr. Wallace MacMullen, the pastor, until 1909. From 1909 to 1912 he was pastor of the Mount Hope Church in New York City.

By this time those large opportunities which have been so characteristic of his life began knocking at his

door. During 1912 and 1913 he was agent of the Board
of Foreign Missions of the Methodist Episcopal Church
in Jerusalem. This was his first contact with the Near
East and in this early period he revealed that quiet sympathy with varied racial groups which has been so characteristic of his whole life. He was executive secretary
of the Newark District Church Society from 1913 to
1914.

On February 14, 1914 Arlo Ayres Brown was married to Grace Hurst Lindale. It is the simple statement
of truth to say that Mrs. Brown has made an unusual
and notable contribution to her husband's success. Her
artistic sense and meticulous good taste have made their
home a place of rare and gracious charm. And she has
given to that home a quality of simple distinction and
cordial friendliness which many generations of students
have deeply appreciated.

Dr. Brown's interest in matters of education was
sharpening all the while and from 1914 to 1921 he was
the effective superintendent of teacher training in the
Board of Sunday Schools of the Methodist Episcopal
Church. During this period he entered upon experiences and formed friendships with men in the field of
education of the utmost significance of his whole life.

The World War of 1914 to 1918 found him ready for
service. He enlisted in the training school for Army
Chaplains June 1, 1918. He was commissioned first
lieutenant chaplain 318th Engineers, 6th Division,
A.E.F. August 29, 1918, and senior chaplain of the same
June 12, 1919. He was captain chaplain O.R.C. 1921 to
1924, and major chaplain 1924 to 1934.

All the while his mind was broadening and enlarg-
ing its grasp of educational problems and in 1921 he
was made president of the Chattanooga University,

which office he held until 1929. The university pros-
pered under his leadership and he became a familiar
figure at educational gatherings in the South where he
was soon accepted as a friend and a trusted leader.

The next step in his career was one which must have
brought particular gratification to him as it was a source
of the deepest satisfaction to his friends all over the
church. In 1929 Drew University called him to its presidency and Drew Forest, which years before had witnessed his arrival as a new theological student and three
years later had sent him forth with its professional
degree, now received him back as the head of an enlarged and growing institution.

His many-sided educational interests continued. He
was vice-president of the Association of American Colleges 1928 to 1929. He became chairman of the executive committee of the International Council of Religious Education in 1939. He was president of the American Association of Theological Schools 1936 to 1938.
During this period he visited Union Theological Seminary, Yale Divinity School, and other schools as
inspector in connection with the appraisal of American
Theological Schools which took place at that time. He
was president of the Methodist Educational Association
1928 to 1930 and 1939 to 1940. He has rendered very
important service as a member of the Commission on
Conference Courses of Study of the Methodist Episcopal
Church since 1923. He has been a familiar figure as a
member of the University Senate of the Methodist
Episcopal Church and more recently in the Methodist
Board of Education. As a member of the Appraisal
Commitee of the Laymen's Foreign Missionary Inquiry
he made a memorable visit to the great missionary enterprises in India, Burma, China and Japan, 1931 to 1932.

Here in constant and intimate fellowship with Christian leaders in the Orient he had opportunities of the rarest sort in respect of entering into the very life of the Christian Movement in Asia. He is a member of the International Committee of the Young Men's Christian Association, of the Commitee on Public Relations and Chairman of the Program Commitee of the Army and Navy Committee of the Y.M.C.A., the latter being the channel through which the Y.M.C.A. serves men of the armed forces through the United Service Organization. In all these relationships at home and abroad he has become the intimate and trusted comrade of the leaders of his own and many other Christian communions.

During his busy life as an administrator of important educational activities and institutions he has found time to write and publish *Studies in Christian Living* 1914, *Primer of Teacher Training* 1916, a *History of Religious Education in Recent Times* (perhaps his most characteristic contribution to the literature of the field) 1923, *Youth and Christian Living* 1929. He was the co-author of *Life in the Making,* published in 1917.

President Brown has brought to Drew University a mind richly fertilized by the widest experience and the richest contact with men and movements. His simple friendliness and his unruffled urbanity have made him something more intimate and human than an effective administrator without diminishing his constant and understanding command of the essential features of the vastly varied situations with which he has had to deal.

He has been a delegate to the General Conferences of the Methodist Episcopal Church in 1928, 1932 and 1936, of the Uniting Conference in 1939, and of the General Conference of the Methodist Church in 1940. In committee work and on the floor of the General

Conference he has been a significant and influential person. Cool and careful and understanding in his judgment, he has won the respect of his colleagues and has quietly and effectively advanced the causes which have won his interest and compelled his loyalty.

During the thirteen years of his presidency of Drew University many advances have been made in material prosperity, in scholarly activity and in intellectual impact upon the American community. The endowment of the institution has increased from $2,294,000 to $5,879,000, not including the principal of the Rose Scholarship Fund and the principal assets of the Wendel Foundation, totaling approximately $4,000,000. Also, $680,000 has been spent on new buildings and campus improvements, especially the Lenox S. Rose Memorial Library, which combines beauty and serviceableness in an unusual degree.

President Brown has a cosmopolitan mind ready to accept what is true whatever its source, not easily subject to party labels, and devotedly loyal to the Christian ideal which gives direction to his life.

L. H. H.

ARLO AYRES BROWN: b. Sunbeam, Ill., Apr. 15, 1883; A.B., Northwestern Univ., 1903; B.D., Drew, 1907; Union Theol. Sem. 1908-11; Northwestern Univ. 1919-21; D.D., Cornell Coll. Iowa, 1921; LL.D., Syracuse Univ., 1927; Litt. D., Univ. of Chattanooga, 1929; LL.D., Northwestern, 1938; L.H.D., Boston Univ., 1939; m. Grace Hurst Lindale, Feb. 14, 1914; ord. dea., 1907; ord. eld., 1909; entered New York Conf., 1907; assoc. pastor, Madison Av. Ch., New York, N. Y., 1907-09; pastor, Mount Hope Ch., New York, N. Y., 1909-12; agt., Bd. of Foreign Missions, Jerusalem, 1912-13; exec. sec. Newark Dist. Ch. Soc., 1913-14; supt. teacher training, Bd. of Sunday Schs., 1914-21; Holston Conf., 1921; president, Univ. of Chattanooga, 1921-29; Newark Conf., 1929; president, Drew, 1929; 1st. lt., and chaplain, 318th Engrs., 6th Div., A.E.F., Aug. 29, 1918; sr. chaplain, Dec. 21, 1918; capt., Mar. 26, 1919; hon. discharged June 12, 1919; captain chaplain, O.R.C., 1921-24; major chaplain, 1924-34; Chr., International Council of Religious Education; Secretary, Board of Managers, Methodist Hospital (Brooklyn); Vice-Pres., Morris-Sussex Area Council, Boy Scouts of America; International Committee, Army and Navy Committee,

Public Relations Committee, YMCA; Commission on Courses of Study, Methodist Church, since 1922; Board of Education, Methodist Church, since 1940; University Senate, Methodist Church, 1923-40; Vice-Pres., Association of American Colleges, 1928-29; Book Committee, Methodist Episcopal Church, 1928-30; Pres., American Association of Theological Schools, 1936-38; Pres., Methodist Educational Association, 1927-29, 1939-40; Appraisal Commn. of Laymen's Foreign Missions Inquiry, 1931-32; Phi Beta Kappa; del., gen. conf., 1928, 1932, 1936, 1940 (Uniting Conf., 1939); pub. *Studies in Christian Living,* 1914; *Primer of Teacher Training,* 1916; *A History of Religious Education in Recent Times,* 1923; *Youth and Christian Living,* 1929; co-author, *Life in the Making,* 1917; address, Drew Forest, Madison, N. J.

The Rev. BERNARD HARRISON NADAL

A.B., A.M., D.D.

Professor of Historical Theology, 1867-1870;
Acting President 1870.

PRESIDENT McCLINTOCK'S immediate successor in the presidency was Bernard H. Nadal, though he served only six months and had the title of acting president. Possibly he would have been the actual successor, though it was his own idea that Professor Foster would be the wiser choice, "because Foster had more influence with Mr. Drew than any other man in the church and could secure further endowment as no one else could." As it happened the lot fell upon Foster, and Dr. Nadal's promising connection with Drew was cut short by his sudden death, within a few months. Nadal was born in Talbot County, Md., in 1812, and was a contemporary of McClintock and Foster. His father came to America from the south of France to escape from being trained as a Roman Catholic priest. His mother was a devoted Methodist whose father, a prosperous planter, manumitted his many slaves for conscientious reasons. Nadal, after an apprenticeship of 4 years as a saddler, was con-

PLATE II—FACULTY

BERNARD H. NADAL, 1867-1870   JAMES STRONG, 1868-1894
DANIEL P. KIDDER, 1871-1881   JOHN MILEY, 1873-1895
GEORGE R. CROOKS, 1880-1897   SAMUEL F. UPHAM, 1881-1904

verted and entered the ministry in 1835, joining Baltimore Conference, and riding his circuit in a saddle
which he had made. He had begun to educate himself,
and persevered with the process while serving churches
in Maryland, Virginia and Pennsylvania. His appointment in the latter state was Carlisle, seat of Dickinson
College, and while in that college town he earned in
two years the degree of bachelor of arts and won the
good opinion of Professor John McClintock and others
who were to wield strong influence in Methodist education. For three years he taught *belles lettres* in Indiana
Asbury University (DePauw) returning to the itiner-
ancy to hold a succession of great pastorates in Foundry
Church, and Wesley Chapel, Washington; First Church,
New Haven; and Sands Street, Brooklyn. In Washington he was chaplain of the Senate. Dr. McClintock,
casting about for timber out of which to build the first
Drew faculty, laid his hand on Dr. Nadal, having confidence in his hard-earned but solid educational attainments, his zeal for self-improvement, his experience in
the most exacting pulpits, and his wide acquaintance
and popularity throughout Methodism. He was the
first professor of Historical Theology, a title which has
since been improved to "Church History." But again
death interposed. In March 1870 President McClintock
died and Dr. Nadal was named as acting president. In
that capacity he wrote to young Hurst in Germany offering him his chair of Church History. Hurst accepted,
and thus was unconsciously brought into the line of
succession. But a month later, Dr. Nadal, also, passed
away, leaving the presidency to Dr. Foster, whose brief
tenure was ended within a few months by his election
to the episcopacy, 1872.

Dr. Nadal's connection with Drew lasted but three

years—not long enough to enable him to make the contribution which his learning and his personality warranted. He was the first choice of President McClintock, who probably counted on his gracious manner, fine taste, and breadth of culture to supply an essential element in the training of the young minister. Furthermore he was widely known for his brilliant writings in the church press, and was in great demand as a preacher and occasional orator. His connection with the Methodist college in Indiana moreover, was a link with a section from which Drew hoped to draw students. For while a good deal had been said about the need of a seminary in the vicinity of New York City, it had never been in the mind of its projectors that Drew should be a distinctively local or sectional school. From the beginning it appealed to the nation-wide denomination for patronage, and it has continued for three quarters of a century to attract students from all sections of the Union and indeed from foreign lands. A colleague of his in the early days at Indiana Asbury speaks of "the sunny atmosphere which he brought with him and in which he lived," and adds, "he enjoyed that peculiar popularity among his students which belongs only to the teacher who possesses the heart to enter deeply into sympathy with young men, and also the power to inspire them with his own devotion to earnest work." L. M. Vernon, one of his first pupils at Drew, testifies, "The lectures which he delivered to his students were not the dry details of science; they were the warm outbreakings of great truths which lived in his heart." He speaks also of his "classical elegance and fertility of diction." Dr. Buttz, his youngest colleague here, was impressed by his habit of "doing everything thoroughly," and continues "the breadth and accuracy of his knowledge, his power of communicating truth with clearness and force, united with skill in criticising the productions of others, were well calculated to secure for him the eminence which he attained as a professor." Dr. Nadal's light was too soon extinguished for him to illumine this history of the teachers of Drew. He belongs rather to the morning stars that shone in our sky before the great constellation—the "Big Five" appeared above the horizon.

BERNARD HARRISON NADAL: b. Talbot Co., Md., Mar. 27, 1812; A.B., Dickinson Coll., 1848; A.M., 1848; D.D., 1857; m. Jane Mays, 1841; entered Baltimore Conf., 1835; ass't pastor, Luray Circuit, Va., 1835-36; pastor, Saint Mary's Circuit, Md., 1836-37; Bladensburg, Md., 1837-38; City Station, Baltimore, Md., 1838-40; Lewisburg, Va., 1840-42; Lexington, Va., 1842-44; Columbia St., Baltimore, Md., 1844-46; Central Pennsylvania Conf., 1846; Carlisle, Pa., 1846-48; Baltimore Female Coll., 1848-49; Baltimore Conf., 1849; High St., Baltimore, Md., 1849-51; City Station, Baltimore, Md., 1851-53; supernumerary, 1853-54; professor, Indiana Asbury Univ., 1854-57; supt., Roanoke District, 1857-58; Foundry, Washington, D. C., 1858-60; New York East Conf., 1860; First, New Haven, Conn., 1862-64; Baltimore Conf., 1864; Wesley Chapel, Washington, D. C., 1864-66; Philadelphia Conf., 1866; Trinity, Philadelphia, Pa., 1866-67; professor, Historical Theology, Drew, 1867-70; acting president, Drew, 1870; pub., *The New Life Dawning,* with a biographical sketch, edited by Dr. H. A. Buttz; contr., relig. periodicals; d. June 20, 1870.

The Rev. LYNN HAROLD HOUGH

A.B., B.D., Th.D., Litt.D., D.D., LL.D., J.U.D.

Lecturer on Preaching, 1920-29; *Professor of Homiletics,* 1930-33; *Professor of Homiletics and Comprehensive Scholarship,* 1933-37; *Professor of Homiletics and the Christian Criticism of Life,* 1937—; *Dean,* 1934—

METHODIST CLERGYMAN distinguished as a preacher, author, teacher, and educational administator. Born in Cadiz, his boyhood and youth were spent in Ohio until after his graduation (with honors) from Scio College

(A.B., 1898). Coming to Drew Theological Seminary
in 1898, he has been intimately connected with the life
of Drew ever since, although his responsibilities kept
him away from the campus, except for occasional lectures, for many years. Seeking breadth as well as depth
in cultural and religious training, he allowed himself
seven years for the completion of the B.D. degree in
1905, and by so doing laid the foundations for a career
distinguished in English and classical literature as well
as in religion. In 1919 he was awarded the Th.D. degree
by Drew Theological Seminary. Of honorary degrees
he has received the following: D.D., Mount Union-Scio
College, 1912; D.D., Garrett Biblical Institute, 1918;
Litt.D., Allegheny College, 1922; LL.D., Albion College, 1923; D.D., Wesleyan University, 1924; LL.D.,
University of Detroit, 1928; L.H.D., University of Vermont, 1932; LL.D., University of Pittsburgh, 1935;
J.U.D., Boston University, 1939.

No biographical sketch of Dean Hough would be
adequate which did not cite the contributions to his
brilliant career of service made by his mother, Mrs.
Eunice R. G. Hough, and his wife, Blanche Horton
Trowbridge Hough. From his seminary days in Drew
Theological Seminary on through several of his years
as dean his mother was homemaker and counsellor.
Herself for years the teacher of a Men's Bible Class at
Central Church in Detroit, her insight into character
and her gracious charm made her a lady beloved by all
who knew her. She was called to her reward in 1937.

On October 13, 1936 Dean Hough married Blanche
Horton Trowbridge who had already enjoyed the
unique privilege of serving as a missionary for twenty-
five years, first in Turkey and later in Cairo, Egypt. A
citizen of the world and a lady of keen intellect and un-

usual social graces, she has greatly enriched the life of Drew Forest through her hospitality and sympathetic interest in students and every phase of campus life.

Dean Hough's career includes the following: pastorates—Arcola, N. J., 1898-1904; First Church, Cranford, N. J., 1904-06; King's Park, N. Y., 1906-07; Third Church, Long Island City, N. Y., 1907-09; Summerfield Church, Brooklyn, N. Y., 1902-12; Mt. Vernon Place Church, Baltimore, Md., 1912-14; Central Church, Detroit, Mich., 1920-28; American Presbyterian Church, Montreal, Canada, 1929-30. Teaching—professor of Historical Theology, Garrett Biblical Institute, 1914-19; professor of Homiletics and the Christian Criticism of Life, Drew Theological Seminary since 1929. He gave an annual series of lectures on Homiletics at Drew from 1920 to 1929. In educational administration he served as president of Northwestern University in 1919-20 and has been dean of Drew Theological Seminary since 1934. The site for the Chicago campus of Northwestern was bought under his leadership, thereby laying a foundation for one of the most significant developments in higher education in the United States. In Drew Theological Seminary graduate study has been lifted to a higher plane by his untiring efforts. A man of comprehensive scholarship and exacting standards for his own intellectual work, he has applied the same rigorous standards to every phase of the Seminary's work. He has also given much time to deepening and extending the worldwide influence of the institution.

Dean Hough has held membership in the following annual conferences of the Methodist Episcopal Church: New York East 1906; Baltimore 1912; West Ohio 1914; Rock River 1918; Detroit 1920-28; New York East 1931- . From 1928 to 1930 he was a minister of the

United Church of Canada while serving the great American Presbyterian Church of Montreal. He was a member of the General Conference of his church in 1936 and 1940, and of the Uniting Conference of Methodism in 1939. As a debater in the General Conference he has had few equals and no superiors. Scholar though he is, he has always taken a keen interest and active part in the practical affairs of his denomination, giving special attention to the work of the Board of Publication of which he is a member. He is president of the Association of Methodist Theological Schools.

While ardent in love and loyalty for his own church, he has been very active in interdenominational movements, serving as president of the Detroit Council of Churches, 1926-28; vice president of the Religious Education Association, 1926-28; and president of The Religious Education Council of Canada, 1929-30. He is a member of the Executive Committee of the Federal Council of Churches of Christ in America.

Few men of his generation have preached so often to students in colleges and universities or have been called upon so often to speak on special occasions and for so many denominations. As an example of the service which he has rendered, he has preached the Thanksgiving sermon at St. Bartholomew's, New York City, on three occasions. In Boston he has preached during Holy Week in the Cathedral and also in other lenten periods. He preached in the Cathedral at Washington in the spring of 1942. During a number of different years he has had five-day engagements at Kings Chapel in Boston, and on many occasions he has spoken at the Sunday Evening Club in Chicago. Sound learning, wealth of illustration not only from literature but also from every-day life, clarity of thought and beauty of expression,

together with passion for the truth of the Gospel of
Jesus Christ, these with other factors have made him
one of America's greatest preachers.

His main scholarly interest has been in the field of
Critical Humanism in which he is recognized as the
outstanding American authority, succeeding to the
leadership of the late Irving Babbitt and the late Paul
Elmer More.

However, this bare recital of facts gives but a partial
picture of the wide range of his activities and the
catholicity of his spirit. He has been a member of:
Society of Biblical Literature and Exegesis; Chicago
Society of Biblical Research; Society of Midland Authors; Board of Sponsors, *Christianity and Crisis;* Board
of Publication, *Christendom;* American Society of
Church History; National Association of Biblical Instructors; English-Speaking Union; Clergy Association
of New and York and Neighborhood; Academy of
Political Science; Ohio Society of New York; Editorial
Board, *Religion in Life.*

Of unique significance has been his contribution to
international understanding and good will. In 1918 he
was sent to Great Britain to interpret the moral and
spiritual aims of World War I, and he has preached in
City Temple, London, for twelve different summers.
In June 1942 he flew to England upon invitation of the
British Ministry of Information and Dr. Leslie Weather-
head, to preach for two months to the congregation of
the City Temple, London. He has preached in many
other British pulpits, and in 1938 preached the League
of Nations sermon at the Cathedral of St. Pierre in
Geneva. In 1923 before the British Wesleyan Conference he delivered the Fernley Lecture on Evangelical
Humanism, and only last year he delivered the Fred J.

Cato Lecture before the General Conference of the Methodist Church of Australasia, in Melbourne, taking as his subject "Adventures in Understanding."

Fortunately Dean Hough is at the height of his powers at the time this biographical sketch is being written. His career has been unique, brilliant, and of far-reaching significance. Drew has every reason for pride in his achievements and gratitude that he has been able to put so much of his talent and power into the life and work of his Alma Mater.

A. A. B.

LYNN HAROLD HOUGH: b. Cadiz, O., Sept. 10, 1877; A.B., Scio Coll., 1898; B.D., Drew, 1905; Th.D., 1919; New York Univ.; D.D., Mount Union-Scio College, 1912; D.D.; Garrett Bibl. Inst., 1918; Litt. D., Allegheny Coll. 1922; LL.D., Albion Coll., 1923; D.D., Wesleyan Univ., 1924; LL.D., Univ. of Detroit, 1928; L.H.D., Univ. of Vermont, 1932; LL.D., Univ. of Pittsburgh, 1935; J.U.D., Boston Univ., 1939; m. Blanche Horton Trowbridge, October 13, 1936; ord. dea., 1906; ord. eld., 1909; entered New York East Conf., 1906; pastor, Arcola, N. J., 1898-1904; First Ch., Cranford, N. J., 1904-06; King's Park, N. Y., 1906-07; Third Ch., Long Island City, N. Y., 1907-09; Summerfield Ch. Brooklyn, N. C., 1909-12; Baltimore Conf., 1912; Mt. Vernon Place Ch., Baltimore, Md., 1912-14; professor, Historical Theology, Garrett Bibl. Inst., 1914-19; president, Northwestern Univ., 1919-20; Detroit Conf., 1920; Central Ch., Detroit, Mich., 1920-28; lecturer, Preaching, Drew, 1920-30; American Presbyterian Ch., Montreal, 1928-30; professor, Homiletics, Drew, 1930-33; professor, Homiletics and Comprehensive Scholarship, Drew, 1933-37; professor, Homiletics and the Christian Criticism of Life, 1937 to date; dean, Drew Theological Seminary since 1934; president, Detroit Council of Chs., 1926-28; vice-president, Religious Education Ass'n., 1926-28; Soc. Bibl. Lit. and Exegesis; Chicago Soc. Bibl. Research; Nat. Voters' League (dir.); Soc. Midland Authors; president, Religious Education Council of Canada, 1929-30; pub., *Athanasius, the Hero,* 1906; *The Lure of Books,* 1911; *The Theology of a Preacher,* 1912; *The Men of the Gospels,* 1913; *The Quest for Wonder,* 1915; *In the Valley of Decision,* 1916; *The Man of Power,* 1916; *The Little Old Lady,* 1917; *Living Book in a Living Age,* 1918; *The Significance of the Protestant Reformation,* 1918; *The Clean Sword,* 1918; *The Productive Beliefs* (Cole lectures, Vanderbilt Univ.), 1919; *Flying Over London,* 1919; *The Eyes of Faith,* 1920; *The Opinions of John Clearfield,* 1921; *Life and History,* 1922; *The Strategy of the Devotional Life,* 1922; *The Inevitable Book,* 1922; *A Little Book of Sermons,* 1922; *Twelve Merry Fishermen,* 1923; *Synthetic Christianity* (Merrick lectures, Ohio Wesleyan Univ.), 1923; *The Imperial Voice,* 1924; *The Lion in His Den,* 1925; *Evangelical Humanism* (Fernley lecture, Lincoln, England), 1925;

Adventures in the Minds of Men,
1927; *Imperishable Dreams,* 1929; *The
Artist and the Critic* (Samuel Harris
lectures, Bangor Theol. Sem.), 1930;
Personality and Science (Ayer lectures,
Colgate-Rochester Div. Sch.), 1930;
The University of Experience, 1932;
Vital Control (Forest Essays), 1934;
The Church and Civilization, 1934;
The Great Evangel (Sam P. Jones
lectures, Emory Univ.), 1936; *The
Civilized Mind* (Forest Essays), 1937;
Free Men (Forest Essays), 1939; *The
Christian Criticism of Life,* 1941;
Adventures in Understanding (Fred
J. Cato Lecture, General Conf. of
Methodist Church of Australasia),
1941; *Patterns of the Mind,* 1942;
editorial bd., *Religion in Life,* and
editorial com. of *Intercollegian* and
Far Horizons; lecturer on theol., lit.
and philos. topics; sent to Great
Britain to interpret the moral and
spiritual aims of the war, by the
Lindgren foundation of Northwestern
Univ., 1918; writer, Sunday School
Lesson Expositions; contr. ed., *The
Christian Advocate;* editor and contr.
to *"Whither Christianity,"* 1929; bd.
of sponsors, *Christianity and Crisis;*
exec. com., Federal Council of Chs. of
Christ in America; bd. of publication,
Christendom; bd. of publication, The
Methodist Ch.; pres., Ass'n. of Metho-
dist Theological Schs.; mem., Ameri-
can Soc. of Ch. History; Pi Gamma
Mu; National Ass'n. of Biblical
Instructors; English-Speaking Union;
Clergy Ass'n of New York and
Neighborhood; Acad. of Political Sci-
ence; Ohio Soc. of New York, Kappa
Chi; Sigma Chi; address, Drew Forest,
Madison, N. J.

JAMES STRONG

A.B., A.M., S.T.D., LL.D.

Professor of Exegetical Theology, 1868-1894.

JAMES STRONG was the first full professor of the "Big
Five"—Strong, Crooks, Upham, Miley, and Buttz—who
for nearly a quarter of a century constituted Drew's
famous team of teachers, and in some respects he was
unique among his able and brilliant colleagues, since
he was a layman among ministers. In fact he had commenced to study medicine before he took up "the theological languages." Even after he had graduated vale-
dictorian at Wesleyan University in 1844 he had organized a railroad company and built the line; had been
mayor of his home town on Long Island, and had taught
Biblical literature and been acting president of the

short-lived Troy University. But John McClintock recognized a scholar when he saw him, and when in 1868 John Wesley Lindsay of Genesee Wesleyan Seminary declined his election to the chair of Exegetical Theology in the Drew set-up, he offered it to this versatile layman. It was no leap in the dark. He had already measured Strong's caliber and worked with him as joint-editor of the monumental *Cyclopedia of Biblical, Theological and Ecclesiastical Literature,* better known as "McClintock and Strong." (In fact the senior editor's untimely death left the major part of the burden of that vast undertaking on the competent shoulders of his partner.) In Drew Seminary Dr. Strong had found his element. As Dr. J. M. Buckley once said of him, "He knew something about everything and he knew everything about the things he gave himself to." He gave everything to his job of knowing the Scriptures and opening their content to the young men in his classes. Fifteen years before he came to Drew a powerful article from his pen had appeared in *The Christian Advocate* of Dec. 22, 1853, on the imperative need of a training school for Methodist preachers in the vicinity of New York City. This was before Garrett and Boston had come into being, and at a time when the tide of Methodist opinion set strongly against such blasphemous innovations as would seem to substitute "man-made" preachers for "God-made" itinerants like Francis Asbury, Jesse Lee and Peter Cartwright. The editor, Dr. Bond, was sharply rebuked by many correspondents for admitting such a corrupting article to his columns; and one writer sought to break its force by ridicule, suggesting that the proposed school be named "Central Salvation Seminary," and that one teacher should have the degree of "P.P.R."—professor of Plenty of Religion.

But Dr. Strong laughed last! He not only lived to see the school established along the lines which he had laid down, but he enjoyed the supreme satisfaction of being a part of it and contributing to it of his own extraordinary enthusiasm and abundant learning. His achievements enhanced its reputation from the first. In those days American Methodist scholarship was under suspicion. The older churches, not too friendly to this upstart sect, were inclined to view its literary productions somewhat as the English of an earlier day had regarded all literature of the New World. "Who reads an American book!" might have had an echo here in "Who values a Methodist book?" So, when the Harpers (a good Methodist house in those days) published the great *Cyclopedia,* bearing the names of two Methodists, it must have been a shock to some people in Cambridge, Princeton and New Haven to learn that its compilers, John McClintock and James Strong, were both professors in the infant Methodist seminary in New Jersey which Daniel Drew had set up—a Nazareth out of which no good thing could be expected to come. And in that procreant brain of James Strong another great idea was germinating. He would compile a Biblical Concordance which should displace all other concordances, even Alexander Cruden's masterpiece. It should contain every occurrence of every word in the English Scriptures, not excepting adverbs, prepositions and articles, even down to "a," "an" and "the." Furthermore, it should enable the student, however unskilled in the Biblical tongues, to identify the Hebrew or Greek original of each English word, and to know its pronunciation and its definition. It should be absolutely exhaustive, as its name *Strong's Exhaustive Concordance* implies, and such it must forever remain as long as the Holy Book is read and studied. This is James Strong's monument. It tells of his inventive faculty, his organizing mind, his boundless energy, and his capacity for unremitting toil. "At night in his library," says Dr. Buckley, "he worked like a plow-horse, but in the lecture room he was as frisky as a colt. No one ever went to sleep in his classes unless he was out of health or an imbecile." Indeed he was so full of matter on every subject that wily students were known to take advantage of his eagerness to impart information. Early in a recitation period some one would innocently ask a question which would set the professor off on an excursion which not only afforded immediate interest and information, but which consumed time that he might otherwise have employed in asking awkward questions of students who were inadequately prepared with answers. Outside of his special field—the Bible, its languages, literature and lands—he indulged several minor interests, notably hymnology, on which he was probably the first to lecture at Drew. He traveled much in Europe and the Holy Land. His publications were numerous, beside the *Cyclopedia* and the *Concordance,* by which he will be longest remembered. Nor was he wholly a bookman. He lived in no ivory tower. He took an active part in reform movements in the denomination. With his friend Dr. Crooks he worked with energy and persistence as a leader in the movement to win for Methodist laymen a voice in the government of the church. And when victory was won and laymen took their seats in the General Conference of 1872, the Newark Conference elected him as one of its first lay delegates.

Such was the second member of the "Big Five," a link between the founders and the builders of Drew. Enthusiastic, scholarly, vivacious, industrious, a personality which no student could ever forget, a man of letters whose name will be known as long as interest in the English Bible endures.

Physically Dr. Strong was above medium stature, with a well-knit frame. His movements were agile and graceful. His countenance was pleasing, though for the most part concealed by an abundant growth of silky hair, which in his later years was a long beard, wavy, somewhat forked and snow-white. A picturesque and arresting personality.

JAMES STRONG: b. New York, N. Y., Aug. 14, 1822; Lowville N. Y. Acad.; A.B., Wesleyan Univ., 1844; A.M., 1847; S.T.D., 1856; LL.D., 1881; m. Marcia A. Dustin, July 18, 1845; teacher, Languages, Troy Conf. Acad., 1844-46; justice of the peace, Flushing, N. Y., 1848-52; president, Flushing Railroad Co., 1852-55; president, Corporation of the Village of Flushing, 1855; professor, Biblical Literature and acting president, Troy Univ., 1858-63; professor Exegetical Theology, Drew, 1868-94; del., Gen. Conf., 1872; mem., Anglo-American Bible Revision Comm., 1871-81; mem., Palestine Exploration Soc., 1872; pub., *English Harmony and Exposition of the Gospels*, 1852; *Manual of the Gospels*, 1853; *Sunday School Question Books* (5 vols.), 1854-60; *Greek Harmony of the Gospels*, 1854; *Epitome of Greek Grammar*, 1856; *Epitome of Hebrew Grammar*, 1857; *Theological Compend for Advanced Scholars*, 1859; *Epitome of Chaldee Grammar*, 1869; *A Year with Christ in the Old Testament*, 1869; *Tables of Biblical Chronology*, 1875; *Greek in a Nutshell*, 1876; *An Explication and Vindication of Solomon's Song*, 1889; *The Student's Commentary—The Book of Psalms*, edited by Dr. H. A. Buttz, 1896; *Doctrine of a Future Life*, 1892; *Sketches of Jewish Life in the First Century*, 1892; *Exhaustive Concordance of the Bible*, 1895; editor, (with J. McClintock) *Cyclopedia of Biblical, Theological, and Ecclesiastical Literature*, 1867-86; *Daniel and Esther*, (Lange's Commentary), 1876; Stier's *Words of the Lord Jesus*, 1863; contr., relig. periodicals; d. Aug. 7, 1894.

The Rev. DANIEL PARISH KIDDER

A.B., A.M., D.D., LL.D.
Professor of Practical Theology, 1871-1881.

DR. DANIEL PARISH KIDDER had been a member of the original faculty of Garrett Biblical Institute for fifteen years, when in 1871 President Foster invited him to come to Madison to take the chair of Practical Theology, left vacant by the death of President McClintock. He was then forty-one years old and had made a distinguished name for himself in the church. Born in western New York of the old New England stock, he early showed intellectual gifts and was teaching in public schools at the age of 14. Though his family had no liking for Methodism, the lad attended Genesee Wesleyan Seminary at Lima, New York, where he was soundly converted and joined the Methodist Episcopal Church. After a few months in Hamilton College, to please his parents, he transferred to Wesleyan University, graduating in 1836. He had entered Genesee Conference on trial, when in 1838, Bishop Waugh sent him to Brazil as a missionary. His two years' sojourn bore fruit in two notable volumes on Brazil, which contained the best account of these "good neighbors" that had been printed in English. Two pastorates in Paterson and Trenton were highly successful, when interrupted by his election in 1844 as secretary of the Sunday School Union. He held this office for three quadrenniums, and by unrelenting industry succeeded in raising in some measure the low standards of the old fashioned Sunday School. Some of his published opinions reveal his wise analysis of the institution and cast foregleams along the line of progress followed by his brilliant successor, John H. Vincent. Meanwhile, the Garrett Biblical Institute was beginning to take form, and from its inception Dr. Kidder's counsel was constantly sought by Eliza Garrett's legal adviser and by President Dempster, who sought him for the faculty. Here he had a notable career as a teacher and counselor of young men. It is not strange that Dr. Foster, who had known him intimately during his residence in Evanston as president of Northwestern University, should turn to him to take McClintock's vacant chair. Conditions, however, as they developed at Madison were in some respects unfavorable to the highest success. Within a year President Foster had become Bishop Foster, to be replaced by a new president, John F. Hurst, a much younger man and a comparative stranger. Before the new order at Drew was well established, came the Wall Street hurricane of '73 which swept away the Drew endowment and left the Seminary treasury bare. President Hurst threw all his strength into the Herculean task of making good the loss. He unloaded upon Dr. Kidder the great mass of executive detail which he was unable to handle. Perhaps this produced a certain friction between the two good men. Moreover the new professor had moved into the house which Mr. Drew had built for the McClintock family. President Hurst regarded it as the "presidential" residence and acted upon that theory somewhat to the discomfort of its occupant, who, however, gracefully accepted the situation and effected the exchange of domiciles. Yet none of these things disturbed the calm dignity of Dr. Kidder, though it is probable that the added executive responsibilities and the general anxiety on the campus as to where the next month's salary, if any, would come from, did not tend to make his classroom work any more efficient. Yet many of his students have testified to the value of his instruction and the kindly interest and sympathy with which he entered into their personal problems. His own missionary experience in South America, though brief, intensified his interest in missions and in young men from the foreign field and in those students who were preparing for foreign service. When he retired in 1881 and became secretary of the Board of Education, President Buttz said that by his books and teachings he had "virtually founded the department of practical theology in the Methodist Episcopal Church." Dignified and somewhat formal in manner, he was a stickler for etiquette, and his students used to tell many amusing stories about his politeness, even to vagrant domestic animals which crossed his path. But no one discounted his thoroughness as an instructor. This student comment could be multiplied many times: "As a teacher he was painstaking and thorough; his pupils must not only understand, but remember; he was a driller."

(See *Biography of the Rev. Daniel Parish Kidder, D.D., LL.D.,* by his son-in-law, Rev. G. E. Strobridge, D.D., New York, 1894.)

DANIEL PARISH KIDDER: b. Darien, N. Y., Oct. 18, 1815; Hamilton Coll., 1833-34; A.B., Wesleyan Univ., 1836; A.M., 1839; D.D., 1855; McKendree Coll., 1851; LL.D, Grant Memorial Univ., 1883; m. (1) Cynthia H. Russell, 1836, m. (2) Harriett Smith, 1842; entered Genesee Conf., 1836; pastor, Rochester, N. Y., 1836-37; missionary, Brazil, 1837-41; New Jersey Conf., 1841; Paterson, N. J., 1841-43; Trenton, N. J., 1843-44; corr. sec'y, Sunday School Union, 1844-56; professor, Practical Theology, Drew, 1871-81; librarian, Drew, 1872-80; sec'y, Board of Education, Methodist Episcopal Church, 1880-87; del., Gen. Conf., 1852, 1868; mem., Centenary Methodist Comm., 1866; mem., Evangelical Alliance, 1873; pub., *Mormonism and the Mormons,* 1842; *Sketches of Residence and Travels in Brazil,* 1845; *Senior Classes in Sunday Schools,* 1851; *A Treatise on Homiletics, designed to illustrate The True Theory and Practice of Preaching the Gospel,* 1864; *The Christian Pastorate; its Character, Responsibilities, and Duties,* 1871; *Helps to Prayer;* translated from the Portuguese, *Demonstration of the Necessity of Abolishing a Constrained Clerical Celibacy,* 1844; editor, *Catechisms of the Methodist Episcopal Church,* Nos. 1, 2, 3, 1852; *Sunday School Advocate,* 1844-56; Sunday sch. books, 1844-56; co-author, *Brazil and the Brazilians,* 1857; contr., Kiddle and Schem's *Cyclopedia of Education,* and *McClintock and Strong's Cyclopedia;* relig. periodicals; d. July 29, 1891.

JOHN MILEY

A.B., A.M., DD., LL.D.

Professor, Systematic Theology, 1873-95.

A PORTRAIT OF JOHN MILEY still hangs in the Systematic Theology Seminar Room at Drew. It is eminently fitting that this should be so. Of the men who taught theology at Drew for the first fifty years of its history, none was more distinctively the systematic theologian. Miley did not have the range of scholarship of McClintock, nor yet the verbal felicity of Foster, and he was certainly far from the sheer vitality, brilliance, and originality which were to come with his immediate successor, Olin A. Curtis. But he brought to the teaching of theology at Drew a strength and solidity of mind which expressed themselves in his "system" and still remain its characteristic marks.

The portrait is always a surprise to those who had known Miley only through his writings. These are severe in style, legalistic in temper: everywhere they bespeak the logician, interested much more in the coherence of the argument than in literary grace and finish. There are pages in both his *Systematic Theology* and his *Atonement* which are drier than dry: they are nothing less than arid. Yet by every testimony, the man must have had qualities which the books fail to reveal. The mind of Miley may be in the books, but his heart and soul are in the portrait. The face is a benign face. This is no befuddled Savonarola; no dour John Knox; no dictatorial Calvin. One can well believe that these eyes often twinkled with a quiet humor, and that the classroom sessions where this man presided were not always overweighted with solemnity.

In actual fact, the deductions from the portrait have ample support in the traditions that have gathered around the name of this man, and in the memories of him cherished by aging residents of Madison and by the few students—all too few—still living, who sat in his classes. He lived with his two daughters in what is now known as "The Rogers' Dormitory" (how are the mighty fallen!). One can almost see for oneself the sturdy figure, clad in stormy weather in a greatcoat still further supplemented by an Inverness cape, emerging from the front door and walking with measured step to the classroom in Mead Hall. He served as the campus clock, a Drew Kant in respect of punctuality. "When we saw him crossing the campus, we knew the hour for class had arrived. No watch was necessary. He was practically never absent from class, and he was never late."

The story lingers of the huge enjoyment with which he watched from behind a convenient tree a bashful new student from a Maryland farm, uncouth, bewhiskered, and of unsuspected strength, turn in wrath upon a group of three tormentors, throw one of them to the ground, deposit the other two on the prostrate form, seat himself atop of the squirming pile, and roar out his determination to make jelly of the lot if they did not "leave him be." One likes that story—and suspects that the amused professor perceived a somewhat concrete illustration of his favorite theme of "distributive" justice!

Miley was true to a theological tradition in his love of walking. *Solvitur ambulando.* He was observant of Nature's changing moods, with somewhat of a Wordsworthian eye, and those who knew him testify that he as he walked he gathered richly "the harvest of a quiet eye." But his chief relaxation was quoits. It is a persistent legend that he was the best quoits-player on the campus. He had an uncanny skill in scoring "ringers," and this in spite of the fact that he invariably played in his long "Prince Albert" coat—his one sad violation of quoits history! One confesses with much less pride that he also played croquet, although it is a satisfaction to know that he played it less expertly than his colleague, Samuel F. Upham. Skill in croquet is no masculine virtue: its implications are lawns, ladies, and leisure. But skill in quoits is another matter: the game is redolent of the lusty virility of pioneer days. For the understanding mind, the clang of the horse-shoe against the stake echoes "embattled farmers." It brings up visions of horny-handed men who loved the feel of iron, visions of the shod hooves of great horses, of the ringing blows of the blacksmith's forge. From such stock came John Miley, and with such men he played as a boy in Ohio.

Report declares him a sympathetic teacher, almost maternally patient with the student who went haltingly in his way. He frequently called for verbal recitations on dictated notes. He refused to accept as final a student's "Not prepared, sir." Instead, he began to ask questions, says Henry C. Whitney, in a way that suggested the answer to even the least discerning. "When the *dual* recitation was finished, the Doctor would smilingly observe, 'There, I thought that you and I together could manage this—for one of us, you see, was prepared.' "

One would never suspect from Miley's books that he was either a very interesting or a very inspiring preacher. But here again the tradition belies the inference. No less a critic than James M. Buckley used to put him in the same class with Bishop Simpson as a "great occasion" preacher. He served a number of conspicuous churches before coming to Drew. His increasing absorption in abstract thinking tended to weaken his pulpit power, but S. G. Ayres recalls a baccalaureate sermon by Miley on the subject, "The Supreme Excellence of Jesus Christ," and he says of it: "It was one of the greatest sermons I ever heard. He took us from height to height, and finally brought us to the very throne of God."

Dr. Curtis regarded Miley's two volumes as one of the most substantial and well-knit statements of the Arminian theology produced in the nineteenth century, and required his own students to master them. For years they were in the Conference Course of Study. Their choice for this purpose was a deep satisfaction to Miley. "It is a great honor," he said, "to be selected as the theologian of the Church." In his treatment of the Atonement, he departed somewhat from the usual Methodist view. He made a classic statement of the so-called Governmental or Rectoral theory. The theory was first broached by Hugo Grotius, and had been taken over by Arminius. It had a place in both Anglican and Wesleyan theology in the eighteenth century, but it can hardly be said to loom largely in the teaching of Wesley himself. The Arminianism of early Methodist theology is seen rather in the emphasis on free grace and on the universality of the Atonement than in any Rectoralism. Undoubtedly the legalistic cast of Miley's own mind is one chief explanation of his attraction to the emphasis on Moral Government and its necessities characteristic of the thinking of Grotius, himself a great international jurist.

None will question that John Miley has a secure place among the stalwarts of American theology of whatsoever school. He stands with Hodge and Strong and Warfield, with Little and Raymond and Sheldon, with Dwight and Channing and Bushnell, and they have no occasion to be ashamed of his company. In respect of loyalty to Scripture, evangelical insight, and structural coherence, he worthily perpetuates the tradition established by the early English Methodist theologians, Benson, Watson, and Pope, with whom, indeed, he is strangely one in spirit and in mental style.

The few remaining students who heard Miley's last lecture will still tell you about it, and will insist on its complete appropriateness. He died the next day, which is perhaps the chief reason for the lingering memory of that last session. He had lectured on "The Angels of God"—and shortly he heard the sound of their coming, and was not afraid. The modern theologian would probably prefer to close his career, if he could have the choice, with a theme upon which he could speak with more certainty; but given Miley's time and place and the accepted view of the universe, and it is easy to understand why his students should have regarded that last lecture as at once a climax, a premonition, and an assurance.

E. L.

JOHN MILEY: b. Butler Co., O., Dec. 25, 1813; A.B., Augusta Coll., ——, A.M., ——; D.D., Ohio Wesleyan Univ., 1858, LL.D., 1881; m. Olive C. Patterson; entered Ohio Conf., 1838; pastor, Batavia, O., 1838-39; Western, Cincinnati, O., 1839-40; Hamilton, O., 1840-41; Chillicothe, O., 1841-43; Columbus, O., 1843-45; Zanesville, O., 1845-47; Wesley Chapel, Cincinnati, O., 1847-48; Wesley Female Coll., 1848-50; Morris Chapel, Cincinnati, O., 1850-52; New York East Conf., 1852; Pacific St., Brooklyn, N. Y., 1852-54; South Second St., Brooklyn, N. Y., 1854-56; Sands St., Brooklyn, N. Y., 1856-58; Danbury, Conn., 1858-60; Forsyth St., New York, N. Y., 1860-62; Bridgeport, Conn., 1862-64; New Rochelle, N. Y., 1864-66; New York Conf., 1866; First, Newburgh, N. Y., 1866-69; Sing Sing, N. Y., 1869-72; Saint Paul's, Peekskill, N. Y., 1872-73; professor, Systematic Theology, Drew, 1873-95; fraternal del., Gen. Conf.,

Methodist Episcopal Church, South, 1887; del., Gen. Conf., 1864, 1872, 1876, 1888, 1892; del., Centennial Methodist Conf., 1884; pub., *Class-* *meetings,* 1893; *The Atonement in Christ,* 1880; *Systematic Theology,* 1893; contr., relig. periodicals; d. Dec. 13, 1895.

The Rev. GEORGE RICHARD CROOKS
A.B., A.M., D.D., LL.D.

Professor of Historical Theology, 1880-1897.

DR. CROOKS would have been a charter member of the faculty if Dr. McClintock and Mr. Drew had had their way. For he had won his spurs as a scholar and leader of men, and was hand in glove with McClintock, whom he had known from boyhood in Philadelphia and with whom he had collaborated on a series of classical text-books when they were colleagues on the faculty of Dickinson College. But in 1867 Dr. Crooks was in his editorial shirtsleeves in New York, fighting one of the fiercest ecclesiastical battles in Methodist history. Eventually victory wrought a revolution in the polity of the church. For it broke the ministerial monopoly of power by admitting laymen—male laymen—to membership in the General Conference. (It took another fight, a generation later, to "get the women in.") Scholar that he was, he had proved himself a first-class fighting man by his editorship of *The Methodist,* in New York, the doughty unofficial rival of the official weekly—*The Christian Advocate,* which stood for the status quo, and took a sound beating. The editor had already worked his way up to the first rank in the ministry, and had written several books of recognized worth, while serving pastorates in Philadelphia, Wilmington, New York East and New York Conferences, when, like the poet Whittier.

"He left the Muses' haunts
    To turn the crank of an opinion-mill."
The battle won, he returned to the pastorate, where he
found abundant employment for his rare pulpit gifts.
But, no sooner was a teaching chair at Drew vacated by
the call of Dr. Hurst to the episcopal office in 1880, than
he was invited to take his place as professor of Historical
Theology. His friends McClintock, Nadal and Foster
were gone, but James Strong, who had fought by his
side in the laymen's battle, was still at Madison. This
was Dr. Crooks' rightful niche. Twenty-five years before
as a young man he had supported John Dempster and
other forward-looking men in their struggle to legalize
the establishment of schools like Drew where young
Methodist men might be trained for the ministry. And
now his opportunity had come to put all his acquisitions
of ripe experience and life-long study into just such an
institution. He had had full teaching practice at Dickinson; the text-books which he had helped to prepare
showed that he had mastered the science of imparting
knowledge; fruitful years in charge of churches small
and great had given him intimate acquaintance with
the conditions under which his pupils would have to do
their work when "the great iron wheel" of the itiner-
ancy commenced to revolve. Moreover, he was a conspicuous figure in Methodism; not a "has been," but
mature, vital, vigorous, at the very top of his powers.
Everything that he had been he could put into this
teaching job. This he proceeded to do. And he had
the time of his life. As a lecturer he was the farthest
possible removed from dullness. He is described as
"painstaking, conscientious, energetic and successful."
Though in his 60s he had not settled down to a fixed
set of opinions. Of a progressive, even radical temper,

he kept his mind open toward the newer movements of thought, read with discrimination all the newer literature in his field, and kept his pupils in touch with the times. He was anything but the drillmaster type of pedagogue. One says, "He had a rare gift of imparting knowledge *and* inspiration"—gifts that do not always occur in pairs! His lectures smelled neither of the lamp nor of the barrel. They were constantly worked over and freshened by contact with new sources and by the maturing of the teacher's own reflections. The ardor with which he toiled up to the very last to increase his own stock of knowledge reminds one of Browning's "Grammarian"—

> So, with the throttling hands of death at strife,
>   Ground he at grammar;
> Still, through the rattle, parts of speech were rife:
>   While he could stammer
> He settled *Hoti's* business—let it be!—
>   Properly based *Oun*—
> Gave us the doctrine of the enclitic *De*,
>   Dead from the waist down.

In these years also he found time to write the life of Bishop Simpson and to edit his sermons. Before he came to Drew he had produced his fine *Life of McClintock*. The vision of what his bosom friend the great first president would be doing, if he were still at the helm, must often have risen before Dr. Crooks as he walked beneath these oaks and looked into the faces of the earnest youth in his lecture room. He could not help dwelling upon the pioneer's plans for the development of the school, and he was continually suggesting ways in which the lofty ideals of the founders might be realized and suited to the changing conditions. Can you not see him now? A short man, inclined to stoutness, ruddy of countenance, a sort of John Bull; but gracious in manner, an enthusiast for his church, but not blind to its faults, and doing his best, as long as life lasted, to train its ministers to be worthy of the high vocation wherewith they were called.

GEORGE RICHARD CROOKS: b. Philadelphia, Pa., Feb. 3, 1822; A.B., Dickinson Coll., 1840; A.M., 1843; D.D., 1857; LL.D., 1865; m. Susan Frances Emory, July 10, 1946; entered Philadelphia Conf., 1843; principal, Dickinson Coll. Grammar Sch., 1843-46; adjunct professor, Latin and Greek, Dickinson Coll., 1846-48; pastor, Dauphin, Pa., 1848-50; Pottstown, Pa., 1850-51; Philadelphia, Pa., Trinity, 1851-53; Philadelphia, Pa., Saint John's, 1853-55; Wilmington, Del., Saint Paul's, 1855-57; New York East Conf., 1857; New York, N. Y., Seventeenth St., 1857-59; Brooklyn, N. Y., Washington Ave., 1859-61; Brooklyn, N. Y., Sands St., 1861-63; New York, N. Y., Seventeenth St., 1863-66; Flushing, N. Y., 1866-69; Mamaroneck, N. Y., 1869-70; supernumerary, 1870-76; New York Conf., 1876; North Tarrytown, N. Y., 1876- 79; Peekskill, N. Y., Saint Paul's, 1879-80; professor, Historical Theology, Drew, 1880-97; del., Gen. Conf., 1856; mem., Methodist Centenary Comm., 1866; Ecumenical Meth. Conf., 1881; Centennial Methodist Conf., 1884; Anglo-American Comm. of Revision; American Church History Soc.; American Acad. of Theol.; New Jersey Historical Soc.; pub., *Butler's Analogy, with Analysis and Notes*, 1852; *Life and Letters of Dr. John McClintock*, 1876; *Sermons of Bishop Simpson*, 1885; *Life of Bishop Simpson*, 1890; *The Story of the Christian Church*; co-author, *First Book in Latin*, 1846; *First Book in Greek*, 1847; *Latin-English School Lexicon*, 1858; *Theological Encyclopedia and Methodology*, 1884; ed. with J. F. Hurst, Biblical and Theological Library, 1875-1895; editor, *The Methodist*, 1860-75; d. Feb. 2, 1897.

The Rev. SAMUEL FOSTER UPHAM
A.B., A.M., D.D., LL.D.
Professor of Practical Theology, 1881-1904.

DR. SAMUEL F. UPHAM, who succeeded Professor Daniel P. Kidder to the chair of Practical Theology in Drew Theological Seminary, for more than twenty-three years (1881 to 1904) served with distinction in his department, training men to preach the Gospel of Jesus

Christ, drawing upon his own experience as a successful preacher and pastor for twenty-five years in New England and New York. Judged by present academic standards he was not a great scholar, but he had by inheritance and training, coupled with a rich and bouyant religious experience, those gifts of wit and practical wisdom that made him a great teacher in the art of making sermons and in the techniques of delivery. He knew from experience in the rural field as well as in the great cities the various kinds of work the preacher had to do and the moral and spiritual struggles he had to face in the pastorate.

He had a remarkable gift of illustrating the lessons he wished to impress upon the members of his classes, or the audience he was addressing, whether from the pulpit or from the platform. His repertoire of wholesome stories, brimming over with wit and wisdom, was inexhaustible. The movement of his eyebrows, the twitching of his lips, and the swing of his arm, all answered to the quick activity of the mind and ebullient wit of his soul. So he became one of the greatest pulpit orators of his day, as he was one of the ablest public speakers upon the rostrum of a political gathering.

He was an ardent member of the Republican party and was a popular speaker in every Presidential campaign while he was a professor at Drew.

His passing to the realm of the immortals, in 1904, left a lonesome place in Drew Forest, and a deep sense of loss in the hearts of the Drew men who had sat in his classes, and learned so many lessons of how to preach and practice the Gospel, he so greatly loved and defended. He kept us alert to the dangers confronting us in modern trends in theology and morality.

He told this story of old Father Taylor, of Boston,

who used to keep the boys straight in their theology. One Monday morning at the preachers meeting a young theolog came up to Father Taylor .and said:—"Father Taylor, science has proven there can be no physical resurrection of the human body. There is only a limited amount of phosphorus in the earth, and it takes a certain amount of it to make a human body; at the time of the final resurrection there will not be enough phosphorus to make bodies for those who have died—from Adam to now—let alone those who will live and die from now until the judgment day; therefore, there can be no physical resurrection of the body." Father Taylor replied—"Young man, that argument does not worry me in the least. The good Book says, 'The dead in Christ shall rise first'—we Christians will be all right; you infidels will have to scurry around for your own phosphorus."

His wit and wisdom were at high tide when he criticized the senior's sermons in chapel. I well remember when Arthur D. Berry of the class of 1898 had preached from the great text, at the basis of Calvinism, in Romans, which Dr. Henry A. Buttz used to *exegete* into an Arminian text—when he, Dr. Berry, lambasted Calvinism throughout the sermon. Dr. Rogers, in commenting, said he did not like the sermon, as everybody knew that Calvinism was dead; then why should anyone preach against it? When Dr. Upham, who was presiding that morning, took his turn in criticism he said—"I liked that sermon of Brother Berry's. My father would sit up nights to hate Calvinism! Did Dr. Rogers say Calvinism is dead? Well, so much the better, for I believe in punishment after death!" There was great laughter on the part of students and faculty, and none enjoyed the fun more than Dr. Rogers himself.

Dr. Upham was quick to make use of wit in debate. One Monday morning at the Preachers Meeting in New York, Dr. Wm. F. Anderson and Dr. Beattys, then both young liberals in theology, just out of Drew, challenged some of the conservative statements of a dear old gentleman from Princeton who had read a long paper, and these young radicals were rebuked by some of the stalwarts of those days. The young men held their ground and said, among other things, that certain things in the creeds of the church should be rewritten, and the younger generation of preachers should be allowed to think for themselves etc.

Dr. Upham arose and eased the tension by saying: "Methodism was born in freedom of thought. Who objects to Brother Anderson and Brother Beattys having a thinking spell whenever they want to? I agree with them that the creeds should be rewritten—but exactly as they were the first time."

He believed in extemporaneous preaching with thorough preparation. He was not opposed to having students write out their sermons from "a to izzard" as we used to say; but he insisted that the student should become so familiar with his sermon that he could follow the trend of thought it contained as easily as one could find his way to the post office.

He warned against plagiarism, but declared that originality consisted in gleaning from many fields of thought, grinding the grain, kneading the dough, and baking your own loaf to share with the hearers hungry for the living word. He said, if a preacher believed that all he had to do was to open his mouth and let the Lord fill it—"He will fill it with wind if you don't study."

He believed a sermon should have *points*. His general pattern for a sermon was; an introduction; several leading points, with one or more subsidiary ideas and illustrations; and then, the conclusion with what he called the "arousements." He humorously illustrated the framework of a sermon by an analogy, "It should have points like an old horse on whose hips you could hang your hat." But he added—"You must have plenty of meat on the bones, or the people will not take it."

He was himself an example for excellence of what he taught. He read volumes of great sermons and essays on preaching, and kept abreast of important public affairs and current events; yet he maintained a unique originality in his lectures, his sermons, and in his platform addresses.

He illustrated how to be original in sermonizing, as follows:

A man at the foundry designs a new original cookstove. He gathers iron from many sources, some old plowshares, some old horseshoes, the scrap iron from old discarded stoves, etc., and melts them all in the blast furnace, and pours the liquid iron into a new mould of his designing, and puts together the frame, the plates, the doors, the fire grate and the oven racks; and then he has an original stove. So the preacher must gather thoughts and words and great ideas from many sources and fuse them in the crucible of his own brain by emotional thought, and then make for the congregation an original sermon.

Dr. Upham was also a master in the art of sermon delivery. He insisted on the student cultivating the grace of delivery as well as the substance and matter of the sermon. He told us we must be like a fisherman who chooses the best bait, or lure, and then casts his line with hook and bait in the most attractive way to catch the fish. I can see him now as he illustrated by his gestures, with his arms, as though he were casting a line in a New England trout stream, or lake, and then he would change his manner and say: "What would you think of a man who, impatient with his lack of luck, would suddenly smite the water with his rod and shout in an angry voice: "Dirn you! Bite!" And then he would remark to the class, "I have seen men act like that in preaching."

The men of Drew who had the privilege of sitting in his classroom four days a week for three years, imbibing and assimilating the wit and wisdom that flowed from his lips, as from a perennial fountain, have carried his line through all the earth, his words to the end of the world.

E. L. E.

SAMUEL FOSTER UPHAM: b. Duxbury, Mass., May 19, 1834; A.B., Wesleyan Univ., 1856; A.M., 1858; LL.D., 1898; D.D., Mount Union Coll., 1872; LL.D., Hamline Univ., 1889; m. Lucy Graves Smith, April 15, 1857; ord. dea., 1838; ord. eld., 1860; entered Providence Conf., 1856; pastor, Central, Taunton, Mass., 1856-58; First, Pawtucket, R. I., 1858-60; Fourth St., New Bedford, Mass., 1860-62; Bristol, R. I., 1862-64; New England Conf., 1864; Saint Paul's, Lowell, Mass., 1864-67; Winthrop St., Boston, Mass., 1870-73; Lynn Common, Lynn, Mass., 1873-76; Trinity, Springfield, Mass., 1876-79; Grace, Boston, Mass., 1879- 81; professor, Practical Theology, Drew, 1881-1904; librarian, Drew, 1881-91; del., Gen. Conf., 1880, 1888, 1896, 1900, 1904; mem., Christian Comm'n., 1862; chaplain, Mass. legislature, 1865; mem., gen. missionary com., M.E. Ch., 1882-1902; mem., Methodist Centennial Conf., 1884; sec'y., Comm. on the Constitutional Law of the Church, 1896-1900; chairman, Comm. on the Revision of the Methodist Hymnal, 1900-04; trustee, Wesleyan Univ., 1871-1904; trustee, Wilbraham Acad. (Mass.), 1877-1904; mem., New England Soc., N. Y.; d. Oct. 5, 1904.

The Rev. ROBERT WILLIAM ROGERS
A.B., Ph.D., Litt.D., D.D., LL.D.

Professor of Hebrew and Old Testament Exegesis, 1893-1929; Professor Emeritus and Lecturer on History of the Ancient Orient, 1929-1930.

ROBERT ROGERS, age 29, a tall, slender, sharp-featured, thin-lipped schoolman, came into the Drew faculty just as the hoary patriarch, James Strong, was succumbing to the infirmities of age. It marked the beginning of a new era. The "Big Five," who had reigned in the Forest for a quarter of a century, was breaking up. The *novus homo* had a promising pedigree, biologically and academically. The Rogers family was already remarkable for the number of educators on its rolls. The latest—and greatest—showed an awakened interest in the study of Hebrew when a mere boy in Philadelphia. This is Dr. Rogers' account of the incident which determined his course of life. Though the story has been told before, it must be told again and again, and in his own words:

"When I was a boy, not yet 15, I read in *Self-Culture,* a volume by Prof. John Stuart Blackie of Edinburgh, that Job in the Old Testament was the greatest book in all literature. I determined to read it for myself, and can remember to this day the Sunday afternoon when I lay on the floor in my father's house and read the book of Job through to the end. There was much that was beyond me, and that a second and third reading failed to clear up. Someone told me that what I needed was a commentary. So I went to Leary's second hand bookstore and bought Lange's learned *Commentary on Job*. But I had not read very far in it before I came against words from the Hebrew with which of course I could do nothing. Undismayed I sought help from the neighboring Lutheran minister. This man admitted that he had lost all the Hebrew he had ever had, but loaned me his grammar, lexicon and Old Testament in Hebrew. With these tools I set to work to find out what was in the book of Job, that made the great Edinburgh professor characterize it as the greatest literary production of the ages. Strange that I should have begun my study of the Bible at Job instead of Genesis, but so it happened! Well, I kept at it, studying Hebrew by myself while I was preparing for college, and by the time I was ready to enter, I knew as much of Hebrew as of Latin and Greek—and I might add that I received the prize for the best entrance paper in Latin.

"From those beginnings on that Sunday afternoon when I lay on the floor, trying to comprehend the book of Job, I can trace the whole course of my life and studies. That was fifty years ago. I have never strayed from that line. My whole activity as a student has been concerned with the study of Hebrew and the related languages and the life and literature of the peoples who spoke those languages."

The boy was indeed father of the man. Hungry for learning, he was always seeking it wherever there were stores of it in the Old World. When found and mastered, he put it to service for mankind in the form of books which were true to the existing state of knowledge, and yet expressed in language which the general

PLATE III—FACULTY

ROBERT W. ROGERS, 1893-1929   CHARLES F. SITTERLY, 1892-1935
OLIN A. CURTIS, 1896-1914   JOHN A. FAULKNER, 1897-1931
EDWIN L. EARP, 1909-1938   WILLIAM J. THOMPSON, 1911-1935

public could understand and with which the most
learned could find no fault. This gift of presenting
the results of his own and others' researches into the
ancient past in such form as to engage the attention
of the public made his lectures on Assyriology as
fascinating as a tale of adventure. Not only university
audiences, but pastors in Annual Conferences, and
much more miscellaneous groups, listened eagerly as
the dim figures of the past moved before them in color,
action and life under the magic touch of the master.

Robert Rogers' graduation at the University of
Pennsylvania was only the beginning. He had heard
of a new fountain of knowledge, and promptly joined
the select body of ambitious young scholars who
flocked to Johns Hopkins for advanced study. Before
he was 26 he had been teaching the Biblical languages
and Semitic history at Haverford and Dickinson. Not
yet 30, he was nominated with others for the chair
which Dr. Strong had filled since 1868, and—wonder
of wonders!—he was elected over the veteran nominees.
Within two years he was off for Germany to delve deeper
into things Semitic. There he earned his doctorate at
Leipzig, possibly the first Methodist to qualify in that
renowned center of learning. Later he found Oxford
more congenial, and became a familiar figure in the
Bodleian; St. John's College elected him a life member,
and he spent many summers in its cloisters. These
summer sojourns were not vacations! British Orientalists began to recognize that this young American
scholar was an indefatigable worker, and that he had set
himself certain definite and heavy literary tasks for
which he was preparing. His books on Oriental history
began to attract attention on both sides of the Atlantic.
He was elected to learned societies, invited to lecture at

Harvard, Princeton and Columbia, and honored with the degree of Doctor of Literature by the University of Dublin and—most prized of all his honors—by Oxford, where he was regarded as an adopted son.   Dr. Sayce, the Oxford savant, admitted him to the circle of his personal friends, and visited him at his home in Drew Forest.

But it was Drew—not Oxford—that outranked everything in "The Rabbi's" enthusiasms.   Everything that could be done to reproduce in his students the romantic interest in the studies which possessed him he did with all his might and main.   When it became apparent that interest in the study of Hebrew was definitely on the wane among the students, the fact was to him inexplicable.   And when the subject was actually dropped from the prescribed courses of study at the seminary he felt that the glory had indeed departed.   No amount of instruction in Comparative Religions, or the Social Implications and Applications of the Gospel, or even The Christian Criticism of Life seemed to him to outweigh in their importance and value to the future minister the identical words which fell from the lips of the Hebrew sages, prophets, priests and kings.   He could never be persuaded that the change was for the better, and he continued to offer his courses in the Semitic languages long after their popularity—such as it was—had ceased.   The boys knew the "Rabbi" didn't like it, but they were proud of the "Rabbi" just the same.   Possibly it was the fact that they no longer had to take his Hebrew under compulsion, that saved the day for him.   As the years rolled by he too had become an institution, and the students gloried in him, Hebrew or no Hebrew.   With his senior colleague, the president, he had inherited much of the respect, not to say the awe, with which a previous generation had universally regarded the "Big Five." For no one could forget that in this modest scholar the Seminary possessed a man whose work had made the name of Drew known wherever pure learning was honored. His last years were shadowed by a painful and progressive illness, which aged him prematurely and for which no relief could be found. When he could no longer meet his classes and must forego his annual visits to Oxford, he asked for release from the chair which he had occupied with such distinction for 36 years, eleven more than the tenure of his predecessor, Dr. Strong. It was hoped that a period of restful retirement on his Pennsylvania farm would prolong his life and enable him to resume his activities in some degree. The trustees continued him as professor emeritus and lecturer on the History of the Ancient Orient. But his sun was setting. The loving care of his wife, who did not long survive him, ministered to him tenderly in the closing months, and he was mightily cheered by the knowledge that their son and daughter were following in his footsteps as tireless scholars and inspiring teachers.

ROBERT WILLIAM ROGERS: b. Philadelphia, Pa., Feb. 14, 1864; A.B., U. Penn., 1886; Litt. D., 1925; A.B., Johns Hopkins, 1887; Ph.D., Haverford, 1890; D.D., Wesleyan U., 1894; Ph.D., Leipzig, 1895; LL.D., Baker U., 1899; LL.D., Nebraska Wesleyan U., 1899; Litt.D., Dickinson, 1908; Litt.D., Univ., Dublin, 1914; Litt.D., Oxford, 1923; m. Ida Virginia Ziegler, June 3, 1891; ord. deacon, 1891; ord. elder, 1894; entered Philadelphia Conference, 1890; instructor, Greek and Hebrew, Haverford Coll., 1887-1889; professor English Bible and Semetic History, Dickinson Coll., 1890-1893; professor Hebrew and Old Testament Exegesis, Drew, 1893-1929; professor emeritus and lecturer on the History of the Ancient Orient, Drew, 1929-1930; New York East Conference, 1907; lecturer, Harvard Univ., 1908; lecturer Columbia Univ., summer term, 1915-1921; visiting professor, Ancient Oriental Literature, Princeton Univ., 1919-1930; life member, St. John's Coll., Oxford U.; member numerous learned societies American and foreign; F.R.G.S. London; Am. Philosophical Society; Member Congress of Orientalists, Stockholm, 1889, London, 1892, Geneva, 1894, Paris, 1897, Hamburg, 1902, Copenhagen 1908; pub. *Two Texts of Esarhaddon*, 1889; *Catalogue* of MSS, 1890; *Inscriptions of Senna-cherib*, 1893; *Outlines of the History of Early Babylonia*, 1895; *History of Babylonia and Assyria*, 1900, (re-written, 1915); *The Religion of Babylonia and Assyria*, 1909; *Cunei-form Parallels to the Old Testament*, 1912; *The Recovery of the Ancient Orient*, 1912; *History and Literature of the Hebrew People*, 1917; *Great Characters of the Old Testament*, 1920; *Old Testament Lessons—A Lectionary*, 1921; *A History of Ancient Persia from its Earliest Beginnings to the Death of Alexander the Great*, 1929; d. Chadd's Ford, Penn., Dec. 12, 1930.

The Rev. CHARLES FREMONT SITTERLY
A.B., A.M., Ph.D., S.T.D., B.D.

Adjunct-Professor of New Testament Greek and Exegesis of the English Bible, 1892-1895; Professor of Biblical Literature and Exegesis of the English Bible, 1895-1935.

IN 1892 a young preacher who had been pastor of the Methodist Church in Madison and had taken his bachelor's and doctoral degrees at Syracuse University and his B.D. at Drew was elected to a new post—the adjunct professorship of New Testament Greek and Exegesis of the English Bible. He had been preparing himself diligently for this work for several years. He had been one of Dr. Crooks' most promising pupils, and had twice won the fellowships for foreign study which had just been established. Thus he had enjoyed a year at Oxford and another in Germany all these advantages when such opportunities were almost unprecedented in the Methodist educational world. In 1891 he was married to Julia Cobb Buttz, the daughter of President Buttz, and a few months later the young couple set up their lares and penates on the campus which was to be his home and the scene of his varied activities for more than forty years. For he not only gave strict attention to his courses and to the related studies, which bore fruit in several publications, but served as secretary of the Faculty, 1895-1935, and as the president's utility man. He was always liable to be called upon in emergencies for all sorts of teaching or administrative service outside his special field. Whole-souled in his devotion to Drew and to its president, he accepted these assignments, whatever they might be, without hesitation, though at times they must have seriously interrupted his own designs for building up his department. But Dr. Sitterly practised one activity with which no outside assignment could ever interfere. That was his close sympathy with the hard beset individual student and his problems, both educational and personal. The entering junior was quick to recognize that the man to go to for advice and friendly guidance was Dr. Sitterly. There were some of the "Five Demigods" to whom he might have hesitated to open his heart, and there were other barriers, probably unintentional or even imagined, which seemed to surround other teachers. But the door to Dr. Sitterly's heart always stood ajar. Many a young man whom he helped over the hard places would confess to a peculiarly tender feeling toward him for assistance which a perplexed youth can not glean from text-books or the most erudite lectures. It is no reflection upon others or upon his own pedagogic skill, if we place emphasis on this man's Christian brotherliness as his best contribution to the common life in Drew Forest. In a generation which produced such stalwarts as Ezra Squier Tipple, William F. Anderson, Herbert Welch, John L. Nuelsen, and many others, none rated stronger than he. While these won many or all of their laurels off the campus, this promising young man really never left Drew Forest, except for graduate study abroad. His name is bracketed with that of Horace Lincoln Jacobs as holder of one of the first fellowships granted by the seminary for graduate study. Thus he was the first of a line of students who went from Drew to the British and German universities for advanced work. On that long roll of honor one may read such shining names as John L. Nuelsen, Frederick Carl Eiselen, William H. McMaster, Edwin Lewis, Clement D. Rockey, Fred G. Holloway and Malcolm S. Pitt.

There were no dull moments in Professor Sitterly's classes. He abominated the attitude of smug complacency and the willingness to use trite phrases to express age-old but ever-living truths. New students, and old as well, were often shocked by some unconventional putting of a Scriptural passage which the student was translating in a dull, commonplace way. Woe to him who tried to bluff, when unprepared! "I don't know" or "Not prepared," met with a more sympathetic response from the teacher.

"Mr. X—, what is the meaning of ——?"

"I do not know, professor."

"Correct. Thank you. Nobody knows" was Dr. Sitterly's prompt comment.

Alumni who look back through the years can recall many a passage which was made vivid by the keen insight of this unusual teacher. No one on the faculty knew quite so much about the weaknesses and the strong points of individual students as he. He could have filled the chair of Practical Theology with great success, had he chosen to devote his teaching career to the practical rather than to the Biblical field. Apparently he could never quite divest himself of that "cure of souls" to which he had pledged himself when he was ordained a minister of Christ.

Professor Sitterly has had a genius for growing young,

rather than for growing old. Perhaps his zest for new truths and for new ways of stating old truths has played a part in this. His zeal for archaeological research has increased with the years. President Tipple often spoke to his successor about his loyalty and helpfulness. When a restudy of the curriculum was made in 1929-30, no member of the faculty was more interested or more sympathetic toward the experiments which the revision contemplated than this senior member, who might have been disposed to criticise such innovations.

Dr. Sitterly's membership in learned societies and the excellence of his published work are evidence of the extent and accuracy of his scholarship, while his latest volume, *The Building of Drew University,* gathers up with scrupulous care the details of his Alma Mater's history and tells her story with becoming modesty and with the fine loyalty which has characterized his every thought and action since the day, now well-nigh sixty years ago, when he signed the student roll as a member of the Class of 1886.

A. A. B., J. R. J.

CHARLES FREMONT SITTERLY: b. Liverpool, N. Y., June 4, 1861; A.B., Syracuse Univ., 1883; A.M., 1885; Ph.D., 1886; S.T.D., 1900; B.D., Drew, 1886; Grad. Sch., 1886-88; fellow, Univs. of Oxford, Bonn, Heidelberg, Leipzig, Berlin, 1890-92; m. Julia Cobb Buttz, Dec. 22, 1891; ord. dea., 1889; ord. eld., 1889; entered Newark Conf., 1887; pastor, Chester, N. J., 1886-88; Cranford, N. J., 1888-89; Madison, N. J., 1889-90; adjunct professor, New Testament Greek and Exegesis of the English Bible, Drew, 1892-95; professor, Biblical Literature and Exegesis of the English Bible, Drew, 1895-1935; retired, 1935 to date; sec., Faculty, Drew, 1895-1935; del., Gen. Conf., 1920; del., ecumenical conf., 1921; Phi Beta Kappa; Delta Upsilon; assoc., American Soc. of Biblical Literature and Archeology; trustee, Syracuse Univ., 1908-15; visitor for Bd. of Foreign Missions of M.E. Ch. to India, Burma, Malaya, China, Korea, Japan, 1923; lectured at Bombay, Hyderdon, Agra, Calcutta, Lucknow, Darjelling, Peking, Benang, Qwalasumpur, Singapore, Soochow, Nanking, Panyang, Seoul, Shanghai, Foochow, Amoy Swartow, Nagasaki, and Tokio, Japan; pub., *Praxis in Manuscripts of Greek New Testament,* 1898; *Canon, Greek Texts and Manuscripts of the New Testament,* 1914; *Jerusalem to Rome—The Acts* of the Apostles, 1915; Henry Anson Buttz—"His Book," 1922; The Building of Drew University, 1938; co-author, History of English Bible, 1899; contr., relig. periodicals; address, 30 Green Ave., Madison, N. J.

The Rev. OLIN ALFRED CURTIS
A.B., A.M., B.D., S.T.D., LL.D.

Professor of Systematic Theology, 1896-1914; Professor Emeritus and Lecturer on Christian Doctrine, 1914-1918.

FEW men can ever have taught the Christian doctrines as they were taught at Drew for almost twenty years by Olin Alfred Curtis. Classes in Systematic Theology are not regarded in most seminaries as especially exciting occasions, but there was no lack of excitement in classes where this master-teacher was in charge. He was spare of frame, and his health was never robust, but he was charged with an intellectual and spiritual energy which on occasion was almost irresistible. Speech would sometimes come from him with the tempestuous onrush of a mountain torrent, but he could also conduct a classroom recitation with quiet constraint. Both characteristics were seen in conjunction in his famous Martensen Seminar. For a little while, his uncanny power of analysis of the subject presented would suggest a mind completely detached and objective, and then that same mind was likely to come to a sudden glow—"fused with the inert stuff"—and note-taking became both impossible and unnecessary under the devastating onslaught or the impassioned advocacy that followed. Often, at the close of one of his characteristic outbursts, the class remained for moments in perfect silence, and then filed out of the room as men should who for a little while had seen the veil rent asunder and the Holy of Holies authentically disclosed.

There are men still living who will declare that nobody ever made things divine more real to them than did Dr. Curtis. His power to do this was no accident. By great tribulation he had entered the Kingdom. He had known disappointment, bereavement, misunderstanding. He had wrestled in the deep places, and the marks of it were on him. He had, there is good reason to believe, a sense of growing loneliness of spirit in a world, even in a church, to which he seemed at many points an extremist. But if ever a man believed that nothing mattered except the offering of a complete testimony to Jesus Christ, that man was Dr. Curtis. He believed that it had been given to him to see the Christian faith as that total organism of fact and truth which answered to existence as the concave answers to the convex. That being the case, he must tell what he saw; he must tell the meaning of it; he must make clear its overwhelming majesty; he must set forth its significance as the promise of a possible complete and everlasting redemption for every human soul.

And this he did. He did not do it automatically: that would have been utterly impossible to him. He did it as though it were a matter of life and death—as, indeed, it was! He did it by the whole demeanor of his life. He did it by his chapel prayers. Those prayers were not—just prayers. They were events. They were prayers that subdued, prayers that rebuked, prayers that shamed, prayers that made souls tremble, prayers that cleansed, prayers that inspired, prayers that exalted, prayers that thrust back the horizons of smaller minds so that room enough could be made for at least a suggestion of the wonder and the glory of Jesus Christ.

The life that came to so sharp a Christian focus was,
however, a many-sided life. Everything human interested Dr. Curtis, and everything in the world around
him. His passion for baseball was a perpetual surprise
to people who supposed that a theologian lived in a
world of abstractions! He knew the averages of the
great batters and pitchers, and a World Series found him
as enthusiastic as a boy. A baseball game, he declared,
confirmed and illustrated his fundamental philosophy
of personality as individual—social! Besides, baseball
was so distinctively an American game. The crowd in
Times Square, New York, on election night, fascinated
him: he loved to be a part of it. He despised no man,
because he saw in every man—*a man!* He understood
equally John Brown and Robert E. Lee: both alike
represented the moral finality of motive. One of his
intimates was "Old John," a colored workman on the
Drew campus, born in slavery, "salt as life," and of an
antiquity so great that it had become a legend. He
had a patriotism that ran deep and strong. Few men
studied Lincoln as Dr. Curtis studied him, and few men
not professional historians, could have had a more
complete grasp of the movement of American history.
Frail of health as he was, he served as a volunteer navy
chaplain during the Spanish-American War. He was a
great admirer of Theodore Roosevelt, and followed him
into the "Bull Moose" party.

The mountains, in particular the White Mountains,
were his familiar friends, and he wrote of them as not
many have done. His description of the song of the
hermit thrush ought to be in the American Classics.
The very trees spoke to him, and he would tell you what
they said. One morning in the early spring he and
Mrs. Curtis were seen apparently playing hide-and-seek

on the campus: it was learned that they were searching in friendly rivalry for the first hepatica. When his health failed, and he retired, he began the culture of roses in his little garden, and acquired an expert knowledge of the process. He was a lover of great music, and could interpret its message as though it were a language.

There was a curious catholicity about Dr. Curtis' reading. He was scholarly, but never scholastic. His style was as distinctive as Carlyle's, but much more flexible. He possessed an astonishing amount of out-of-the-way literary and historical knowledge. He was well-read in German theology. He made a study of the great modern preachers, and if they were doctrinal preachers, so much the better: for that reason, he placed Liddon, Dale and Bushnell above Brooks, Matheson, and Horton. He exhorted his students to read the great classical novels, and he was equally insistent that they read the classics of devotion. His library, however, was never allowed to get very large. Books that ceased to interest him were quickly disposed of—perhaps given to Dr. Faulkner! On the other hand, he made a practice of having books for which he had a high regard rebound in leather. Bryce, *The American Commonwealth,* the *Institutes* of John Calvin, Harnack, *A History of Dogma,* and Cary's translation of *The Divine Comedy* of Dante, were so treated.

Great in mind, great in heart, great in personal character, great in Christian devotion—this was Olin Alfred Curtis. In his bones was a burning fire, and he could not forbear. The evangelist's passion for souls was upon him. Like his beloved Browning, he was ever a preacher, but he was a priest as well. His class was never just a class: he sharply individualized every member of it. A student in trouble found in him an instant

friend. He loved Drew. He loved the campus. He
loved the traditions of the place. He loved the students.
He loved his work. He loved his native land. He loved
the great and the good of all times. He loved beauty
and sincerity wherever he saw them, and just as intensely
he hated all evil, all pretence, all injustice, all exploit-
ing of man by man. But over and above all else he
loved his Lord, loved him as the Eternal Son of God
made man to suffer and die for the salvation of Olin
Alfred Curtis, and consequently for every other soul.
And there be those living and dead who love their
Lord the better because they marked the so great love
which inspired and sustained the unforgettable man.

E. L.

OLIN ALFRED CURTIS: b. Frankfort,
Me., Dec. 10, 1850; A.B., Lawrence
Univ., 1877; A.M., 1879; S.T.D.,
1886; LL.D., 1905; B.D., Boston
Univ. Sch. of Theol., 1880; Univ. of
Leipzig, 1886-88; Erlangen Univ., 1890;
Marburg Univ., 1893; Edinburgh Univ.,
1894; m. (1) Eva Farlin, Sept., 1880,
m. (2) Ellen Hunt, 1889, m. (3) Ida
Gorham, June, 1906; entered Wisconsin Conf., 1880; pastor, Janesville, Wis.,
Court St., 1880-83; Milwaukee, Wis.,
Summerfield, 1883-86; supernumerary,
1886-88; Rock River Conf., 1888;
Chicago, Ill., 1888-89; professor, Systematic Theology, Boston Univ., Sch.
of Theol., 1889-96; professor, Systematic Theology, Drew, 1896-1914; professor emeritus, Systematic Theology,
and lecturer on Christian Doctrine,
Drew, 1914-18; pub., *Elective Course
of Lectures in Systematic Theology*,
1901; *The Christian Faith Personally
Given in a System of Doctrine*, 1905;
Personal Submission to Jesus Christ,
1910; contr., relig. periodicals; d.
Jan. 8, 1918.

The Rev. JOHN ALFRED FAULKNER
A.B., A.M., B.D., D.D., LL.D.

Professor of Church History, 1897-1931.

WHAT Drew man who knew him can forget that spare,
black-suited figure, hurrying to class with his lectures
under his arm? Who cannot close his eyes and see the

sensitive face, the thinning white hair, the inevitable stand-up collar, and black, loosely-knotted tie, the thick glasses, and the tired eyes behind them? We see him tipping his hat—grasping it at the back—as he meets a colleague's wife. We remember how he would stop, urged by a genuine effort to interest himself in the students' welfare, to inquire about the health, the church, the family of some stripling preacher. Chances are he could not call the student by name, but his tone was brotherly, and his concern sincere. We shall not look upon his like again—Uncle Johnny Faulkner.

As a teacher, Dr. Faulkner was content to be accurate rather than inspiring. He had none of the parlor tricks of the popular lecturer. His high-pitched, gentle voice often sounded weary, and often, be it said in shame, had a soporific effect on the less devoted. "Root, hog, or die" was his motto, publicly stated and privately adhered to. But those students who persevered, indeed found treasure for their rooting. It was not that the master could not be interesting. Once in a great while, he would leave his notes and share with us his learning in lively fashion. But in a moment he would be back to the pedestrian piling up of fact on fact.

Dr. Faulkner lived to know. His library was his workshop, his castle, and his kingdom. You could sense the pride in his modest statement that it was "just a good working library." One remembers a high room, with French windows, and books, books, books,—on the chairs, on the floor, on the desk, and stacked on all sides of the room to the very ceiling. There were scholarly monographs galore, master works in English, French, and German—over twenty-five lives of Luther alone.

And among these books Dr. Faulkner moved as a

master. We sensed that here was his true life. Indeed, he has been known to confess frankly that he missed a class because he became so engrossed in pursuit of an elusive fact.

His store of general learning in Church History was amazing. He was at home in any of the great ages of the Church. Those few times we could beguile him from his notes by questioning him in class revealed to us an amazing background of knowledge. Yet he had his favorite men and periods. The Apostolic Age was to him the great age of Christianity. He studied deep into this period, and had strong convictions about it. He loved the Fathers, and gave us some fine studies of chosen men. The literature on the Methodist Movement is richer because of his work.

But it was in the great religious movements of the sixteenth century that Dr. Faulkner found his most engrossing field of study. To him the great evangelical up-surge of this time was a Reformation, not merely a revolt against the Catholic Church. Luther was his delight. Here he worked in the original sources, reading thousands of pages in the German of Luther's day. One remembers the scorn he had for those who wrote in ignorance and malice against the great reformer.

As a writer, Dr. Faulkner exhibited a meticulous scholarship, joined to a readable, often lively style. And he loved to write. Perhaps Dr. Rogers' characterization of him as one who believed that a university was a place in which men wrote books was a bit extreme—but much of his best went into his writing. He never neglected the human and personal side of Church History: some of his best books are studies of individual men.

His book reviews were more valuable than some

books. Into the reviewing of a book went careful reading, then possibly hours of the checking of statements,
then judicious summaries, or sometimes scornful castiga-
tion. Those lists of errata that Dr. Faulkner included
in his reviews should have been as whips on the back
of a careless author. Into all his written work went a
meticulous search for fact, a courage to challenge
accepted statements, coupled with humble belief in the
truths of revelation, and deference to the Biblical
record.

In judging his theological position, one needs to know
of his earlier days. Dr. Faulkner himself recognized
that time and the veering winds of doctrine had played
him a strange trick. When he was young, those in
authority considered him more than a bit radical—perhaps hardly safe. Indeed, he once intimated that his
appointment was questioned in some quarters, and
heads were shaken. But age found him regarded as
ultra-conservative in his theology. Not a subtle or
profound thinker was he, perhaps, but graced with
humility, courage, and faith, and rooted in a vast knowledge of fact, he held the faith once and for all delivered
to the saints. The supernatural was no stumbling-
block to him. Miracle needed not to be explained away,
but accepted as revelation and defended.

Dr. Faulkner's personal religion was very personal
indeed. There seemed to be between him and God
a very intimate fellowship. This is the germ of truth
under those anecdotes of his talks with the Almighty
about the contents of the morning papers. God was
very real to him, and we dare assert that he was precious
to God. And can we not be certain of what he is doing
now? Is there anyone to whom the phrase "the communion of saints" meant more? Whom would he search

out first in that "sounding labor-house vast of being"—
Athanasius, Luther, Paul? He knew and loved these
and many more. His work on earth is done, but his
influence lives on in the books he has written, in the
deep respect for fact he implanted, in the long, steady
drive of his devotion to the winning of knowledge.
Well did he say of himself, "There is only one John
Alfred Faulkner."

H. J. S.

JOHN ALFRED FAULKNER: b. Grand Pré, N. S., July 14, 1857; A.B., Acadia Coll., 1878; A.M., 1890; D.D., 1902; B.D., Drew, 1881; Andover Theological Sem., 1881-82; D.D., Wesleyan Univ., 1897; Univ. of Leipzig, 1902-03; Univ. of Bonn, 1904; LL.D., Pennsylvania Coll., 1919; m. Helen M. Underwood, July 28, 1887; ord. dea., 1883; ord. eld., 1887; entered Wyoming Conf., 1883; pastor, Beach Lake, Pa., 1883-84; Yatesville, Pa., 1884-85; Court St., Scranton, Pa., 1885-87; Taylor, Pa., 1887-92; Great Bend, Pa., 1892-94; Chenango St., Binghamton, N. Y., 1894-97; professor, Church History, Drew, 1897-1931; Stone lecturer, Princeton Theol. Sem., 1923; pub., *The Methodist* (Story of the Churches Series), 1903; *Cyprian: the Churchman* (Men of the Kingdom Series), 1906; *Erasmus: the Scholar* (Men of the Kingdom Series), 1908; *Crises in the Early Church*, 1912; *Wesley as a Sociologist, Theologian, Churchman*, 1918; *Value of the Study of Church History*, 1920; *Modernism and the Christian Faith*, 1921; *Miraculous Birth of Our Lord*, 1924; *Burning Questions in Historic Christianity*, 1930; co-author, Hurst's *Short History of the Christian Church*, 1893; Hurst's *History of the Christian Church*, 1897-1900; art., in *A New History of Methodism*, London, 1909; art., *Methodism*, in *New International Encyclopedia*, 1903; contr., theol. reviews, etc.; d. Sept. 6, 1931.

The Rev. EDWIN LEE EARP

A.B., B.D., Ph.D.

Professor of Christian Sociology, 1909-1938.

HIS father was a Sunday School superintendent with
consistencies thereunto belonging. His mother's verbal
portrait is Proverbs XXXI. Stalwart laymen of Howard
County, Maryland, were neighbors with whom Methodist pastors prayed, to whom they preached and

together held protracted meetings. He was soundly
converted in his fourteenth year. Therewith began
his worship in primitive simplicity and his good fight
of faith with heroic ardor.

The nine Colonial colleges, all church-related, sustain
the high correlation between education and religion.
Spiritually quickened and talented, this youth matric-
ulated in Dickinson College. Drew Theological Seminary and New York University. From them he received
respectively A.B., B.D., A.M. capped with Ph.D.
from Leipzig University. Defraying his own educational
expenses indicates he was not sent, but *went* to temples
of knowledge.

"As iron sharpeneth iron, so man sharpeneth the
contenance of his friend," Giddings appraises as the
earliest and greatest discovery in sociology. It has
demonstration in large families; conspicuously in
church by John Wesley, in state by Benjamin Franklin,
each the fifteenth child. Dr. Earp was the tenth child
in a family of apostolic size. Home, church and school
liberally prepared him for optimum service.

His "hunger" theory in sociology prevailing would
incite historians loyal to their motto, *Super omnia
veritas* (Beyond all else, the truth), to rewrite history.
This theory, rooted and grounded in the revelation of
God in Christ, forecasts its author's professorship, Christian Sociology, the first so named in the United States.

Like an ant he gathered from without, like a spider
he spun from within, then spread the fabric of his
lectures before his class. He assigned readings on the
"inherited wisdom of the ages," stripped of detected
error, and enjoined "a decent respect for the opinions
of mankind." What is retained of readings and lectures must not be alien, like a gold inlay, but a part of

the brain corpus, affording a forthright affirmative to "sayest thou this thyself?" He sternly opposed burrowing, like a mole, to nowhere and pointed approvingly to the homing pigeon. The goal sought is a full-orbed man who is a sociologist, reproducing his kind and promoting society betterment as standardized in the Sermon on the Mount.

"As adversaries do in law, strive mightily, but eat and drink as friends," so did his fighting intellect in faculty meetings and his comradery after. With Professor Robert W. Rogers, both Doctors of Philosophy of European universities, a foreign scholarly imprimatur was stamped upon Drew graduate courses.

His rural policy influenced the Home Missionary Program of the Methodist church. He fruitfully lectured in southern summer schools and on the Pacific coast. He was a national counsellor of the Y.M.C.A. In its reorganization and years following he was chairman of its committee on "Town and Country." He was American representative at its conference in Europe, 1930, and was elected its president.

Not the public porch but Plato on it made the Academy. Neither plain nor ornate rooms, but Gildersleeve and Sylvester in them was the prototype of American graduate schools. "Not the bee-hive, but the bees make honey." Accordingly, more to be desired than fine gold is a plenary personality. Joy dominates Dr. Earp's. His first birth prodigally dowered him with *joie de vivre*. His second birth made "December as pleasant as May." The color and fragrance of his Autumn surpass his Spring. Horace vows no one is free from joy-killing envy. If true, Dr. Earp's is encysted. His rejoicing with those who rejoice embraces colleagues exulting on their topmost rung. Many a classroom story had he, but a frown for those who recalled the story and forgot what it clarified. The morphology of sociology he would parallel with philosophy, matching "lovers of wisdom," with "lovers of socius." Never did he teach the Easter music of sociology with a Lenten Friday face. "No profit grows where is no pleasure ta'en."

To mathematicians' estimate of 10,042,000,000 to one, nature displays intelligence, he oversubscribed. Wordsworth-like, his heart leaps up as he beholds a rainbow. Beyond its iridescence he presses to the Covenant-making God. His grandfather, uncle and brother bore the name of the prophet Amos. Dr. Earp follows this fig-mulberry grower of Tekoa avocationally in gardening. "First the blade," "the full corn in the ear," freshest vegetables; afterward, a gala feast at which guests dine not eat, converse not talk, are glad of others, good and jubliant over their superlative best.

His ear is melodiously attuned to his native, "My Maryland." His flag bears the defense inscription, "Don't tread on me." Attacked, the rattlesnake uncoils and darts with protruding sting of death. He dwells not in an "ivory tower," but among people as one who serves. From top to bottom of the social pyramid, all are his kin. To them he is kind, well-neighbors, pities and relieves. Associates say of him what Paul says of Onesiphorus, "Many a time he braced me up."

The "Who's Who" in a certain area in ancient Greece presented themselves to be crowned. A teacher, who followed his pupils' fortunes attended. Zeus crowned *him*, for he was the secret of the greatness of the great. Professor Edwin L. Earp, in the presence of his students, acclaimed as a learned sociologist with "aptness to teach," would evoke tremendous applause.

Sociology includes the family. Mrs. Earp is a daughter of the late James W. Pearsall, one-time treasure of Drew Theological Seminary and all-time benefactor of Methodism. Her wifely cooperation in student welfare and hospitality to them was as an honeycomb dripping without stint.

The universal collecting instinct induced pre-adolescent Edwin to collect canes. Only one of 1,937 boys collected canes. Dr. Earp, a collector of canes, withstands Tarde's "Imitation" and invites the title, "individualist." The countries whence they came, their utility and former holders tell-tale the collector's character. Most boys cease collecting, or change the object collected. Dr. Earp's hands on the "collecting" plow, true to his tenacity, remain thereon to the end of the furrow. He now has fifty more canes than a centipede can use in a single outing. This supply of a support in old age would be ample for Methuselah. Beloved, in the last lap of life's journey be your experience: "Thy rod and thy staff, they comfort me."

W. J. T.

EDWIN LEE EARP: b. Illchester, Md., Oct. 26, 1867; A.B., Dickinson, 1895; A.M., New York Univ., 1897; B.D., Drew, 1898; fellow, Univ. of Berlin, 1898-99; Ph.D., Leipzig, 1901; m. Lina Gibb Pearsall, May 1, 1901; ord. dea., 1892; ord. eld., 1897; entered Newark Conf., 1900; pastor, Ridgewood, N. J., 1895-97; Community Ch., East Madison, N. J., 1897-98; St. James, Newark, N. J.,1900-02; Grace, N. Plainfield, N. J., 1902-04; professor, Sociology, Syracuse Univ., 1904-09; professor, Christian Sociology, Drew, 1909-38; Phi Beta Kappa; Nat. Council, YMCA, 1924-30; pres., World's Conf. on Town and Country Work, YMCA, Dassel, Germany, 1930; pub., *Die Relative Volstaendigkeit und Hinlaenglikeit der Entwicklungs Ethik und der Christlichen Ethik,* 1901; *Social Aspects of Religious Institutions,* 1908; *The Social Engineer,* 1911; *Rural Church Movement,* 1914; *A Community Study,* 1917; *The Rural Church Serving the Community,* 1918; *Rural Social Organization,* 1921; *Biblical Backgrounds for our Rural Message,* 1922; art., "What Workingmen Might Reasonably Expect from the Church" in the *Socialized Church,* 1909; contr., religious and sociological periodicals; address, Cross Ave., Basking Ridge, N. J.

The Rev. WILLIAM JOSEPH THOMPSON
B.S., A.M., B.D., Ph.D., D.D., LL.D.

Professor of Religious Psychology and Pedagogy,
1911-1935.

PROFESSOR WILLIAM J. THOMPSON, retired in 1935 after twenty-four years of effective teaching, is now living with his family at 610 Park Avenue, New York City, where they have lived for a number of years since moving from 7 East 63d Street just off Central Park, where resided for many years a former treasurer and trustee of Drew, Mr. John S. McLean, whose charming and accomplished daughter, Mary Stover McLean, Professor Thompson married in 1898. They have two daughters who have won distinction by their achievements; Juliet Woolford, an artist who has written an illustrated book on "Old Roumania," and, in collaboration with her sister—a book on "French Riviera Villages"; Virginia, an historian, who has written a number of books requiring long and careful research:—*Dupleix and his Letters,* for which she received a decoration from the French Government; also a book on *Indo-China*—one on *Thailand;* in cooperation with Professor R. Emerson of Harvard and Professor L. A. Mills—*Government and Nationalism in South East Asia;* also, *Malaya,* soon to be published.

Professor Thompson was born on the Eastern Shore Maryland, the eldest son of an Irish Methodist and his American wife, in the home at Woolford Creek that had been in her family since 1660. His father was born in Dromora, County Down, Ireland. When he came to this country as a local preacher he joined the Methodist Protestant Church in Maryland. William lived in the environment of Methodist preachers and was early converted under their powerful preaching. He can remember to this day the names of more than a hundred members of the Maryland Conference of his father's denomination.

His academic preparation for his most successful career, both as a preacher and as a professor of Religious Psychology and Pedagogy, is on record. With a retentive memory and a scientific mind he imbibed and assimilated material for thought and produced sermons, lectures and essays which show he was alert and diligent in his studies at the University of Pennsylvania, at Drew, at Harvard, and at New York University.

When in the pastorate his preaching was topical (He says, "I wish it had been expository"), his delivery pleasing, forceful and persuasive.

He loved the people to whom he ministered and visited among them with comfort and cheer for all. During the summer of 1890 on his first charge in Trinity Church, Washington, D. C., he made 442 calls.

An indefatigable worker, he came to the new chair of Religious Psychology and Pedagogy at Drew when theological education was expanding to the fields of social science. His lecture courses were popular with the students, and his seminars never lacked numbers to fill the alloted quota.

His seminar dinners, held near the close of each year, were always great events. He had a guest speaker of distinction; and after a bountiful dinner, at which his gracious lady presided, he gave each guest, including the students' wives, a pair of easy fitting slippers, emblematic, as he said, of the domestic tranquility at the parsonage, the manse, and the rectory.

So highly esteemed by his colleagues on the faculty,

he was chosen to prepare memoirs for Professor Hannan and Professor Faulkner; and also to present the portraits of Professor Robert W. Rogers, Professor F. Watson Hannan, and Professor Edwin L. Earp to the trustees for permanent placement on the walls of the dining hall among the Drew worthies.

Professor Thompson's interest in Christian education ranged wider than the theological field. His researches in religious education show that nine of the Colonial colleges of America were founded under Christian auspices. The University of Pennsylvania was a seeming exception, but by careful and painstaking research he found, to his satisfaction, that it was founded not by Benjamin Franklin, as currently reported, but by the Rev. George Whitefield. Professor Thompson led in a movement that resulted in the erection of a bronze statue of Whitefield on the campus of the University, bearing the inscription:

"I. The Reverend George Whitefield, Bachelor of Arts, 1736, Pembroke College, Oxford.

"II. Humble Disciple of Jesus Christ, Eloquent Preacher of the Gospel.

"III. Zealous advocate and patron of higher education in the American Colonies. The Charity School of 1740, the beginning of the University of Pennsylvania, was a fruit of his ministry.

"IV. The University of Pennsylvania held its first sessions in the building erected for his congregation and was aided by his collections, guided by his counsel, inspired by his life.

"V. 'I knew him intimately upwards of thirty years. His Integrity, Disinterestedness and Indefatigable Zeal in prosecuting every Good

Work, I have never seen equalled and shall
never see excelled.'—Benjamin Franklin.

"VI. In veneration of his memory this monument
has been erected by Alumni of this University
who are ministers and laymen of the Methodist Church of which he was a founder."

His interests in education outside the campus of
Drew are varied. He is a trustee of Western Maryland
College, and Yenching University in Peiping, China,
and plays an active part in their affairs. He has been
for many years a trustee of the Methodist Hospital in
Brooklyn, New York. He is also active in the Alumni
Association of New York University and keeps up his
interest in Phi Beta Kappa.

He was given a year's leave of absence in 1921 to visit
and study the foreign missionary fields of the church.
With his family he visited all the leading missions,
except Africa, and met many of his former students of
Drew in those world fields of missionary enterprise. In
1926 he and President Ezra Squier Tipple erected a
bronze tablet in Aldersgate Street, London, in commemoration of John Wesley's heart-warming experience.

Like the great Dr. Osler of medical fame, Professor
Thompson has a "southern exposure" to his nature,
and his hands are ever open wide to give to worthy
causes, and in this regard he has the consent and example of his gracious and well-beloved companion, who
has out-distanced him in answering the calls of the
needy.

He has an Hibernian sense of humor, and, whenever
he enters a group of friends in the house, the clubroom,
or in the church they are at once put at their ease by
the friendliness of his manner, and by the wit and wisdom that emanate from his radiant personality.

He likes to hear a good story and can relate some good ones. The following is one he tells on himself: One Sunday morning, soon after his installation as professor at Drew, he was at a church in a New England town where he was asked to address the Sunday School before the preaching service. He thought he would put a test of the efficacy of religious training to one of the bright boys, so he wrote on a slip of paper the name of the boy—thus—"Johnny Blank is a good boy." This slip he held in one hand, and in the other a five-dollar bill. He then called Johnny to the front and asked him to choose which he would take—repeating as he did so the proverb: "A good name is rather to be chosen than great riches." The boy took the five-dollar bill, to the discomfiture of the professor, the great embarrassment of the boy's mother, and the amusement of the audience. She insisted on her son returning the bill, but the professor said, "No! You made your choice —it is yours." He went into the pulpit to preach and while the collection was being taken he whispered to the pastor by his side—"For goodness sake lend me five dollars; I have not enough to pay my fare back to New York." After the service the mother, to protect the "good name" of her son, made him return the money to the professor.

When he knocks at the pearly gates (may that be long deferred) I would like St. Peter to find pinned to the lapel of his white robe this note of recommendation from his many friends: A good preacher and faithful pastor; a successful teacher and learned professor; a brilliant essayist and contributor to religious periodicals; a faithful friend and brother to all kinds of people in need.

E. L. E.

WILLIAM JOSEPH THOMPSON: b. Woolford's Creek, Md., Sept. 22, 1864; B.S., Univ. of Pennsylvana, 1884; B.D., Drew, 1892; A.M., Harvard Univ., 1901; Ph.D., New York Univ., 1910; D.D., Dickinson Coll., 1906; LL.D., Hamline Univ., 1913; m. Mary Stover McLean, June 14, 1898; ord. dea., 1889; ord. eld., 1891; entered Baltimore Conf., 1887; junior pastor, Hampstead Ct., Md.. 1887-89; Walkersville, Md., 1892; Fourth St. (Trinity), Washington, D. C., 1892-93; Kensington, Md., 1893-94; New England Conf., 1894; Grace, Worcester, Mass., 1894-99; Newtonville, Mass., 1899-1904; New York East Conf., 1904; Simpson, Brooklyn, N. Y., 1904-10; corr. sec., New York East Conf. Endowment Fund Comm'n., 1910-12; professor, Religous Psychology and Pedagogy, Drew, 1911-34; assoc. supt., Brooklyn and L. I. Ch. Soc., 1935-40; del., Gen. Conf., 1924; Bd. of Sunday Schs.; trustee, Western Maryland Coll., Yenching Univ., Peiping, China; Meth. Hospital, Brooklyn, N. Y.; Brooklyn Clerical Union; Southern Soc.; Soc. Colonial Wars; Phi Beta Kappa; Alpha Kappa; Sons of the Revolution; pres., Alumni of Grad. Sch. of N. Y. Univ.; contr., religous press; address, 610 Park Ave., New York, N. Y.

The Rev. WALLACE MacMULLEN
S.T.D.

Professor of Homiletics, 1913-1918.

A MINISTER'S SON, himself a minister, coming from notable pastorates to tell other men how to be preachers and pastors—this is the picture presented by Wallace MacMullen, when at the age of fifty-three, he left the pulpit for the teacher's chair. Men sometimes ask pastors who have gone into educational work, "Why did you leave the ministry?" But the answer is easy in the case of a man like Dr. MacMullen; he had not left the ministry, he had taken the ministry with him into the classroom, and there, to a chosen congregation, meeting not once but several times each week, he continued to minister in the things of the Spirit to eager minds and hearts.

Some had come from college with a touch of intellectual arrogance. The pulpit to them was to be primarily a platform from which they could convey their superior

PLATE IV—FACULTY

WALLACE MACMULLEN, 1913-1918   F. WATSON HANNAN, 1913-1929
EDMUND D. SOPER, 1914-1919   OSCAR M. BUCK, 1920-1941
EDWIN LEWIS, 1916—   HARLAN P. BEACH, 1921-1929

learning to an uninstructed people; and this man led such to see that the supreme achievement of a sermon was not to inform but to inspire; not to convey some new facts about God's world but to bring God Himself near. He explained to them the priestly function of the minister (not by the performance of some ancient rite but by "speaking the truth in love") to become in very fact a mediator between God and man, to lessen the distance between the finite and the Infinite.

Some had the crude notion that because they had gained a genuine experience of God's grace and a genuine desire to serve Him, they had but to open their mouths and the Lord would fill them! This man taught the value of industry, of diligence in study, of commandeering the best in literature, in art, in history, and bringing them all into subjection to Jesus Christ. He made clear to them that while the Master might feed a multitude with only five loaves and two fishes, He would use a human hand to bring the loaves and the fishes to be blessed and multiplied.

Some came with careless and slovenly habits, and this man unfolded to them the worth of propriety and dignity. God, as He led them to see, was not glorified by slouchiness or flamboyance in dress, by boorishness of behavior, or by rough and unfinished speech. The oil of the sanctuary was to be beaten oil; the best the minister had or could attain in conduct and in utterance was not too good for the house of God and the purpose of God.

Dr. MacMullen himself "had a beautiful voice (as a student he sang in the seminary quartet), a fine presence, and such literary acumen that he was adviser to the Browning Society," as one of his students writes. He lived, thought, and spoke on a high plane. He

reminded one somewhat of Phillips Brooks, who, with
full appreciation of human weakness and human need,
spoke as if from the clean air of a mountain-top. This
indeed is the true prophet—not the man who sees chiefly
the faults of men and speaks chiefly in denunciation,
but the man who regards the sermon not as an oration,
or an essay, or a treatise, not as a discourse or a diatribe,
but as a message from God. Preaching to that man is as
glorious a privilege as John Wesley thought it! Dr.
MacMullen would have endorsed Ruskin's definition of
the sermon: "A half-hour to raise the dead." That explains what one of his students called his "pastoral slant
toward preaching." It was not a performance, to be
estimated or rewarded by cheap applause, but an offering to the Most High. Dr. MacMullen's classes, sharing
the experiences of his own ministry, admiring him for
his success, found in him an example of what they
wished to be and "learned by contagion."

After all, is not real teaching a process of self-giving?
Just as the law of God is no arbitrary fiat but the for-
mulated expression of what God is in Himself, so the
best instruction is but the projection of the instructor.
The teacher can not be separated from the man.

The tributes to Professor MacMullen are numerous
and heartfelt. One speaks of that natural dignity
"beneath which was a very warm heart and a spirit of
sincere friendliness." Another characterizes him as "a
courteous and thoughtful friend." Still another remarks
upon "his gracious personality, 'every inch a gentleman,' " and adds, "He was always kind, courteous, sympathetic, understanding, and genuinely Christian." One
of his most famous pupils calls him "a perfect exemplar
of the blending of the gentleman with the Christian.
He was a man of great modesty, of personal charm be-

yond measure, and with a true brotherly regard for all his students."

There will be noticed in this chorus of praise the repeated occurrence of the word "gracious." And it occurs again and yet again when men speak of what the MacMullen home meant to the campus life. "Its culture, its graciousness, its fine Christian spirit, were a constant lift." It "was completely delightful. Some of my happiest student memories are of hours spent under the aegis of Professor MacMullen and his gracious and beautiful wife." "Mrs. MacMullen was a woman of infinite charm and graciousness." To have left such an impression is matter for everlasting gratitude.

About Dr. MacMullen there has always been a certain natural distinction, in utterance, in manner, and in nobility of character. He has had a real sense of humor (what Irishman could help it?) but is prevailingly serious. Gentle, refined, unselfish, high-minded, he has served well his generation by the will of God—a son of Drew and a builder of Drew of whom his Alma Mater may justly be proud.

H. W.

WALLACE MACMULLEN: b. Dublin, Ireland, Aug. 31, 1860; dip. Drew, 1888; S.T.D., Wesleyan Univ., 1897; m. (1) Annie Hutchinson, 1888; (2) Laura E. Neal, June 7, 1899; ord. dea., 1888; ord. eld., 1890; entered New England Conf., 1888; pastor, Springfield, Mass., Trinity, 1888-93; Philadelphia Conf., 1893; Philadelphia, Pa., Grace, 1893-98; Philadelphia, Pa., Park Ave., 1898-1902; New York Conf., 1902; New York, N. Y., Madison Ave., 1902-13; professor, Homiletics, Drew, 1913-18; supt., New York District, N. Y. Conf., 1918-25; pastor, New York, N. Y., Metropolitan Temple, 1925-39; del. Gen. Conf., 1920, 1924; trustee, Drew, 1900-13; Board of Foreign Missions, N. Y. City Soc.; Deaconess Bd. N. Y.; Gen. Deaconess Bd.; Bd. of Edn. of N. Y., and N. Y. East Conf.; Dir. Fed. of Chs.; Exec. Comm. and Comm'n. on Internat. Justice and Goodwill of Federal Council; pub., *Captain of our Faith*, 1904; contr., relig. periodicals. Address, 3681 Broadway, New York City.

The Rev. FREDERICK WATSON HANNAN
A.B., B.D., S.T.D.

*Associate Professor of Pastoral Theology, 1913-1914;
Lecturer on Biblical Theology, 1913-1914; Professor of
Biblical Theology and Homiletics, 1914-1929.*

ELOQUENCE, partial to Ireland, sponsored him. Rocke-
feller riches in one scale was balanced in the other by
Hannan poverty. Through shanty, patched clothes,
scant meals, Lady Poverty disciplined him. His parents
emigrated from County Roscommon, Ireland, to Sulli-
van County, New York. His father, Michael Hannan,
died in Watson's infancy. The church of both parents,
Roman Catholic, too distant, the mother countenanced
their five children attending the near-by Methodist
church. There followed Watson's conversion, call to the
ministry, preparation at Centenary Collegiate Institute,
Wesleyan University, Drew Theological Seminary. He
financed his way through them and graduated from each
with distinction. The New York East Conference admitted him and he proceeded from responsibility to
greater responsibility.

Attitudes, emotions, mentality and action, in volumes
of flesh, he studied. Seriously and in caricature he
sketched people with bewitching accuracy. His large
diversified library speaks the wideness of his reading.
Contents of his bulging storehouse on demand sprang
like nimble servitors to the tip of his tongue. The
"Book of Books" was a Kimberley mine into which he
sank his intellectual shafts and by uncanny divination
explored rewarding veins. He brought forth Kohinoor
values, undreamed marvels "both of the wisdom and
knowledge of God."

Dr. Hannan believed a new creature in Christ automatically renders first aid to the man wounded en route from Jerusalem to Jericho, mounts him on the four-footed ambulance, later pays the hospital bill. His preaching priority was, first, individual conversion, next, social regeneration. His view point is that of Bunyan in Mr. Badman. "There are bad times, and bad times they will be until men are better, for they are bad men that make bad times. If, therefore, men would mend, so would the times."

Words "smooth as satin" did not fit his speech. About 93 per cent of New Testament words are Anglo-Saxon, probably his average. Latinized words he used sparingly. Slang and clap-trap sermon topics were electrocuted. Strong verbs, lofty adjectives and kindred adverbs were his verbal currency in negotiating large satisfactions of the abundant life. He chose words with judicious care. Sentences, he pruned, modified, amplified until every word weighed a pound, what Calvin wished for his, and expressed clearly, precisely and forcefully what he meant and effected that for which he toiled and prayed.

Two-thirds of the Scriptures are poetic. Dr. Hannan was poetic. His "Hospital Hymn" is sung at every commencement of the nurses of the Methodist Hospital, Brooklyn. Amid poetry's timeless universals he kept his feet prosaically on earth. As intimately as one talks over the fence to his neighbor, he preached to his congregations that spirit with spirit may interfuse.

He stood firmly on his feet without recourse to the forward pleading pose. He confined himself to the "strike" gesture, though provident in its use. At the conclusion of a week-of-prayer sermon in Simpson Church, Brooklyn, the congregation banded into discus-

sion groups; shortly, their spokesmen reported, "all hit."
"So fight I, not as one that beateth the air." O, Hannan,
would you were living in such an hour as this to accu-
rately hurl verbal death bombs at savage Hitler and his
savage cohorts, therewith hasten complete purgation of
their foul contagion, "That thy way may be known upon
earth, thy saving health among all nations."

He was not wanting in Irish wit and humor. Never
did he employ either to "court a grin," but to shame
wrong doers, quicken right doers, or refresh hearers
with momentary relaxation. A congenial group amidst
his scintillations, at times, held their sides with laughter.

He knew water without heat is hard, useless as water;
accordingly, heeded cold logic's need of melting emo-
tion to move "I know" to "I do." Justice's incendiaries
of "wrath to come" were extinguished by repentance
he agitated in offenders. Hovering specters he dispersed
with faith in the Power and Presence for you is more
than all that can be against you. He kindled feelings
with "God first loved you." As on a flute with seven
stops of the Spirit he made divine melody in human
hearts. The very same Gospel notes, from another's
lips falling flat, from his become God's spell—a balm of
life. So winsome his personality that his deliverances
before Methodist colleges and summer institutes lured
candidates for the ministry to where he taught. Ever
since the completion of the Biblical canon, the Church
has esteemed experience of God, understanding human
nature, knowledge of the Scriptures with anchorage in
the Saviorhood and Lordship of Christ as prime requi-
sites of a minister. These Dr. Hannan had.

His lynx-eyed discernment of his times, sharpening
students' wisdom-teeth to penetrate hard parish problems, consummate originality and imagination, superla-

tive homiletic craftsmanship adjoined to the showman-
ship of Barnum would have licensed him to ride in a
chariot drawn by peacocks. He shunned publicity for
anonymity. One ego-exhibit was equivalent to seven
abominations. F. Watson Hannan, a very great expository preacher of the present generation, walked humbly
before God and men.

Be it written by one often in their home that back
of Dr. Hannan's professorial and ministerial career,
Mrs. Hannan was a *camarilla*—a power behind the
throne.

Dr. Hannan speaks:

"The difficulties of the Old Testament as compared
with the Bible as a whole are like freckles on a giant;
they may mar his beauty a little, but do not affect his
strength."

"—has a capacity for suspicion which is excelled
only by his genius for misrepresentation, and his inabil-
ity to distinguish between form and substance keeps
pace with his zeal for intellectual dishonesty."

"Companionate marriages are only a legal relief for
sex gluttons. But its legal respectability does not save
its moral absurdity and social disaster resulting in a
large group of disillusioned second-hand bargain folks,
dear at half price."   W. J. T.

FREDERICK WATSON HANNAN: b. Co-
checton, N. Y., May 4, 1866; grad.
Collegiate Inst., Hackettstown, N. J.,
1886; A.B., Wesleyan Univ., 1890;
D.D., 1907; B.D., Drew, 1893; m.
Anna Louise Danes, Mar. 20, 1895;
ord. dea., 1890; ord. eld., 1894; entered
New York East Conf., 1893; pastor,
Bayport and Blue Point, N. Y., 1893-
94; First, Meriden, Conn., 1894-98;
First, Waterbury, Conn., 1898-1901;
Bushwick Ave., Brooklyn, N. Y., 1901-
09; New York Ave., Brooklyn, N. Y.,
1909-13; assoc. professor, Pastoral
Theology, Drew, 1913-14; lecturer,
Biblical Theology, Drew, 1913-14; pro-
fessor, Biblical Theology and Homilet-
ics, Drew, 1914-29; Gen. Conf. Comm'n
on Courses of Study; Phi Beta
Kappa; pub., *First Principles for
Young Christians*, 1907; *Pupil's Guide
Book of Homiletics*, 1911; *The Sunday
School, an Evangelistic Opportunity*,
1920; *Evangelism for the New Age*,
1921; d. Feb. 11, 1929.

The Rev. EDMUND DAVISON SOPER
A.B., B.D., D.D., LL.D.

Professor of Missions and Comparative Religions,
1914-1919.

EDMUND DAVISON SOPER was foreordained to be a teacher of Missions. He was born in the right place—on the "foreign field"; the cosmopolitan mind, the world outlook, came to him almost without effort. He was born of the right parents—an able and heroic father and mother who were among the first Protestant messengers to Japan; and Missions were in his blood. He was born at the right time—when the new epoch in Foreign Missions was about to open—when Chaplain McCabe was calling for his impossible million, when the Student Volunteer Movement and the World Student Christian Federation and the Ecumenical Missionary Conferences and the National Christian Councils were just beyond the horizon. And he had the right training—from Dickinson to Drew, with its strong missionary tradition, into student work for the Y.M.C.A., then into the Missionary Education Movement, and then into a professor's chair.

With this rich and varied experience, with ripened powers, and with a record of unvarying success behind him, Professor Soper at Drew came quickly to a position of recognized influence and usefulness. His services were by no means limited to the classroom. Highly acceptable as a preacher and platform speaker, with a warm welcome at institutes and assemblies, associated with a notable group of the younger theologians of the country in basic religious discussions, he readily became

known and valued in wider circles. He was identified
with the World Church movements of the day, at Edinburgh and Lausanne, and by travel in the Far East in
connection with the Methodist Centenary.

Yet, after all, the professor's chair was his throne of
power. To it he brought natural qualifications for the
teaching process. He had, first of all, an eager and
inquiring mind which led to thorough research. He
had a sense of order, neatness, and beauty. He possessed
that lucidity of statement which denotes clear thinking
on the part of the instructor and promotes clear thinking on the part of the student. He was not handicapped
by vagueness or obscurity of thought or by that curse of
the classroom—the technical jargon of the specialist.
With little interest in the modern technique of religious
education, he was absorbed in the content of his subject.

He had thought through the current intellectual and
moral difficulties of the youth of the day, and could
treat them with understanding and sympathy. He was
definite without being dogmatic, progressive but not
radical. His temper was irenic rather than provocative,
conciliatory without compromise. He was more anxious
to show essential agreements than to win superficial victories over men of straw.

In a word, he was a superb teacher, excelled, perhaps,
by no other in his field. He was one of those professors
who exemplify not only diligence and learning but that
something more which distinguishes the man from the
mere scholar and which touches students with a mag-
netic and kindling power. He met that noblest and
most severe test of the teacher, "Has he kindled a fire in
any soul?" Himself deprived of the opportunity for a
life-work abroad, he multiplied himself by awaking and
preparing others.

One of his most thoughtful students has summed up his characteristics as a teacher in this way: "Wealth of material; rather a marvelous historical memory and appreciation of values in history; an interest and enthusiasm which is boundless and which fascinates indifferent students; ability to meet the popular mind in simple presentations which are nevertheless intellectually sound; deep belief in his message; love for teaching; and incessant reading of the best materials for his work."

Dr. Soper has that important gift, a sense of humor, and it is coupled with a certain continuing boyishness which makes him a captivating personality. His winsomeness, however, which assures him friends everywhere, is based on a deep earnestness and his love for that which is pleasant does not impair his dominant interest in that which is best.

H. W.

EDMUND DAVISON SOPER: b. Tokyo, Japan, July 18, 1876; A.B., Dickinson Coll., 1898; D.D., 1913; LL.D., 1927; B.D., Drew, 1905; LL.D., Syracuse Univ., 1931; Ohio Northern Univ., 1935; De Pauw Univ., 1935; m. (1) Miriam Alice Belt, June 15, 1905; m. (2) Moneta Troxel, November 10, 1939; ord. dea., 1905; ord. eld., 1905; entered Newark Conf., 1905; Japan Conf., 1905; New York East Conf., 1907; N. E. Ohio Conf., 1913; N. Y. East Conf., 1915; North Carolina Conf. of M. E. Church, South, 1927; Ohio Conf., 1929 to date; student sec., State YMCA, Pennsylvania, 1898-1901; field sec., Missonary Education Movement, 1905-10; professor, Missions and Comparative Religions, Ohio Wesleyan Univ., 1910-14; professor, Missions and Comparative Religions, Drew, 1914-19; professor, History of Religion, Northwestern Univ., 1919-25; vice-president and dean, Sch. of Relig., Duke Univ., 1925-28; president, Ohio Wesleyan Univ., 1928-38; professor, History of Religion, Garrett Bibl. Inst., 1938—; president, Methodist Ed'n. Ass'n., 1932-33; president, Ass'n. American Colleges, 1933-34; Phi Beta Kappa; pub., *The Faiths of Mankind,* 1918; *The Religions of Mankind,* 1921; *What May I Believe?,* 1927; *Lausanne —the Will to Understand,* 1928; address, 1202 Maple Ave., Evanston, Illinois.

The Rev. OSCAR MacMILLAN BUCK
A.B., A.M., B.D., D.D.

Professor of Missions and Comparative Religions,
1920-1941.

ONE DAY PROFESSOR BUCK told me that he loved to keep by his bedside a portfolio containing views of the Himalayas. The resting of his eyes on their majestic strength, deep peace and eternal whiteness silenced all questionings and put to rest all the carking cares and grim forebodings that may have invaded his mind during the day from the tortured and troubled world. The Himalayas not only ministered peace to his soul but also stood for India and its teeming multitudes, for whose spiritual growth and development he consecrated all his energies. While he gladly recognized and treasured the many beautiful things in the religious heritage of Hinduism, he was deeply convinced of the fact that without the spiritual democracy of Christianity and the power of the risen Christ in the souls of men the fetters preventing India's political and social progress could not be broken. How to introduce Christ and make Him winning and real to this mighty land with its deeply ingrained religious prejudices, its caste system and anti-social practices was ever to him an all-absorbing concern. His writings show the development and progress of his thought on this major missionary issue. Though many of his co-workers did not share his views on the new methods needed for this task, he held to his own with courtesy yet with tenacity so that more and more others came to share his convictions.

To his life-task as missionary in India, teacher of

religions in Ohio Wesleyan and Drew, the summer conferences at Chautauqua, Silver Bay and the schools of the
Conference Courses of Study, Professor Buck brought
an unusual combination of experiences and gifts. From
his devoted father and mother he derived noble examples of true missionary devotion. His early education
in India's schools, his knowledge of some of her languages, his close acquaintance with her great cities and
intimate experience of her villages gave him that first-
hand understanding of a great people's way of life and
thought which in a unique way enabled him to understand her problems and minister to the deep-seated
needs of her soul.

To all this Dr. Buck by his assiduous self-discipline
and private prayer added a deeply devotional spirit,
rooted and grounded in Christ. Nothing revealed this
more clearly than his morning addresses in Drew
Chapel. They showed that spiritual glow which irradi-
ated his mind and spirit when Christ was his theme. I
recall one talk which he gave on Jesus' interest in *little*
things. His imagination played luminously on those
scenes and incidents in Christ's ministry where *little*
things are mentioned. It was the *lowly* sparrows and
the flowers of the field that the Master Teacher urged
his followers to consider to preserve their freedom from
care and anxiety. He selected the *tiny* mustard seed to
set forth the majestic potencies of the Kingdom of God.
The *little* child in the midst, not anyone from court
circles, scribal schools or Pharisaic conclaves illustrated
the qualities of character essential in the members of the
Kingdom. It was with Zacchaeus, a man of *little* stature,
that Jesus stayed in Jericho; when He left him in the
morning the despised taxgatherer felt that he had become big and important, a Son of Abraham, worthy of

a place in the new movement.   To the Great Shepherd
the flock was a *little* flock and its members were *little*
ones. The giving of a cup of cold water to one of these
little ones in the name of the Master merited Heaven's
richest reward. A deep vein of mysticism, poetry and
imagination in his nature enabled Professor Buck to
penetrate deeply into the Master's oriental mind and to
discover there pearls hidden from the eyes of others. It
was this quality that especially endeared him to India's
village folk and made him such an appealing evangelist.

Oscar Buck maintained a spiritual glow by a deep,
intimate and abiding fellowship with his Lord and
Master. It has been well said that if you have morale
you do not everlastingly talk about it. When you crush
underfoot the concealed mint on a hill-side path you do
not need anyone to tell you the source of the fragrance.
He carried everywhere the *"euodia,"* or sweet fragrance,
of Christ.

He maintained this glow of spirit, also, by constant
and studious reading of the Gospels and by keeping
himself abreast of the most recent interpretations by
Christian scholars. I frequently used to talk over with
him Dr. Manson's illuminating studies of the gospels
in the *Mission and Message of Jesus.*   Arnold Toyn-
bee's voluminous historical studies gave increased zest
to his profound belief in Christianity's world program.
He kept in close touch with India and her problems by
his correspondence and readings of her newspapers and
books.

His enthusiasm was by no means without discrimination. It was my good fortune to sit by his side in chapel
and we often sang from the same hymn book.   When a
certain hymn was given out, he would invariably close
the book and stand in silence. Crucifixion was a most

terrible experience and one which no congregation should be asked to express in song its willingness to undergo. This he felt no one could do until one was actually face to face with a cross.

Though he had sharp likes and dislikes and unhesitatingly expressed disapproval and criticism when they were deserved, he possessed in an unusual degree the gift of appreciation. He did not allow this to flow like a hidden river underground, unseen and unexpressed but rather he directed its waters to those for whom it was felt.

A man's inner worth and fortitude is severely tested when he knows that he has been stricken by a disease for which a real cure has not perhaps been found. With calm courage and infinite patience he co-operated with his skilled medical adviser, Dr. Atchley, at the Presbyterian Hospital in New York. Much as he valued the sympathy and help of doctor and friends, he drew his greatest comfort from the inner circle of his home where his wife and two daughters attended lovingly and unfailingly to his needs during his long fight with the disease that brought about a swift and sudden ending to his earthly life.

His students through the years and his fellow-laborers on the faculty will treasure his memory and friendship and will be one in their judgment that no one gave so gladly and loyally to the life and welfare of Drew Theological Seminary as did Oscar MacMillan Buck.

J. N. D.

OSCAR MACMILLAN BUCK: b. Cawnpore, United Provinces, India, Feb. 9, 1885; A.B., Ohio Wesleyan Univ., 1905; M.A., 1908; D.D., 1925; D.D., Drew, 1908; Grad. Sch., 1908-09; m. Berenice Marie Baker, June 20, 1908; ord. dea., 1909; ord. eld., 1909; entered N. Y. East Conf., 1909; pastor, East Meadow, N. Y., 1909; North India Conf., 1909; professor, Bible, Bareilly Theol. Sem., India, 1909-13; Illinois Conf., 1913; Philo, Ill., 1913-14; Rock River

Conf., 1914; Manhattan, Ill., 1914-15; professor, Missions and Comparative Religions, Ohio Wesleyan Univ., 1915-19; North-East Ohio Conf., 1916; professor, Missions and Comparative Religions, Drew, 1919-41; N. Y. East Conf., 1920; on leave of absence to visit India and other mission fields, 1925-26; sec., Commn. on Christian Higher Edn. in India, 1930-31; pub., *Working with Christ for India,* 1922; *Out of their own mouths,* 1926; *Our Asiatic Christ,* 1927; *India Looks to Her Future,* 1930; *Christianity Tested,* 1934; co-author, *India—Beloved of Heaven,* 1918; d. Madison, N. J., Feb. 10, 1941.

The Rev. JOHN NEWTON DAVIES
B.A., B.D., S.T.D.

Visiting Professor of New Testament Greek Exegesis, 1919-1926; Professor 1926—.

DURING HIS twenty-three years as professor of New Testament Greek Exegesis at Drew Theological Seminary, Professor John Newton Davies has carried on his work with a quiet distinction which has aroused in his students the profoundest appreciation. We will quote from eager tributes written by a number of men who entered deeply into the activities of his department:

"He always appeared supremely anxious that the New Testament should be allowed to speak for itself; and he saw clearly that the way to this desirable end is through painstaking, careful and exact study of its language."

"He has one of the most scintillating and yet one of the deepest minds with which I ever have had contact."

"Professor Davies unites linguistic and technical competence with an appreciation of literary and religious values and the ability to interpret them."

"I used to sit spell-bound as I watched him turn on, one by one, the hidden lights that made old, familiar words glow with implications of which I had never dreamed."

"A factor that stands out in my memory was the incisiveness of his interpretations. He could not only bring out hidden meanings, but he could bring out old and new meanings with a freshness and sharpness that would stab one with the sense of discovering a new pearl."

"Scholarly, patient, and kind, with a delightful sense of humor, he was a great teacher and a grand man."

"Dr. Davies never expected more of his students than he did of himself. I learned to love to work from him."

"Looking back, I would say that Dr. Davies in his teaching excelled in his ability to take a Greek word and break it up until every possible meaning could be seen; above all, in his zeal in teaching his subject, reflecting a profound and compelling faith in God and Jesus Christ and instilling a faith and an experience in his pupils."

"He is unsurpassed in the arduous and fruitful labor of word study. It was an unforgettable experience to watch the eager curiosity and consummate skill with which Dr. Davies drew forth the rich meaning of the great words of the New Testament."

In the full ripeness of his powers and with many graces of literary excellence Professor Davies carries on his own high tradition as a teacher of the New Testament at Drew today.

L. H. H.

JOHN NEWTON DAVIES: b. Denbigh, North Wales, Feb. 25, 1881; A.B., Univ. of Wales, 1902; B.D., Didsbury Wesleyan Coll., 1905; S.T.D., Syracuse Univ., 1926; m. Sarah Anne Parry, Aug. 24, 1909; ord. Wesleyan Methodist Ch., 1909; entered British Wesleyan Conf., 1905; pastor, Cardiff, Wales, 1907-13; Lannceston, Eng., 1913-16; Liverpool, England, 1916-19; visiting professor, New Testament Greek Exegesis, Drew, 1919-26; professor, New Testament Greek Exegesis, 1926——; pub., *Rightly Dividing the Word,* 1929; contr., *Abingdon Bible Commentary;* contr., relig. periodicals; address, 41 Pomeroy Rd., Madison, N. J.

The Rev. EDWIN LEWIS
A.B., B.D., Th.D., D.D.

*Instructor in Systematic Theology, 1916-1918; Adjunct
Professor, 1918-1920; Professor, 1920—.*

EDWIN LEWIS was born in England. He came to Canada
at the age of nineteen in 1900. Mount Allison University in Canada, Drew Theological Seminary, Middlebury College, the United Free Church College in Glasgow, and the New York State College account for his
formal education. He was connected with the Newfoundland Conference of the Methodist Church of
Canada for four years. He was a member of the North
Dakota Conference for six years. He has been a member of the Troy Conference since 1911. On January
5, 1904 Dr. Lewis married Louise Newhook Frost. He
represented his Conference as a delegate to the General
Conference of the Methodist Episcopal Church in 1928,
1932 and 1936. Including his missionary work in
Canada and his supply appointments he had something
like nineteen years of experience in the pastorate, a
fact of much significance for his religious leadership.
He came under the spell of that brilliant and dynamic
theologian, Dr. Olin A. Curtis, as a student at Drew.
When Dr. Curtis' health failed, Dr. Lewis' record and
his personality made him the natural person to carry on
the work of the department of Systematic Theology
at Drew. After preliminary service he became full
professor in 1920.

Prof. Lewis' connection with the *Abingdon Bible
Commentary* as co-editor and contributor was of the
closest. His hand was felt upon this significant work in

endless ways.   He has been a prodigious worker.   One volume after another has come from his prolific pen. He was claimed in his earlier years by the men whose loyalty to what they called liberal theological ideals sometimes led them to underestimate essential elements of historic Christianity.   They were pleased with such a volume as *Jesus Christ and the Human Quest* and rather failed to see that a more historic position than their own was implicit in his thinking.   Dr. Lewis came to the Great Divide about the time of the publication of the Layman's Missionary Report.   Professor Hocking's curious forgetfulness of some of his own most characteristic teaching in the name of uncritical gregariousness profoundly disturbed Dr. Lewis.   He wrote a brilliant criticism of Dr. Hocking's new position.   And soon *A Christian Manifesto* came like a call to battle. Since that time he has been in the forefront of the theological defenders of the historic Christian faith.   It is not always realized that just as there was an implicit evangelical center in his earlier thought, so there is an implicit liberalism in his forceful dialectic for classical Christianity.

Dr. Edwin Lewis is first of all a meticulous theological scholar.   It is not merely that he possesses, as the *London Times* said of him, "What is obviously a very thorough knowledge of modern theological writing"; that he writes as the *Manchester Guardian* declared "not as a timid obscurantist but as a Christian scholar who knows what these (science and philosophy) are saying," but that his whole intellectual life from its linguistic basis through all the matters involved in the history of thought is that of a sure-footed thinker who masters his materials as a completely scientific technician before he uses them for purposes of dialectic.   The most microscopic scholar

who tried to catch him napping would have a bad
experience. He would meet such a one on his own
level with easy and quiet mastery. Then Professor
Lewis knows how to use the English language with discrimination and force and distinction. Recently one of
the leaders of American religious thought spoke of the
years of intimate and disciplined study of the great
masterpieces of English literature which must lie back
of the style of writing which Dr. Lewis has made his
own. His mind has been fertilized and his style has
been enriched by the best which has been thought and
said in the good old English speech. Now in the fulness
of his prime as a thinker and a teacher something has
entered into his processes of interpretation which can
only be called prophetic fire. As that influential
British scholar Dr. R. Newton Flew said in reviewing
one of Dr. Lewis' most characteristic books, it "is enough
to send most of us to our knees." The great evangel
has become a fire blazing in his mind, glowing in his
conscience and burning in his words. It is this combination of technical scholarship, of rich and discriminating
learning, of literary excellence and spiritual fire which
has given him his unique place among American teachers
of theology. And this combination of qualities and
disciplined powers helps to explain the fashion in which
a cautious Englishman like Dr. George Jackson called
one of his books "The powerful document that it is."

For over a quarter of a century Dr. Lewis has put the
impress of his mind upon the students of Drew Theological Seminary. When he visited the mission fields of the
Far East he found his own students everywhere. When
he lectures at any of the conferences which are within
the boundaries of the former Methodist Episcopal church
he finds himself entering upon a reunion with a group

of men in each conference who formerly sat in his classroom. He has had an essential part in making the Drew of today what it is and in establishing the quality of the intellectual and spiritual accent which Drew men carry with them all about the world. A prodigious worker, his books will remain when his voice is silent. These books have already carried his fame and his influence all around the English speaking world. In Drew Forest he remains the understanding friend, the wise teacher, the intimate comrade in the things of the mind, and the gracious guide to thoughts about Christ which are truly Christian.

L. H. H.

EDWIN LEWIS: b. Newbury, Eng., Apr. 18, 1881; Univ. of Mt. Allison, 1903; dip., Drew, 1908; B.D., 1909; Th.D., 1918; fellow, United Free Church Coll., Glasgow, 1909; Middlebury Coll., 1911; A.B., New York State Coll. for Teachers, 1915; D.D., Dickinson Coll., 1926; m. Louise Newhook Frost, Jan. 5, 1904; came to America, 1904; naturalized citizen of U. S., 1916; ord. dea., 1904; ord. eld., 1910; entered Newfoundland Conf., 1900; pastor Newfoundland Methodist Church of Canada, 1900-04; North Dakota Conf., 1904; Velva, N. D., 1904-05; Parsippany, N. J., 1906-09; Troy Conf., 1910; North Chatham and Niverville, N. Y., 1910-13; First, Rensselaer, N. Y., 1913-16; instructor, English, N. Y., State Coll. for Teachers, 1915-16; instructor, Systematic Theology and N. T. Greek, Drew, 1916-18; adjunct professor, Systematic Theology, 1918-20; professor, Systematic Theology, 1920-29; professor, Systematic Theology and Philosophy of Religion, 1929—; del., Gen. Conf., 1928, 1932, 1936; pub., *Jesus Christ and the Human Quest*, 1924; *A Manual of Christian Beliefs*, 1927; *God and Ourselves*, 1931; *Great Christian Teachings*, 1933; *A Christian Manifesto*, 1934; *The Faith We Declare* (Fondren lectures), 1939; *A Philosophy of the Christian Revelation*, 1940; *A New Heaven and A New Earth* (Quillian lectures), 1941; *The Practice of the Christian Life*, 1942; *Christian Truth for Christian Living*, 1942; joint ed. and contr., *The Miracles of the New Testament* and *The New Testament and Christian Doctrine*, Abingdon Bible Commentary; chs., *A Survey of the Leaders and Literature in the Conflict Between Christianity and Its Opponents* (Drawbridge, Common Objections to Christianity), 1933; *The Contemporary Note in Theology* (Schofield, The Church Looks Ahead), 1933; *Aldersgate the Motive Power of the Church* (Clark, What Happened At Aldersgate?), 1938; *The Resurrection of Our Lord* (Henson, Sermons by the Sea), 1938; *Constructive Statement from the Standpoint of the Evangelical Churches* (Dunkerley and Headlam, The Ministry and the Sacraments), 1937 (pub. of Edinburgh Conf., 1937); contr. on theol. and lit. topics; address, Drew Forest, Madison, N. J.

The Rev. HARLAN PAGE BEACH
A.B., A.M., D.D.

Professor of Missions, 1921-1929.

HARLAN P. BEACH was a Yale man of the Class of '78, the class of which the late President Taft was a member. They were in the same boarding club together, of which young Beach was the steward. This intimate association with Mr. Taft continued through life and on a number of occasions the members of the class met with the President in the White House to renew the old memories.

I knew Dr. Beach first when he was the educational secretary of the Student Volunteer Movement, a position which he occupied from 1895 to 1906. My memory pictures him as a vigorous man of large frame, most ingratiating and in dead earnest about his work. He seemed positively to enjoy his task. This probably helps to explain why he came to be the very embodiment of mission study and missionary preparation just at the time when the chief interest of American Christian college students was foreign missions. It was the time of the greatest ascendancy of John R. Mott and Robert E. Speer in the love and admiration of college students. They were still young men and no great gathering was considered complete without them. Now it was in that period that Harlan Beach was giving direction to the educational policy of the Volunteer Movement. He was the man for the place—no one in America at that time could be compared with him in fitness for such a position. And withal he had a most contagious sense of humor. Beach once told a group that he was in the habit of adding up the years it would take to fit

a man for the foreign field in view of the increasing
demands made for well prepared candidates. He now
found that to be really trained a man would have to be
something over seventy years of age before a Board would
be justified in sending him! During this period Beach
began to write, mostly text books for students in our
American colleges. My memory carries me back particularly to *Dawn on the Hills of T'ang*, a study of
China, where he had spent a term of service as a
missionary.

It was after this experience in the Student Volunteer
Movement that Dr. Beach was called to Yale as professor
of Missions in the Divinity School. This was the first
chair of Missions in America, I understand, and Professor Beach made it a throne. He had of course a
splendid opportunity, but he made the most of it. He
found at Yale the Day Missions Library which gave him
a field for his research work. The endowment of his
chair also carried with it the stipulation that he should
spend every third or fourth year in travel in mission
lands. This led to extensive first hand investigations
in every part of the world and gave Beach increasingly
the reputation of being the greatest authority in
America on the world mission of the church.

During this period at Yale Dr. Beach gave himself to
missionary statistics and the geography of missions. This
kind of study was much needed in America and he
opened up the science of missions in our country following the methods of Professor Gustav Warneck of the
University of Halle, Germany. Warneck was a man of
prodigious learning and was critical of any work that
did not come up to the high levels which he himself
had established. Beach profited greatly by the friendship and criticism of Professor Warneck, and also of

Professor Julius Richter, of Berlin. There was a mutual interchange, however, and the giving was not all on one side. Dear old Professor Warneck found it difficult to appreciate the British and American ways of looking at mission philosophy. Beach's sense of humor came into play when he commented on this one-sided view of Warneck. He said that of course Professor Warneck could not see anything except from the German angle for he had never been outside of Germany until he went to heaven—an event which had occurred only a short time before.

While Professor Beach was at Yale he came to have a powerful influence in the work of the Foreign Missions Conference of North America. He wanted complete and exact statistics, and lifted the work of the Conference to new levels of accuracy and efficiency. I remember at one of these gatherings he lamented the fact that one missionary had failed to send in his report on time because for some unaccountable reason a cow had destroyed the manuscript. Beach made the suggestion that the brother in question should secure a revolving door to his study, but this, said he, might not be effective if it should happen to be a three-cornered cow!

Dr. Beach rounded out a very full and happy career as professor at Drew from 1921 to '29. I did not see him during those years but word came of his unfailing acceptability and of his genial, kindly spirit. Such was Harlan P. Beach, bless his name! All who knew him here will want to greet him when they reach heaven, where the fires of geniality will surely be burning a little brighter because "Uncle Harlan" is there.

E. D. S.

HARLAN PAGE BEACH: b. South Orange, N. J., Apr. 4, 1854; A.B., Yale Univ., 1878; A.M., 1901; Andover Theol. Sem., 1883; D.D., Amherst Coll., 1913; m. Lucy L. Ward, June 29, 1883; ord., 1883; entered Congregational Ch., 1883; teacher, Phillips Andover Acad., 1878-80; missionary, Tong Chon, China, 1883-90; pastor, Minneapolis, Minn., 1890-92; teacher and dir., Sch. for Christian Workers, Springfield, Mass., 1892-95; educ. sec., Student Volunteer Movement for For. Missions, 1895-1906; professor, Theory and Practice of Missions, Yale Univ., 1906-21; professor, Missions, Drew, 1921-29; fellow, Royal Geographical Soc.; Phi Beta Kappa; pub., *The Cross in the Land of the Trident*, 1895; *Knights of the Labarum*, 1896; *Dawn on the Hills of T'ang*, 1898; *Geography and the Atlas of Protestant Missions*, 1901, 1903; *Princely Men of the Heavenly Kingdom*, 1903; *India and Christian Opportunity*, 1904; *Renaissant Latin America*, 1916; *Missions as a Cultural Factor in the Pacific*, 1927; co-author, *World Atlas of Christian Missions*, 1911, 1925; *World Statistics of Christian Missions*, 1916; dir., *Missionary Review of the World*; bibliographical contr., International Review of Missions; d. Mar. 4, 1933.

The Rev.
WILLIAM GIRDLESTONE SHELLABEAR
D.D.

Instructor in Arabic and Lecturer on Mohammedanism, 1920-1921; Professor of Oriental Languages, 1921-1925.

DR. SHELLABEAR'S career is unique among the Teachers of Drew. British born, he was educated for military service, and went to Malaysia as a Royal Engineer officer. Singapore, even then the crossroads of the world, was a meeting-place of many races. There Captain Shellabear developed a marked aptitude for languages. By way of the West London Mission a missionary fire was kindled in his heart and he entered the Bengal, India, conference. Stationed in Singapore, he developed the Missionary Press there. Soon he was writing and printing as well as preaching in the Malay. He translated the Bible into the vernacular, and wrote the authoritative grammar of the language. The long list of his original and translated works, which is appended

PLATE V—FACULTY

WILLIAM H. NESI, 1921-1925   WILLIAM G. SHELLABEAR, 1920-1925
WILLIAM M. GILBERT, 1923—   GEORGE W. BRIGGS, 1925—
J. NEWTON DAVIES, 1919—   FRANK G. LANKARD, 1929-1936

to this sketch in evidence of his ability and industry. His term of residence at Drew brought to the campus a great traveler, a great scholar, a great linguist. His instruction and lectures were of especial value to those students who were contemplating service in Southeastern Asia or in any field which would bring them in contact with Mohammedanism.

WILLIAM GIRDLESTONE SHELLABEAR: b. Wells, Norfolk, England, Aug. 27, 1862; Haileybury Coll., 1876-79; Royal Military Academy, Woolwich, 1880-82; lieut., Royal Engineers, 1882-1890; School of Military Engineering, Chatham, 1882-85; D.D., Ohio Wesleyan Univ., 1913; m. (1) Fanny Maria Kealy, July 30, 1890; m. (2) Elizabeth Emmeline Ferris, Feb. 16, 1897; m. (3) Emma Naomi Ruth, June 3, 1924; ord. dea., 1894; ord. eld., 1894; West London Mission, 1890; entered Bengal Conf., 1891; Malay Mission, Singapore, 1891; agt., Methodist Publishing House, Singapore, S. S., 1890-1900; Malaysia Mission Conf., 1893; sup't., Singapore Dist., 1896-1902; chief reviser, Malay Bible, 1900-11; sup't., Federated Malay States Dist., 1908-13; translator, Baba Malay New Testament, 1912-14; sup't., Malacca Dist., 1913-16; instructor, Arabic, and lecturer, Mohammedanism, Drew, 1920-21; professor, Oriental Languages, Drew, 1921-25; prof., Mohammedan Dept., Kennedy Sch. of Missions, 1925-35; retired, 1935; del., Gen. Conf., 1916; Asso. Ed., Moslem World, 1922; president, Royal Asiatic Soc. Straits Branch, 1914-15; pub., The Triglot Vocabulary (English, Malay, Chinese), 1891; The Malay Methodist Hymnal (10 eds.), 1891-1924; The Malay Annals (4 eds.), 1898-1920; Practical Malay Grammar (4 eds.), 1899-1921; Malay-English Vocabulary (3 eds.), 1902-25; The Gospels and Acts in Malay, 1896-1904; Pilgrim's Progress in Baba Malay; 1905; 104 Sunday School Lessons on the Life of Christ (3 eds.), 1906-30; A Collection of 1349 Malay Proverbs (2 eds.), 1906-29; Philosophy of the Plan of Salvation (3 eds.), 1907-32; Autobiography of Munshi Abdullah, 1907; Hang Tuah, 1908-09; Complete Revision of the Malay New Testament, 1910; Complete Revision of the Malay Old Testament, 1912; Complete Revision of the Malaysia Chinese Hymnal, 1913; New Testament in Baba Malay, 1913; English-Malay Dictionary, 1916; History of Methodism in Malay, 1921; English Translation of Autobiography of Munshi Abdullah, 1918; New Testament and Psalms in Romanized Malay (2 eds.), 1927-29; Malay verses on the Life of Jesus (2 eds.), 1931-35; Malay verses on the Kingdom of God (2 eds.), 1934-38; address, 185 Girard Ave., Hartford, Conn.

The Rev. WILLIAM HOMER NESI
A.B., B.D.

Professor of Italian Language and Literature and French,
1921-1925.

IN THE YEARS immediately following the First World War the Seminary responded promptly to what many believed to be the call of a New Europe for a missionary effort by American evangelical Christianity. The liberal appropriations from the Centenary funds for theological education made it possible for Drew to expand its facilities for preparing young men for such service, especially in Italy and France, which were represented as fields white for the harvest. Accordingly ample courses in European languages were planned under carefully selected teachers. One of the ablest of these was Mr. Nesi, a Florentine, son of a Protestant pastor, who had been well trained in Rome and Switzerland, had been a Methodist pastor in Italian cities, and had taught in the Methodist Theological School in Rome of which Dr. Walling Clark, Dr. Buttz's son-in-law, was president. As a soldier in the Italian forces he had attained a captaincy and been decorated for valor in the World War. Coming to this country on an errand for the Red Cross, he was impressed that this was the place for him and his family. They soon joined him. He found pastoral work with the Italian congregation of Five Points Mission in New York, and at Dr. Tipple's invitation accepted the professorship at Drew. Here he quickly made friends and a prospect of large usefulness seemed to be opening before him when he was stricken with a fatal malady. His funeral was one of the most impressive that ever took place on the Campus. One who knew him well describes him as "a rare jewel as a scholar, preacher and teacher."

WILLIAM HOMER NESI: b. Florence, Italy, Feb. 7, 1881; A.B., Rome State Coll., 1899; B.A., Univ. of Neuchatel, 1904; B.D., 1907; Grad. Sch., Drew, 1922-25; m. Eva Violet Pickering, July 16, 1908; ord. dea., 1906; ord. eld., 1908; entered Italy Conf., 1903; pastor, Pavia, Italy, 1906-07; dir., Florence Prep. Sch., 1907-08; professor, Rome Theol. Sem., 1908-11; pastor, Modena, Italy, 1911-12; professor, Rome Theol. Sem., 1912-15; Italian military service, 1915-19; New York Conf., 1922; professor, Italian Literature and French, Drew, 1921-25; ass't. pastor, Five Points Mission, New York, N. Y., 1922-25; pub., *Il profeta Amos* (The Prophet Amos, with critical commentary); *La loi selon St. Paul* (The Law according to St. Paul); Medal for Military Valor, 1917; Comm'n for Revison of the Italian Bible; d. April 14, 1925.

The Rev. WILLIAM MARSHALL GILBERT
A.B., S.T.B., D.D.

Professor of Home Missions, 1923-29; *Professor of Home Missions and Field Work Supervision,* 1929—.

AN AUTHORITY in the field of Home Missions and professor in that field at Drew Theological Seminary since 1923. He was born in Monmouth, Illinois, August 24, 1879, and after graduation from the Monmouth High School took the following earned degrees: A.B., Cornell College (Iowa) 1904; S.T.B., Boston University School of Theology, 1909. His Alma Mater, Cornell College, conferred upon him the honorary degree, Doctor of Divinity, in 1920.

On December 31, 1908 he married Harriet Harmon Herrick who has very capably taken an active part in the churches and institutions which he has served.

His ministerial career began in the Central Illinois Conference where he served as pastor of the following churches: Fairview, 1903-04; Madison Avenue, Peoria,

Illinois, 1904-06.   While attending the Boston University School of Theology he was pastor of Edgeworth Chapel (Congregationalist), Malden, Mass., 1906-08. From 1908 to 1913 he served as pastor of the Methodist Episcopal Church of Cliftondale, Mass., becoming a member of the New England Conference in 1910.

In 1913 he had the unusual opportunity of being associated with Dr. Helms at the Morgan Memorial in Boston, the center of the Goodwill Industries which have been operated in many cities under the direction of Dr. Helms.   This work he conducted until 1917 when he went to the pastorate of First Methodist Episcopal Church, Boston, 1917-20.   His experiences at the Morgan Memorial and First Church were especially valuable in preparing him for work in the Home Missions field of Methodism, and he served as Director of the Bureau of Foreign Speaking Work for the Board of Missions and Church Extension of the Methodist Episcopal Church 1920-23.

Aided by the Missionary Centenary Movement of the Church, Drew Theological Seminary established a School of Missions to which Dr. Gilbert came as professor of Home Missions in 1923.   Later the School of Missions expanded its program to include Religious Education, taking as its name the College of Religious Education and Missions, an undergraduate college with courses leading to the A.B. degree.   In 1929 Dr. Gilbert's responsibilities were increased by adding to his duties Field Work Supervision.   In 1935 the College of Religious Education and Missions concentrated upon graduate work and hence merged with Drew Theological Seminary which gave the Drew University graduate degrees, B.D., M.A., and Ph.D., Professor Gilbert continuing his work under the new program.   He transferred into the Newark Conference from the New England Conference in 1924.

Dr. Gilbert served as lecturer on Home Missions under the auspices of the Laymen's Missionary Movement in 1916, also in the Home Missions Council on the Committee on New Americans, and as Secretary of the Commission of Foreign Language Work, created by the General Conference of 1920, for the quadrennium 1920-24. He edited *Social Pioneering*, 1928. In 1937-38 he used his year of sabbatical leave in visiting mission fields in the Far East.

Such a bare recital of facts does little justice to so colorful and useful a career. In field work supervision and in conducting field trips àt Drew he has blazed a trail for other seminaries to follow. His wide range of practical experience, particularly in ministering to the spiritual needs of cities, has made him a most valuable teacher and counsellor of young men. His contacts outside the campus have been notable. He served as Worshipful Master of his Masonic Lodge in Madison and later as Grand Chaplain of the Grand Lodge of New Jersey. He was president of the local Rotary Club, later a District Governor, and held membership on the International Rotary's Committee on Youth Service. As a speaker, to men's groups especially, he has won high esteem, and few ministers have achieved so much influence in these circles. Since 1938 he has been chairman of the Madison Chapter of the Red Cross, carrying in addition to his regular duties at Drew, unusual responsibilities in Civilian Defense.　　　A. A. B.

WILLIAM MARSHALL GILBERT: b. Monmouth, Ill., Aug. 24, 1879; A.B., Cornell Coll., Iowa, 1904; D.D., 1920; S.T.B., Boston Univ. Sch. of Theol., 1909; m. Harriet Harmon Herrick, Dec. 31, 1908; ord. dea., 1907; ord. eld., 1910; entered Central Illinois Conf., 1904; pastor, Fairview, Ill.,

1903-04; Peoria, Ill., Madison Ave., 1904-06; Edgeworth Chapel (Cong'l.), Malden, Mass., 1906-08; New England Conf., 1909; Cliftondale, Mass., 1908-13; Morgan Memorial, Boston, Mass., 1913-17; First, Boston, Mass., 1917-20; dir., Bureau of Foreign Speaking Work, Bd. of Home Missions and Church Ext., 1920-23; professor, Home Missions, Drew, 1923-29; Newark Conf., 1924; professor, Home Missions and Field, Work Supervison, Drew, 1929——; lecturer, Home Missions, Laymen's Missionary Movement, 1916; Home Missions Council; sec., Comm'n. of Foreign Language Work of the General Conf., 1920-24; editor, *Social Pioneering*, 1928; *Gilbert Genealogy*, 1930; address, 296 Woodland Rd., Madison, N. J.

The Rev. GEORGE WESTON BRIGGS
A.B., M.S.C.

Professor of Sanskrit Language and Literature, 1925-1929; Professor of History of Religions, 1929——.

ABOUT ONCE in a generation there emerges in each mission field a scholar—one who approaches his work as a pupil or learner and who pursues advanced study and acquires knowledge in some special field. In the Methodist Mission in India from 1903 to 1925, George Weston Briggs easily holds this place. During these years in India and more recently as professor of Sanskrit Language and Literature and later as professor of the History of Religions in Drew University, he has combined the pursuit of knowledge with the practical bearings of his studies on the Christian approach to Hinduism. He does this in a way which makes him unique among missionary scholars. Before he went to India, his training was that of the usual bachelor of science and master of science from a great university. But, from the moment of his arrival in India, he saw that a missionary must understand his country, not only the manners and customs of the people with whom he is dealing but also their language, history, literature and philosophy. This, in his case, applies especially to

Hinduism. These studies were regarded by him as the basis for the understanding of India. Only on such a foundation, he felt could the missionary know what to say to Hindus concerning Christ and how to say it.

During his very first term in India, he prepared a paper for the All-India district superintendents meeting on the Chamars, the outcast leather-workers, one of the largest of the depressed classes; and, in the preparation of this paper came upon the method he was to use throughout his whole career in India, namely, that in everything he did and wherever he went, he gathered material on his subject. This paper led later to a request to Dr. Briggs from Dr. J. N. Farquar for the preparation of a book on the Doms the lowest of the outcast groups in the middle Ganges country, mostly in Bihar.

All the study which Dr. Briggs did in his first term of service in India he lifted up to graduate study level when he came home on furlough.

With this beginning, Dr. Briggs then utilized his subsequent furloughs to continue his studies, especially in European philosophy and in the Sanskrit language and literature. Teaching at the College of the Pacific in San José for two years, he gave attention to the study and translation of the Bhagavad-Gita and the study of the Vedanta philosophy. Later, while at Goucher College, he went to Johns Hopkins and studied Classical and Vedic Sanskrit under the great scholar, Morris Bloomfield. Fortunately, when he returned to India in 1916, Bishop J. W. Robinson, seeing the importance of the scholarly approach to the outcast problem said, "Finish the Chamars." This work was published in 1920.

In 1922, on his second furlough, he added Avestan,

the early language in Zoroastrianism, to his range of studies. He worked that year with Dr. Franz Boas both in Anthropological Method and in his seminar on General Anthropology. He also studied with Professor A. V. Williams Jackson, taking up advanced Sanskrit, with particular reference to the reading of Sanskrit Commentary. Later, finding himself on a district in India where were located the important monasteries of the Split-Eared Yogis, he gave serious attention to the study of this school of Yoga, and during the next year visited their centers in north and southwest India. In the hot months, when ordinary work was at a standstill, he studied the text books of the sect with the aid of a pundit for several hours every day. In other words, all of his spare time as a missionary was used on scholarly study of his field.

In the fall of 1938, he left Drew University for India for a Sabbatical year, during which he produced his second great book entitled *Gorakhnath and the Kanphata Yogis*. The volume was excellently received in London and is regarded as one of the best books on that phase of the Yoga system. On this visit to India he also renewed his interest in the Doms. In preparation for this, for a year before leaving for India he employed two students to pick out of the libraries in New York City all material that could be found about that caste. In India, in the winter of 1938-39, Professor Briggs spent practically all of his time in field work on the Doms, going to the people for information on anything and everything connected with them. He was spurred on in this anthropological and religious undertaking by discovering that his book on the Chamars was being used in the universities of India in the departments of anthropology.

Dr. Briggs' book on Yoga was written to help the missionary to understand the ascetics of India. So also his book on the Chamars, so also with his volume on the Doms, soon to appear. The object has been to provide for the missionary and others data for an understanding of these outcaste groups. After such a record, one must not think of Professor Briggs' life as one of research for its own sake. He regards his studies and his writings as missionary work of the first importance and the only sound method of approach to the problem of christianizing India. Nor was there neglect of the ordinary missionary tasks, for most of this work was done at add hours when others were busy at various leisure undertakings. He was animated all the time by an attempt to understand the Indians and to let them understand him and his point of view. He never walked from one village to another without talking over these problems with his Indian helpers, getting their experience, their reactions, the results of their work, and whatever lessons were learned for his writing and for the practical approach to the work in the next village.

In his work at Drew, Professor Briggs has had two groups to deal with: one, the ministers who will serve the churches in the United States, and the other, the missionary candidates and the missionaries on furlough. For the minister, his work has been important for a general cultural background, approaching his studies not subjectively but historically and factually. He believes that this approach has a profound bearing on the race problem of America as well.

Professor Briggs regards the study of Sanskrit to be fundamental in the preparation of the missionary to India. Such study puts the missionary at once in touch with the mental processes of the Indian people, gives them basic religious, cultural, social, and philosophical ideas, and a great wealth of technical terms. He feels that nothing is more important in the understanding of a people than to know their languages.

As to his teaching method, he has never asked his students to accept anything merely because he said it, or because it was found in a book, but only after thinking out the problem for themselves. There is always more discussion than lecture. Stating his own points of view as strongly as possible, he never insists on a student agreeing with him, which is always the attitude of the scholar. Professor Briggs has spent a great deal of time in the study of the history of religions, putting his students in touch with the literature of all the great religions, furnishing them with the framework in which the temper and meaning of the religions could be understood. His aim is not the study of comparative religions, but rather to get the student to see what each religion stands for. He tries also to show the historical interrelations of the great religions. It was always fascinating, for example, to hear him tell of "Rita" in the Rig-Veda, the word for "cosmic world order," and its appearance also in Mesopotamia and in Egypt; and of the "Tao" in China as suggested by this concept. Through such word studies, he helps the students to see the basic historical contacts between religions. More important, Dr. Briggs feels that such understanding refutes the notion that religions are unilateral developments, but rather shows that there has been constant interchange of ideas among them. How important for the ecumenical Christian Movement now upon us!

All honor to George Briggs! We now turn our eyes to the East and ask "Whence cometh another?"

R. E. D.

GEORGE WESTON BRIGGS: b. North Branch, Mich., Sept. 21, 1874; B.S., Northwestern Univ., 1902; M.S., 1905; fellow, Sanskrit and Philosophy, Univ. of Calif., 1911-12; fellow, Johns Hopkins Univ., 1914-15; re-elected, 1915-16, but returned to India during year; Columbia, 1922-23; m. (1) Annie Mable Montgomery, July 22, 1903; d. May 19, 1904; (2) Mary Ames Hart, Dec. 24, 1907; teacher, pub. schs., in Mich., 1891-96; ord. dea., 1904; ord. eld., 1904; entered North India Conf., 1904; missionary, India, 1903-25; English Ch., Lucknow, 1904-07; English Ch., Naini Tal, 1907-08; professor, English Literature, Reid Christian Coll., India, 1908-09; district superintendent, Bijnor Dist., 1909-10; assistant professor, mathematics, Coll. of the Pacific, 1912-14, and principal of acad., 1913-14; California Conf., 1913; associate professor, English Bible and Philosophy, Goucher Coll., 1914-15; Baltimore Conf., 1915; Northwest India Conf., 1916; district superintendent, Allahabad Dist., 1916-19; Allahabad and Cawnpore Dists., 1918-19; Cawnpore District, 1918-21; Lucknow Conf., 1924; district superintendent, Gonda Dist., 1924; professor, Sanskrit Language and Literature, Drew, 1925-29; professor, History of Religions, 1929-—; Newark Conf., 1929; lecturer in mathematics in Brothers College, 1928-36; chaplain, Non-Conformist British Troops in India, 1907-08, 1916-18; executive secretary, Representative Council of Missions, United Provinces, India, 1918-21; India Nat. Missionary Council, 1919-21; American Oriental Soc.; American Anthropological Soc.; pub., *The Chamars*, 1920; *Gorakhnath and the Kanphata Yogis*, 1938; contr. relig. and current periodicals; address, 75 Green Village Rd., Madison, N. J.

The Rev. FRANK GLENN LANKARD
A.B., S.T.B., B.D., M.A., Ph.D.

Professor of English Bible, 1929-1931; *Professor of Biblical Literature,* 1932-1936.

METHODIST CLERGYMAN, teacher, author, and dean. Born in Anderson County, Kansas, he holds degrees from the following institutions: B.A., Baker University, 1916; S.T.B., Boston University, 1919; B.D., Garrett Biblical Institute, 1923; M.A., Northwestern University, 1921; Ph.D., Northwestern University, 1926.

On August 7, 1917 he married Myrtle Etna Denlinger who has loyally shared his keen interest in young people and the advancement of their welfare.

His work in the pastorate included the following charges: Community Church of Fremont, New Hampshire, 1916-19; Leaf River, Illinois, 1919-20; Sawyer Avenue, Chicago, Illinois, 1920-22. However, his career has been essentially that of a teacher and dean, serving the University of Chattanooga as associate professor of Biblical Literature and Religious Education, 1922-23, and as professor, 1923-24. He was first an instructor and later assistant professor of Biblical Literature in Northwestern University, 1924-29, when he accepted the invitation to become professor of English Bible in Brothers College of Drew University. He has held this professorship ever since and has also served as dean of Brothers College since 1931. From 1929 to 1936 he taught in Drew Theological Seminary and his college courses have always been open to any seminary students who desired to avail themselves of this privilege.

His Conference relationships in Methodism have been as follows: Kansas Conference, 1915-41; Newark Conference since 1941.

The following books, pamphlets, and articles will show the range of his creative activity to date: *Books—A History of the American Sunday School Curriculum,* 1927; *Difficulties in Religious Thinking,* 1933; *The Wanted Generation,* 1937; *The Bible Speaks to Our Generation,* 1941. *Articles*—The Topical Method in Teaching, 1924; The Educational Method in Religion, 1927; The Vacation Day School Teaches the Church, 1933; The Bible in the Sunday School Curriculum, 1933; Our Evolving Business Ethics, 1934; Business Ethics in the New Age, 1935; What is a Religious Book?, 1937; Can An Ancient Book Teach Any Lessons to a Modern Machine Age?, 1938; The Religious Book Corner of a Layman's Library, 1939; Tension Areas that Need Attention, 1941. *Pamphlets*—Characteristics of the Ideal Teacher of Religion, 1923; Facing the

Future with Religion, 1929; The Bible and the Life and Ideals of the English Speaking People, 1935; The English Bible and British and American Art, 1935; The Church-Related College in a Disordered World, 1941.

He holds membership in the following organizations: National Association of Biblical Instructors (President, 1937); Eastern Association of College Deans and Advisers of Men (President, 1939-40); Society of Biblical Literature and Exegesis; Religious Education Association; American Association of University Professors; Phi Beta Kappa; Phi Delta Kappa; Pi Kappa Delta; Pi Gamma Mu.

He has been very active in Rotary circles, serving as President of the Madison Club in 1939 and as Governor of his Rotary District for the year 1942-43.

As dean of a young, growing college of liberal arts, he has planned and guided the destinies of the college so that it has won rapid recognition as a college of outstanding quality. Students have great affection for him because of his insight into their problems and ability to give them wise counsel. His teaching in Drew Theological Seminary was marked by thorough scholarship and clarity of expression. His influence has gone far beyond the bounds of Drew Forest. Dean Lankard is still a comparatively young man and should be able to give many more years of teaching and administrative service which will benefit every phase of the life of Drew University. **A. A. B.**

FRANK GLENN LANKARD: b. Anderson Co., Kan., Sept. 1, 1892; Univ. of Kansas, 1912-13; B.A., Baker Univ., 1916; S.T.B., Boston Univ., 1919; B.D., Garrett Bibl. Inst., 1923; M.A., Northwestern Univ., 1921; Ph.D., 1926; m. Myrtle Etna Denlinger, Aug. 7, 1917; ord. dea., 1918; ord. eld., 1921; entered Kansas Conf., 1915; pastor, Union Ch. (Community), Fremont, N. H., 1917-19; Leaf River, Ill., 1919-20; Sawyer Ave., Chicago, Ill., 1920-22; assoc. prof., Bibl. Lit. and Relig. Edn., Univ. of Chattanooga, 1922-23; professor, Bibl. Lit. and Religious Edn., Univ. of Chattanooga, 1923-24;

instructor, Bibl. Lit., Northwestern Univ., 1924-25; ass't professor, 1925-29; professor, English Bible, Drew, 1929-36; professor Bibl. Lit., Brothers Coll., 1929; dean, 1931, Nat. Assn. Biblical Instructors, president, 1937; Eastern Assn. of Deans and Advisers of Men, president, 1938-39; Governor, 182nd District, Rotary International, 1942-1943; Phi Beta Kappa, Phi Delta Kappa, Pi Kappa Delta, Pi Gamma Mu; pub., *A History of the American Sunday School Curriculum,* 1927; *Difficulties in Religious Thinking,* 1933; *The Bible and the Life and Ideals of the English Speaking People,* 1935; *The Wanted Generation,* 1937; *The Bible Speaks to Our Generation,* 1941; contr., current periodicals and religious journals; address, 11 Academy Rd., Madison, N. J.

The Rev. JOHN PATERSON
M.A., B.D., Ph.D.

Visiting Professor of Hebrew and Old Testament Exegesis, 1929-1933; *Professor,* 1933—.

SCOTLAND has been the proud possessor of many great Old Testament scholars. Conspicuous among them have been the men who belonged to the particular circle founded by Professor A. B. Davidson of Edinburgh. His own pupils W. Robertson Smith and George Adam Smith were men of most distinguished quality, each a particular star in a brilliant constellation. The tradition was continued by Sir George Adam Smith's able pupil, Professor John Edgar McFadyen who in turn was the teacher of Professor John Paterson, the subject of this sketch. It is Professor Paterson who has brought the great tradition to Drew.

At Glasgow University a group of famous men taught John Paterson. He studied church history under Principal Lindsay, whose study of the Reformation is in every historical library. He studied New Testament under Professor James Denney, whose *Death of Christ* came with something of the force of an explosion upon the world when a pseudo-liberalism was winning victories

PLATE VI—FACULTY

JOHN PATERSON, 1929—

JAMES V. THOMPSON, 1930—

RALPH A. FELTON, 1930—

DORR F. DIEFENDORF, 1921—

NORMAN M. GUY, 1938

GEOFFREY W. STAFFORD, 1937—

on every hand. He studied theology under Professor James Orr who had a place all his own among English-speaking authorities in respect of the Ritschlian theology and whose *Christian View of God and the World* was itself a masterpiece of clear and commanding thinking. He studied Practical Training and Christian Ethics under Professor W. M. Clow. But those who follow this work in the Old Testament most naturally think of his connection with the school of A. B. Davidson through J. E. McFadyen whose interpretation of the book of Job has put preachers all about the world in his debt.

John Paterson was at Glasgow University from 1906 to 1910 when he received the degree M.A. with first class honors in Classics and gained one of the blue ribbons of that universty—the Ferguson Bursary. He proceeded to study both law and divinity, leaving the law after one year. He was awarded the Stevenson Scholarship on entering the United Free Church College in 1910 as the most distinguished student from any of the Scottish Universities. He maintained first place in all subjects except natural science (which he studied under J. Y. Simpson). He received the B.D. from Glasgow University in 1914. He took his Ph.D. in 1929 and was the first person to do so in the department of Old Testament. He had sixteen years experience in Scottish pastorates. He was minister at Penpont, Dumfriesshire from 1915 to 1924 and at Bridgend Church, Dumbarton from 1924 to 1931. On August 22, 1914 he was married to Miss Jane Wilson Wiseman. For twelve years he has occupied the chair of Hebrew and Old Testament Exegesis in Drew Theological Seminary. He was a member of the Glasgow University Oriental Society and in America is a member of the Society of Biblical Literature, the National Association of Biblical Instructors, the American Oriental Society and the American Schools of Oriental Research.

He has published in the *Journal of Biblical Literature* an article dealing with *Divorce and Desertion in the Old Testament;* and in *Religion in Life* articles on *Some Ethical Insights of Prophecy, Religion and Asceticism, The Business of Preaching, The Problem of Pain and The Doctrine of Immortality* and *A Mirror for Preachers.* He is a frequent contributor to the *Christian World Pulpit.*

The man who took up the work of that fascinating and glamorous scholar, Robert W. Rogers, confronted a most difficult task. It says much for Professor Paterson that no one has ever questioned his technical equipment for the great task or the tang and rich personal quality of his teaching. His sound and dependable scholarship has ripened as the years have passed, and the play of his humor and the cut of his wit have quickened the interest of his classes. His deep loyalty to the great sanctions of morals and religion has been constantly evident. If he has brought to Drew a fine tradition of Old Testament scholarship, he has also brought the quiet glowing piety which characterizes Scottish religion at its best.

He is a vital and arresting preacher and has been heard with appreciation not only in his native Scotland and the United States but in Ottawa, Montreal and Halifax. His cordial and understanding interest in his students has given an added quality to all his work.

L. H. H.

JOHN PATERSON: b. Dumfriesshire, Scotland, Sept. 20, 1887; M.A., Glasgow Univ. (with first class honors in Classics), 1910; B.D., 1914; Ph.D., 1929; m. Jane Wilson Wiseman, Aug. 22, 1914; ord. minister, Church of Scotland, 1915; pastor, Penpont Ch., Dumfriesshire, S c o t l a n d , 1915-24: Bridgend Ch., Dumbarton, Scotland, 1924-31; visiting professor, Hebrew and Old Testament Exegesis, Drew, 1930-31; professor, 1931——; representative preacher in Ottawa, Montreal, Halifax, Sydney, Nova Scotia, Canada; contr., Amer. and International theol. journals; address, 29 Academy Circle, Madison, N. J.

The Rev. JAMES VOORHEES THOMPSON

B.A., B.D., Ph.D.

Professor of Administration of Religious Education,
1930——.

METHODIST CLERGYMAN, leader of young people, and distinguished teacher in the field of Religious Education. Born in Rock Springs, Pennsylvania, May 25, 1878, he received his A.B. from Wesleyan University in 1902, his B.D. from Drew Theological Seminary in 1905, and his Ph.D. from Northwestern University in 1928. He married Nora Gray, August 18, 1909. His pastoral service includes Bronxdale Methodist Episcopal Church, New York City, 1903-04, and Christ Methodist Episcopal Church, Pittsburgh, Pa., where he was the first recorded "Minister and Director of Religious Education" in the United States, 1905-07. For the next seven years, 1907-14, he gave his life to teaching, first in Shadyside Academy and later in Peabody High School, both in Pittsburgh, Pa. His success in high school teaching and in religious institutes marked him as a wise leader of youth and in 1912 he became superintendent of the Young People's Department of the Board of Sunday Schools of the Methodist Episcopal Church. This office he held until 1925.

During this period he taught as an instructor in the Department of Religious Education of Boston University in 1918 and served the World's Sunday School Association as a lecturer in Japan, Korea, and China, 1920-21.

His service in the first World War was distinguished. Securing leave of absence from the Methodist Board of Sunday Schools, he entered the Chaplains' Training School at Camp Taylor and became First Lieutenant and Chaplain of the 325th Infantry, 82nd Division, A.E.F., July-October 1918, when he was made Senior Chaplain of the 2nd Army Corps. He was later promoted to the rank of Captain, decorated with the Order of the Silver Palms (France), and made an Officer of the Academy.

From 1925 to 1928 he was associate minister and director of Religious Education of the First Methodist Episcopal Church, Evanston, Illinois. In 1928-29 he was assistant professor of Religious Education and in 1929-30 associate professor of Religious Education at Northwestern University. He accepted in 1930 the invitation to become professor of Administration of Religious Education at his Alma Mater, Drew Theological Seminary, where he continues to teach with distinction. From 1931 to 1935 he was director of the College of Religious Education and Missions. When the program of this College was merged with that of Drew Theological Seminary Dr. Thompson remained in the seminary as professor and also as chairman of the Division of Religious Education. Religious Education has been a study of ever increasing interest and usefulness at Drew under the leadership of Professor Thompson. Not only have the students of the division been inspired and guided by him but he has made his own services and those of others in his division available to many churches, those near to Madison and many at a distance. He has been very much in demand for summer schools of Religious Education, having lectured at Lake Junaluska, North Carolina, twenty-three summers out of the last twenty-seven years.

Mrs. Thompson has also shown great personal interest in students and their open door has welcomed large numbers of Drew men and women every year.

He is the author of the following books and articles: *Handbook for Workers with Young People*, 1921; *The daily Vacation Church School* (with J. E. Stout), 1923; *Studies in Religious Education* (with Lotz and others), 1931; *Orientation in Education* (with Schutte and others), 1932; *Great Biographies* (with Lotz and others), 1938; *The Open Door Series* (guidance pamphlets for adolescents and their leaders).

Professor Thompson joined the Pittsburgh Conference in 1905 and has been a member ever since. He also holds membership in the Religious Education Association, Alpha Delta Phi, and Phi Delta Kappa. He has been for many years active in the work of the International Council of Religious Education. He is a Mason.

In the course of his duties he has given particular attention to weekday religious instruction, having sponsored and guided work in such a school in Madison, New Jersey, for eight years. He is also active in the work of the National Conference of Christians and Jews for which he has directed important research projects. The most important of these was the three-year study of all Protestant Church School materials. This was followed by a study of periodical literature for youth issued by both church and extra-church publishers. These studies are at present being revised and brought up to date.

Professor Thompson has been a loyal friend and counsellor of students, not only an able teacher in his field but one of the recognized leaders of Religious Education in America. He is a man with wide interests who has extended his influence far beyond the confines of his own campus and community.

A. A. B.

JAMES VOORHEES THOMPSON: b. Rock Springs Pa., May 25, 1878; A.B., Wesleyan Univ., 1902; B.D., Drew, 1905; grad. study, Univ. of Pittsburgh, 1912-14; Ph.D., Northwestern Univ., 1928; m. Nora Gray, Aug. 18, 1909; student pastor, Bronxdale M. E. Ch., N. Y. City, 1903-04; asst. minister and dir. religious edn. (first recorded in U. S.), Christ M. E. Ch., Pittsburgh, Pa., 1905-07; ordained ministry M. E. Church, 1907; teacher Shadyside Acad., Pittsburgh, Pa., 1908-12; Peabody High Sch., Pittsburgh, Pa., 1912-14; supt., young people's dept., Bd. of Sunday Schs., M. E. Ch., 1914-25; instructor, dept. of relig. edn., Boston Univ., 1918; agt., World's S. S. Ass'n. and Bd. of Sunday Schs., M. E. Ch. in Japan, Korea, and China, 1920-21, assoc. minister and dir. relig. edn., First M. E. Ch., Evanston, Ill., 1925-28; ass't. professor, Religious Edn., Northwestern Univ., 1928-29; assoc. professor, Relig. Edn., Northwestern Univ., 1929-30; professor, Administration of Relig. Edn., Drew, 1930——; director, Coll. of Relig. Edn. and Missions, Drew, 1931-35; served as corpl., Span.-Am. War, 1898; chaplain, 325th Inf., 82nd Div., A.E.F., June-Oct., 1918; senior chaplain, 2nd Army Corps, Oct., 1918-19; mem., O.R.C.; decorated, captain, Order of the Silver Palms (France), also Officer of Academy; International Council of Relig. Edn.; pub., *Handbook for Workers with Young People*, 1921; *The Daily Vacation Church School* (with J. E. Stout), 1923, *Studies in Religious Education* (with Lotz and others), 1931; *Orientation in Education* (with Schutte and others); 1932; *Great Biographies* (with Lotz and others), 1938; editor and author of "The Open Door Series"; lecturer on religious edn.; address, 11 Glendale Rd., Madison, N. J.

The Rev. DORR FRANK DIEFENDORF
B.D., D.D.

Lecturer on Social Responsibility of the Church and Practical Theology, 1921-1923; Associate Professor of Practical Theology and Applied Christianity, 1933-1934; Professor, 1934——.

DR. HENRY ANSON BUTTZ used to tell of a conversation he once had with a layman from the West whose pastor was a graduate of Drew. The president of the seminary was inquiring how his former student was getting along in the ministry, and the layman hesitantly replied,

"Well, Brother So-and-so has a fine library and spends a
lot of time in it. He is a very studious man and quite
a scholar; but when it comes to preaching, *he can't get
his goods on the sidewalk!*"

Theological learning may seem an enjoyable treasure
to hold in one's mind; but it is really quite worthless
if it is not made accessible to the people who crowd the
sidewalks of life. Applied Christianity is the only kind
of Christianity that counts. When applied, something
happens; lives are changed, society revolutionized.

Dr. Diefendorf's work is the training of prospective
ministers to apply the truths they learn to the conditions
they will face. These conditions consist largely of the
mental and spiritual attitudes found in the minister's
community and especially in his congregation. Some
of this material is ossified, some of it soggy with ignorance and apathy, some of it plastic and durable. Nothing is more vital to the worker than to know how to
handle his material. And nothing, it may be added
emphatically, is more important to the church.

Fortunate are the theological students who have as
their teacher one who has spent years in the ecclesiastical work-shop and knows what he is talking about.
Not alone from his own inherent sense of the greatness
of the Christian ministry, but also from his knowledge
of human nature, from large responsibilities and difficult situations successfully met in important pastorates,
from participation in general church councils Dr. Diefendorf comes to offer the facts and results of his experience, as well as his methods of reasonableness and tact,
to young men who expect to be pastor-preachers. Small
wonder that many of his former students concur in the
statement, "The things I learned from Dr. Diefendorf
are matters of every-day practice."

The method of the Division of Applied Christianity
in developing efficient ministers is a combination of
thorough knowledge of the field, high ideals and practical drills. As in all arts, no limits are set to aspirations
of excellence in the art of shepherding the people, the
art of presenting religious truth persuasively, the art of
leading human beings into communion with God, the
art of conducting public worship so that it will prove
to be not a soporific but an inspiration to decision and
action. Indeed, so insistent is Dr. Diefendorf on correc-
tion of faults, on observance of right demeanor and
right spirit, on accurate, clean-cut preaching, free from
the foggy maze of generalities, that when any member
of his preaching class does a particularly good piece of
work, he is said, in student jargon, to "do a Diefendorf."

But the student is not left to mere hopeful dreaming
of ministerial excellence. His teacher brings him down
to earth from the clouds of wishful thinking, and puts
him and his fellows through chapel rehearsals and classroom maneuvers that are calculated, through mutual
criticisms (students can be so fraternally caustic!) and
through wise direction, to train the "rookie" in the use
of his weapons for future spiritual warfare. And if the
trainee should forget this—which would appear un-
likely—he will do so at his peril. Defeat will be his—
perhaps a lifetime of plodding in the ranks of medi-
ocrity.

The man is always more than his teaching. Facts,
principles, suggestions may be wormed out of a book;
but learners are more than book-worms. Contact with a
strong, sterling, likeable personality is what students
remember with gratitude and enthusiasm. The teaching lives on through the years because the teacher was

alive. When the truth sifts through character, authority is at once accepted, respect and admiration are aroused, emulation kindled.

Everybody knows what a Christian gentleman is, but everybody hastens to say what it means to be one! So many students, as well as others, speak of Dr. Diefendorf in these words that their witness must be accepted as description rather than eulogy. They find in him superior ability without ostentation, good companionship without condescension, unquestioned leadership without self-importance; an authority in knowledge, a servant in spirit.

Dr. Diefendorf's well-known acquaintance with social and economic conditions is happily accompanied by keenness of analysis and prophetic insight into the meaning of world trends. In forecasting the outcome of world movements he has seemed to some of his students to combine an almost uncanny prophetic vision with perfect sanity of judgment. Surely the pulpit needs to understand as never before the signs of the times and the drift of world thought and action.

A liberal in theology, a fervent believer in social salvation, a man of strong convictions, he impresses everyone with his fairness, consideration and courtesy toward opposing views. Light, not heat, is the objective.

His friendliness is marked by a genuine personal interest and great skill in counseling individual students and by such social amenities as are highly prized in seminary days and treasured in memory through many years. Such friendliness is perhaps brought to its finest flower in his home; for here his own cordiality is heightened by the gracious welcome and womanly charm of Mrs. Diefendorf. Together in their home they present not only a memorable picture of hospitality but also a practical demonstration of "applied Christianity!"

R. B. U.

DORR FRANK DIEFENDORF: b. Canajoharie, N. Y., Aug. 9, 1874; Rugby Acad., dip., Drew, 1899; B.D., 1922; D.D., Dickinson Coll., 1919; New York Univ.; m. Mabel A. Runyon, June 15, 1898; ord. dea., 1900; ord. eld., 1904; entered Newark Conf., 1901; pastor, Chatham, N. J., 1901-05; Ridgewood, N. J., 1905-07; Roseville Ch., Newark, N. J., 1907-20; Calvary Ch., East Orange, N. J., 1920-28; contbg. editor, The Christian Advocates, 1928-32; lecturer, Social Responsibility of the Church, and Practical Theology, Drew, 1921-33; assoc. professor, Practical Theology and Applied Christianity, Drew, 1933-34; professor, 1934; M. E. Book Com., 1920-28; Bd. of Foreign Missions, 1920-28; Gen. Com., Dep't. of Research and Education, com. on worship, and Dep't. Internat. Justice and Good Will (Federal Council of Chs.); Council for Clinical Training of Theol. Students; pub., The Christian in Social Relationships, 1922; address, 45 Prospect St., Madison, N. J.

The Rev. NORMAN MILLIGAN GUY
A.B., M.A., D.D.
Professor of Christian Sociology, 1938—.

A METHODIST CLERGYMAN with an unusual range of experience, including pastorates in Newfoundland and Bermuda together with teaching in four collegiate institutions. He was born in Twillingate, Newfoundland, March 27, 1883, and received the A.B. and M.A. in philosophy from Mount Allison University, Sackville, N. B., Canada, in 1912 and 1913 respectively. He received the Master of Arts degree in sociology from Harvard University in 1924, and the D.D. from Pine Hill Divinity Hall, Halifax, N. S., Canada, in 1942. On August 21, 1912, he married Dulcie Moore. In that year also he was ordained a minister of the Methodist Church of Canada. His pastorates include the following: Grand Falls, Newfoundland, 1912-13; George Street Church, St. Johns, Newfoundland, 1914-18; Wesley

Church, Hamilton, Bermuda, 1918-22, 1925-26. During the First World War he was appointed officiating chaplain to His Majesty's Forces in Newfoundland and also in Bermuda. After ten years as a teacher in the public schools of Newfoundland, he served as professor of economics and sociology at Mt. Allison University from 1926 to 1930, as lecturer in sociology and philosophy of religion at Pine Hill Divinity Hall from 1928 to 1930, and from 1930 to 1938 as professor of economics and sociology in Brothers College of Drew University. He has been professor of Christian sociology in Drew Theological Seminary since 1938.

A mere recital of these facts gives little conception of the colorful personality and exceptional gifts of this eminent teacher. His classroom work has been characterized by brilliant presentation of subject matter, openmindedness to the opinions of students, and a passion for clear, constructive thinking. His influence on students outside the classroom has been as great as that within. Young people have found in him a friend, broadminded and warmly sympathetic, never too busy to give gladly all the counsel and direction which a student may request. Mrs. Guy shares his interest in young people and their home has been a center of student activity.

He was transferred from the United Church of Canada to the New York Conference of the Methodist Episcopal Church in 1935 and has made an unusual contribution to the work of the Conference as chairman of the Committee on Social Service.

He is a member of Sigma Phi, Tau Kappa Alpha, American Academy of Political and Social Science, and Kiwanis International, serving as president of the Kiwanis Club in Madison for one year. His writings include the following pamphlets: *The Church, the School, and the Economic Crisis,* 1933; *The Cooperative Movement,* 1938; *The Role of the Church in Economic Change,* 1939; *The Development of Modern Social Consciousness,* 1940.

A. A. B.

NORMAN MILLIGAN GUY: b. Twillingate, Newfoundland, March 27, 1883; A.B., Mt. Allison Univ., Sackville, N. B., Canada, 1912; M.A. (Philosophy), 1913; A.M. (Sociology), Harvard, 1924; D.D., Pine Hill Divinity Hall, Halifax, N. S., Canada, 1942; m. Dulcie Moore, Aug. 22, 1912; ord. minister, Meth. Ch. of Canada, 1912; pastor, Grand Falls, Newfoundland, 1912-14; George St. Ch., St. John's, Newfoundland, 1914-18; Wesley Ch., Hamilton, Bermuda, 1918-22, 1925-26; Federated Ch., Southville, Mass., 1922-25; chairman of the Bermuda District of Meth. Ch., 1918-22, 1925-26; Officiating Chaplain, His Majesty's Forces (Naval), 1914-18; (Army), 1918-22, 1925-26; received into New York Conf., 1935; professor, Economics and Sociology, Mt. Allison Univ., 1926-30; lecturer in Philosophy of Religion and Sociology, Pine Hill Divinity Hall, 1928-30; professor, Economics and Sociology, Brothers College of Drew University, 1930-38; professor, Christian Sociology, Drew Theological Seminary, 1938—; pub. (pamphlets): *The Church, the School, and the Economic Crisis,* 1933; *The Co-operative Movement,* 1938; *The Rôle of the Church in Economic Change,* 1939; *The Development of Modern Social Consciousness,* 1940; mem. Sigma Phi, Tau Kappa Alpha, American Academy of Political and Social Science; address, 2 Green Hill Road, Madison, N. J.

The Rev. RALPH ALMON FELTON

A.B., M.A., Ph.D.

Lecturer on Rural Sociology, 1930-31; *Associate Professor,* 1931-1940; *Professor,* 1940—.

To LAY FLOWERS on the grave of a departed friend and to deliver a memorial eulogy is a simple task in comparison to that of paying a just and deserved tribute to the living. The reason is, I suppose, that in the latter case mere words seem to be so inadequate to convey what one desires. In the case of Professor Ralph Felton this is peculiarly so. It is like trying to describe a dynamo or perhaps better still an airplane in motion; one never seems to see the plane in two places exactly alike. It is constantly moving on and making the changes necessary to meet the new atmospheric conditions in which it soars.

This to me would describe in part at least the professional career of Professor Ralph Felton and in large measure accounts for the amazing contribution that he has made and is still making to the ministry of the town and country church and the missionary cause at home and abroad.

Professor Felton, although he was born in the country and received his early training in the practical experiences of rural life, was led to a conviction of the importance of, and commitment to, the rural ministry while a student in Union Theological Seminary. During this period he spent his summers working in rural churches. This gave him a first-hand contact with various types of rural communities, and the surveys conducted by him, while of great value to the churches and communities where they were made, and later a foundation for much of the thinking and planning for the rural church on a national scale, were most significant in their influence upon Professor Felton himself. They helped to produce him, and through him have been one of the great personality contributions to the cause of the rural church. It is of the nature of genius in man to seek for the meaning of life in this world, to shape his destiny by the same, and to accept the consequences of his will to live for the goals that seem to him most important. Rural life and the rural church constitute the goal of Professor Felton's ministry. To this he has brought a contrite heart and a consecrated life. Someone has said, "There can be no true knowledge of ultimate things, that is to say, of God and man, duty and destiny, that is not born in concern and perfected in commitment." Such a statement explains the unique success that has been achieved by Professor Felton in his chosen career.

To Professor Felton is due in large measure the credit for the organization of summer schools for town and country ministers. During the years he was responsible for the educational division of the Department of Rural Work in the Methodist Church he gave himself with devotion to this summer school idea, which without doubt has been the one outstanding contribution to the improvement of the rural ministry and in turn the most helpful single contribution to the cause of the rural church. These summer schools and institutes have continued as an interdenominational movement, centered primarily in the State Colleges of Agriculture.

In addition to his experiences and contributions to rural life in America, Professor Felton has also given significant leadership to rural life in the foreign field. During the years 1936 to 1938 he spent himself with some 600 Chinese rural pastors in their parishes and helped them develop a forward-looking program for their work.

One of the outstanding experiences as reported by Professor Felton was his contacts with Dr. Kagawa and the opportunity that this presented of going with him, visiting among the Japanese peasants and "discovering how a man could live over again the daily sacrificial life of Jesus of Nazareth."

The things which have impressed Professor Felton as constituting the appeal to men to dedicate their lives to the rural ministry are themselves a high tribute. Briefly stated, they are:

(a) The rural church has the opportunity of determining the church life of the future because the surplus childhood is in the countryside.

(b) Religion must get back into home life, and the rural home is more normal and unified.

(c) The minds of rural people as they live with nature instead of in the competitive machine age are more ready for and appreciative of religious teaching.

(d) Rural community life allows for more personal face-to-face contacts between a pastor and his people.

(e) The spiritual values of church union must be worked out in rural life because the population here is too limited to have a church for every type of believer.

(f) Rural people deal in farming, the basic occupation all over the world.

(g) The rural minister can preach the simple gospel of truth, faith, and love to the small and the great, to the young and the old without opposition or hindrance, "where neighbor joins his neighbor, clear of eye, in praising God beneath the country sky."

It is the human quality in such a ministry that has endeared Professor Felton to all who have come to know him. One has the feeling that while he is dealing with things profound, he is also in the realm of simplicity and reality.

It is toward these ideals that Professor Felton continues to press the cause of the rural church. No one in the United States has made a greater contribution, and the whole church is greatly indebted to him. We look to him for a continuing leadership in this important ministry and desire to express in this very inadequate way our sincere thanks for the high service he has rendered.

M. A. D.

RALPH ALMON FELTON: b. Arkansas City, Kan., July 26, 1882; A.B., Southwestern Coll., 1905; M.A., Columbia Univ., 1913; graduate, Union Theol. Sem., 1913; Univ. of Pennsylvania, 1919-23; Ph.D., Drew, 1933; m. Blanche Shimer, Aug. 19, 1914; ord. dea., 1919; ord. eld., 1930; entered Oklahoma Conf., 1919; taught in rural sch., Hydro, Okla., 1905-06; principal, High Sch., Douglas, Kan., 1906-07; instructor, English and Bible, American Univ., Beirut, Syria, 1907-10; ass't., Dep't. of Church and Country Life, Presbyn. Bd. of National Missions, 1913-19; ednl. dir., Rural Church Dept., Methodist Bd. of Home Missions, 1919-23; extension professor, Rural Social Organization, N. Y. State Coll. of Agriculture, Cornell Univ., 1923-30; lecturer, Rural Sociology, Drew, 1930-31; Wyoming Conf., 1931; assoc. professor, Rural Sociology, Drew, 1931-40; exchange professor, Nanking Union Theol. Sem., Nanking, China, 1936-38; visiting professor, Rural Church, Union Theol. Sem., Seoul, Korea, 1937-38; professor, Rural Sociology, Drew, 1940 to date; Newark Conf., 1941; exec. comm., N. Y. State Library Ass'n., 1927-30; exec. comm., N. Y. State Bd. of P.T.A., 1927-30; exec. comm., N. Y. State Council of Churches; exec. comm., N. Y. State Council of Religious Edn.; sec., organizing comm., Agricultural Missions Foundation; sec., N. J. State Council of Churches, 1933-40; special adviser, National Christian Council of Japan, summer, 1937; Town and Country Joint Comm. of Home Missions Council of North America and Federal Council of the Churches of Christ in America, 1938——; chm., comm. on research, Town and Country Comm., Home Missions Council of North America, 1939——; chr., comm. on comity and cooperation, N. J. State Council of Churches, 1940——; dir,. clinical training, Interseminary Comm. for Training for the Rural Ministry, 1940——; N. J. Comm. on Work Among Migrants, 1940——; sec., comm. on work with Share Croppers, Home Missions Council of North America, 1942——; visiting professor, Rural Church, Union Theol. Sem., Mexico City, Mexico, summers, 1940, 1941; consultant, Cuban Council of Evangelical Churches, summer, 1942; pub., *The Study of a Rural Parish,* 1915; *Serving the Neighborhood,* 1920; *The Epworth League in Rural Community Service,* 1919; *A Christian in the Countryside,* 1925; *Our Templed Hills,* 1926; *Adventures in Service,* 1928; *What's Right with the Rural Church,* 1930; *The Rural Church in the Far East,* 1938; *Local Church Cooperation in Rural Communities,* 1939; *Building the Rural Church* (in Japanese), 1939; *Christianity and Rural Reconstruction in the Far East* (in Chinese), 1940; *The Rural Church in the Far East* (in Korean), 1940; *A Hundred Games* (in Chinese), 1941; *The Rural Church* (in Spanish), 1942; co-author, *The Library of the Open Road,* 1929; *Rural Health,* 1929; lecturer at various State Colls. of Agriculture; began and developed the plan of extension service of theological seminaries in East Asia and Mexico; contr., agricultural and religious periodicals; address, Drew Forest, Madison, N. J.

The Rev. CHRISTOPHER R. NORTH
A.M.

*Visiting Professor of Hebrew and Old Testament
Exegesis, 1929-1931.*

THE RETIREMENT of Professor Rogers on account of failing health created a vacancy which was temporarily filled by bringing over a noted British Orientalist from one of the Wesleyan theological institutions.

CHRISTOPHER R. NORTH: b. England; entered Wesleyan ministry, 1912; tutor in Old Testament Literature, Handsworth College, 1924——; visiting professor, Hebrew and Old Testament Exegesis, Drew, 1929-1931; address, Handsworth Wood, Birmingham, England.

The Rev. FRED DANIEL GEALY
A.B., S.T.B., S.T.M., Ph.D., D.D.

Visiting Professor of Exegesis of the Greek New Testament, 1937-1938.

DR. GEALY, after thorough preparation, taught New Testament in Aoyama Gakuin, Tokyo, the great Methodist school in Japan, for 14 years. Since his return to America he has lectured on Missions and given instruction in a number of Methodist schools, east and west. At Drew he devoted himself to the subject which he taught in Aoyama, and in which he was a stimulating teacher.

FRED DANIEL GEALY: b. Oil City, Pa., May 13, 1894; A.B., Allegheny Coll., 1916; D.D., 1937; S.T.B., Boston Univ., 1919; Universities of Basle and Berlin, 1920-21; S.T.M., Union Sem., 1929; Ph.D., Boston Univ., 1929; Univ. of Chicago, 1937; m. Mildred Gladys Reader, June 26, 1923; ord. dea., 1917; ord. eld., 1921; entered Erie Conf., 1921; pastor, Townville, Pa., 1921-23; professor, New Testament Language and Literature, Aoyama Gakuin, Tokyo, Japan, 1923-36; visiting professor, Missions, Iliff Sch. of Theology, summer, 1937; visiting professor, Exegesis of the Greek New Testament, Drew, 1937-38; visiting professor, Missions, History of Religions and New Testament, Iliff Sch. of Theology, 1938; visiting professor, Missions and New Testament, Southern Meth. Univ., 1939; visiting professor, History of Religions, Iliff Sch. of Theology, summer, 1939; visiting professor, Political and Cultural History of the Far East, Univ. of Denver, summer, 1939; professor, New Testament Greek, Missions, History of Religions, and Church Music, Southern Meth. Univ., Sch. of Theology, 1939—; ed., *Japan Christian Year Book*, 1935, 1936; pub., *The 'Ipsissima Verba'* or the *'Ipsissimus Spiritus'* (in New Testament Studies), 1942; contr., religious and technical journals; address, Southern Meth. Univ., Dallas, Texas.

The Rev. WILLIAM WARREN SWEET
A.B., A.M., B.D., Th.M., Ph.D., Litt.D., D.D.

Lecturer on American Methodism, 1919-1920, Visiting Professor of Church History, 1932-1933; 1934-1935.

No ONE since Abel Stevens has made so wide and so fruitful a study of the Methodist movement in America as Professor Sweet. Born in Kansas, educated in the middle west and at Drew, he has had unusual opportunities of observation and inquiry. As a teacher he has gained a leading place in the faculty of a great university, and as a research scholar and voluminous writer he has sought out and recorded many facts and aspects of Methodist history and biography that heretofore had not been properly illuminated. The long list of his associations and productions, which follows, is without an equal in the record of any Methodist scholar of his generation. Nor is his field narrowly denominational.

His series on the *Makers of Christianity in America* is already far advanced and covers impartially the entire field of American church history. In his three terms as lecturer here, after "Uncle John" Faulkner had passed on, he rendered rare service to his Alma Mater, which was increased when he gave the Biographical Lectures on the Tipple Foundation, which have been published under the title, *Men of Zeal; The Romance of American Methodist Beginnings.*

WILLIAM WARREN SWEET: b. Baldwin, Kan., Feb. 15, 1881; A.B., Ohio Wesleyan Univ., 1902; Litt. D., 1935; B.D., Drew, 1906; Th.M., Crozer Theol. Sem., 1907; A.M., Univ. of Pa., 1907; Ph.D., 1912; D.D., Cornell Coll., 1922; m. Louise M. Neill, May 18, 1906; ord. dea., 1908; ord. eld., 1910; entered Philadelphia Conf., 1906, pastor, Willow Grove, Pa., 1906-08; Langhorne, Pa., 1908-11; instructor, History, Ohio Wesleyan Univ., 1911-12; ass't. professor, 1912-13; North Indiana Conf., 1913; professor, History, DePauw Univ., 1913-27; lecturer, American Methodism, Drew, 1919-20; elected president, West Virginia Wesleyan Coll., but declined, 1926; dean, Coll. of Liberal Arts, DePauw Univ., 1926-27; professor, History of American Christianity, Univ. of Chicago, 1927—; visiting professor, Church History, Drew, 1932-35; Tipple lecturer on Christian Biography, Drew, 1932; cadet sergt., 18th Co., S.A.T.C., Ft. Sheridan, Ill., 1918; dir., War Aims Course, DePauw Univ., 1918; del., Congress on Christian Work in South America, Montevideo, 1925; Phi Beta Kappa; pub., *The Methodist Episcopal Church and the Civil War*, 1912; *Circuit Rider Days in Indiana*, 1916;

A History of Latin America, 1919; *The Rise of Methodism in the West*, 1920; *Circuit Rider Days Along the Ohio*, 1923; *History—a Survey*, 1923; *Our American Churches*, 1924; *The Story of Religions in America*, 1930; *Religion on the American Frontier* (Vol. I, The Baptists), 1931; *Methodism in American History*, 1933; *Men of Zeal*, 1935; *Religion on the American Frontier* (Vol. II, the Presbyterians), 1936; *Indiana Asbury-DePauw University, 1837-1937*, 1937; *Makers of Christianity: John Cotton to Lyman Abbott*, 1937; *Religion on the American Frontier* (Vol. III, The Congregationalists), 1939; *Religion in Colonial America*, 1942; co-author, *History of North Indiana Conference*, 1917; *Community Religion and the Denominational Heritage*, 1930; *A Biographical Guide to the History of Christianity*, 1931; *Religion in Colonial America*, 1942; contr., *Ency. Britannica* (14th edition); *Dictionary of American Biography;* mem., editorial council and contr., *Dictionary of American History;* winner of 1st prize ($1000) offered by *Chicago Tribune*, 1930, for best 500 word history of the U. S.; contr., current periodicals; address, 5805 Dorchester Ave., Chicago, Ill.

The Rev. JAMES MOFFATT
M.A., B.D., Litt.D., D.D., LL.D.

Visiting Professor of English Bible, 1939-1942.

I HAVE KNOWN Dr. James Moffatt ever since he was a freshman at Glasgow University. He was my near neighbor when we were settled as ministers in Scotland, and for many years he has been my colleague at Union Seminary, New York. He has thus been closely associated with me all my life, and he is the sort of man who soon turns acquaintance into warm friendship. It is impossible for me to write of him with any critical detachment. I met him, as it happened, just the day before I was asked for this article, and he spoke of Stevenson's unfinished masterpiece, *Weir of Hermiston,* which was to culminate, he told me, in a heart-rending scene of the grim, conscientious judge passing sentence on his son. We little thought that a callous editor, at that very moment, was assigning us our parts in a similar scene. I have not the fortitude to pass sentence on Dr. Moffatt, and I am glad to think that it is not necessary. A great jury of readers, all over the world, have agreed on their verdict, and I have nothing to do but to endorse it.

Few scholars have ever made their mark so early as Dr. Moffatt. He had only been a few years out of college when he published his *Historical New Testament,* which may be said to have opened the modern period of New Testament criticism in Great Britain. The book was remarkable, not only for its brilliance, but for a wealth of learning which it would have taken most men a long life-time to acquire. It was at once necessary

PLATE VII—FACULTY

HARRY M. TAYLOR, 1937—
JAMES MOFFATT, 1939-1942
ALBERT B. WEGENER, 1914-1935

WILLIAM P. TOLLEY, 1926-1930
STANLEY R. HOPPER, 1935—
F. TAYLOR JONES, 1929—

to confer the venerable honor of Doctor of Divinity on a man who was still in his twenties, and this was a scandal which had never happened before in Scotland. We were assured, however, by those acquainted with the various colleges, that there was not the slightest danger of its being soon repeated. After the success of his first book Dr. Moffatt was launched on a career of authorship which is one of the marvels of modern theology. The number of his books is a secret known only to librarians, and they are all packed full of knowledge, and cover almost the whole range of theological scholarship. A wise student, when he sets himself to work on any subject, should always begin by asking, "What has Moffatt written about this?" Hundreds of men are now happy graduates because they followed this simple rule. How Dr. Moffatt has accomplished such a mass of work is a mystery, I have often tried to fathom it but have never come near succeeding. From all that one can see of him he takes life easily. He has read more detective novels than any man living; he is a musician, a fisherman, and since coming to America has developed a weird passion for baseball. These are his interests in life, and yet between whiles he has managed to produce that long shelf of books, besides the articles and reviews which he throws off by the dozen every month. How does he do it? To add to the mystery his books are never wooden and mechanical. He is a master of literary style and vivid illustration, and in everything he writes there is a note of genuine sympathy. A certain professor, it is said, was so very dull that after a time the other professors noticed it. Dr. Moffatt has never run true to the professorial type, although he has now followed that calling for more than thirty years in a number of colleges. This is no doubt the reason why his books, most of them written for scholars, are read just as eagerly by plain men and women.

The works by which he is best known are his *Introduction to the New Testament* and his translation of the Bible. Although the *Introduction* appeared a generation ago, it is still the standard work on the subject. Every question in New Testament criticism has been fiercely debated since it was written, but hardly any of Dr. Moffatt's conclusions has been seriously disturbed. The translation of the Bible has become almost a classic. It has won this position by its accurate scholarship, but still more by its literary quality. With his delicate sense of language Dr. Moffatt seems always to hit on word or a turn of phrase which everyone can feel to be exactly right. It has been largely this insight into words which has made him great as a commentator. His commentaries on Revelation and Hebrews, to mention only two, are among the best in any language, and of late years he has edited a series, covering the whole of the New Testament. Several of the volumes he has written himself, and the others have been executed on his plan and under his supervision. It is not too much to say that the Moffatt Commentary is the best now available for ordinary use. A good commentary on the New Testament is the one work that is indispensable to a preacher's library, and by supplying it Dr. Moffatt has put the whole Church in his debt, but to discuss all his books (and they are all worth discussing) would carry me far beyond the limits permitted me. It is enough to say that Dr. Moffatt has won for himself a place that is all his own among modern New Testament scholars. The students of Drew University have enjoyed a rare privilege in having him for a short time among their teachers, and whatever else they have learned from him they will carry with them the memory of a gracious personality. His books will mean far more to them by their knowledge that the author, who has done so much to illuminate Christian history, is himself a modest and lovable Christian man.

E. F. S.

JAMES MOFFATT: b. Glasgow, Scotland, July 4, 1870; M. A., Glasgow Univ., 1889; B.D., 1894; D. Litt., 1909; D.D., St. Andrews Univ., 1901; M.A., Oxford, 1915, D.D., 1927; LL.D., Dickinson Coll., 1928; m. Mary Reith, Sept. 29, 1896; came to U. S., 1927; minister of United Free Ch. of Scotland, 1896-1912; Yates professor of Greek, Mansfield, Coll., Oxford, 1911-15; professor, Church History, United Free Ch. Coll., Glasgow, 1915-27; Washburn professor of Church History, Union Th. Sem., 1927-42; visiting professor, English Bible, Drew. 1939-42; Jowett lecturer, London, 1907; Cunningham lecturer, Edinburgh, 1914; Hibbert lecturer, London, 1921; pub., *Historical New Testament*, 1901; *Primer to Novels of George Meredith*, 1909; *Introduction to Literature of New Testament*, 1911; *Theology of the Gospels*, 1912; *The New Testament, a New Translation*, 1913; *The Old Testament, a New Translation*, 1924; *Approach to the New Testament*, 1921; *Hebrews, in the International Critical Commentary*, 1924; *Everyman's Life of Jesus*, 1924; *The Bible in Scots Literature*, 1925; *Presbyterianism*, 1928; *Love in the New Testament*, 1929; *The Day Before Yesterday*, 1930; *Grace in the New Testament*, 1931; *First Five Centuries of the Church, First Corinthians*, 1938; *The Books of the Prophets*, 1939; address, 445 Riverside Drive, New York, N. Y.

The Rev. WILLIAM GEORGE CHANTER
A.B., M.A., S.T.B., D.D.

Visiting Professor of English Bible, 1942—.

DR. CHANTER has been pastor of the College Church in Wesleyan University, Middletown, where his fine spirit and warm religious zeal commended his ministry to many students. His page in *Zion's Herald* has been eagerly read by a large public.

WILLIAM GEORGE CHANTER: b. New Carlisle, P. Q., Canada, July 29, 1884; came to U. S., 1900; A.B., Wesleyan Univ., 1915; S. T. B., Boston U. Sch. of Theology, 1918; M.A., Harvard U., 1920; D.D., Lawrence Coll., 1930;

ent. Meth. ministry, 1910; pastor, Upton, Mass., 1914-1916; Cliftondale, Saugus, Mass., 1918-1919; Howard Fellow, B. U. S. T., 1919-1920; professor, Ethics and Religion, Wesleyan U., 1923-1941; dean of Freshmen, 1927-1928; dean of univ., 1930-1935; pastor, College Church, 1928-1941; visiting professor English Bible, Drew, 1942——; Army Y.M.C.A. in Mesopotamia, 1916-1917; Phi Beta Kappa; British Great War Medal; address: 12 Academy Road, Madison, N. J.

The Rev.

THOMAS S. KIRKPATRICK SCOTT-CRAIG

M.A., B.D.

Visiting Professor of Church History, 1935-1937.

BEFORE DR. STAFFORD's election to this chair, which had been so long and ably filled by Professor Faulkner, the courses in Church History were given by this highly qualified Scottish scholar, who has since found his place in the faculty of Hobart College.

THOMAS S. KIRKPATRICK SCOTT-CRAIG: b. Edinburgh, Scotland, Dec. 13, 1909; George Watson's Coll., 1920-27; M.A., Edinburgh, 1931; B.D., 1934; Ph.D., 1938; Univ. of Zürich, 1933; Univ. of Tübingen 1934-35; came to U. S., 1935; visiting professor, Church History, Drew, 1935-37; guest assistant, New Testament, General Theol. Sem., 1937-38; ass't. professor, English Literature and lecturer, Christianity and Western Civilization, Hobart Coll. and Wm. Smith Coll., 1938—; licentiate, Ch. of Scotland; pub., *Christian Attitudes to War and Peace,* 1938; editor and translator (with R. E. Davies), *Germany's New Religion,* 1937; address, Hobart Coll., Geneva, N. Y.

The Rev. WILLIAM PEARSON TOLLEY

A.B., A.M., B.D., Ph.D., D.D., LL.D., L.H.D.

Instructor of Systematic Theology, 1926-27; Instructor of Philosophy, 1927-29; Assistant to the President, 1927-29; Associate Professor of Philosophy, 1929-30.

WILLIAM P. TOLLEY made his chief contribution to Drew as first dean of Brothers College. He was largely responsible for its character and educational ideals, and he directed its work through its critical first three years. He had important responsibilities also in Drew Theological Seminary. He had the good fortune to work closely with President Tipple during that fine administrator's best days and to be forced early into executive work himself. His position as assistant to the president was not an easy one to fill while illness forced Dr. Tipple's gradual withdrawal from campus affairs in the months preceding his resignation, for the administrative system had been highly centralized. The fact that the educational framework of Brothers College was forged during that difficult period and departed decisively from past models to achieve a strength and distinction of its own is proof of William P. Tolley's genius.

No task the educational world afforded could have been more congenial to him at that time than the organization of a new college of liberal arts, with plenty of funds for its first few years and no hampering traditions. His fundamental educational concepts demanded quality, care for the individual, and breadth of view. He was able to lead his faculty, president, and trustees to make these the student's basic right in the "adventure in excellence." The curriculum and teaching methods which were developed around them were not radical, but they included experimentation with procedures like comprehensive examinations, fields of concentration, survey courses, and divisional organization of the faculty which were proved sound in many established universities after they had been pioneered in Brothers College.

Dean Tolley's faculty always had a sense of excitement. He had at Drew and has retained at Allegheny and at Syracuse an eagerness, a challenge to the staid, which lifts work out of routine. The movements of his mind are logical, but they are fresh and unexpected. William P. Tolley is a teacher's dean or president, a man with extraordinary ability to stimulate other people and to keep them working at their best level. He hates complacency.

His importance to Drew lies not only in what he did while he was here, but in its continuing effect in the sound evolution of the college. He has moved in larger circles since he left Madison, but he cannot have more significant work to do.

F. T. J.

WILLIAM PEARSON TOLLEY: b. Sept. 13, 1900, Honesdale, Pa.; B.A., Syracuse Univ., 1922; M.A., 1924; B.D., Drew, 1925; M.A., Columbia Univ., 1927; Ph.D., 1930; D.D., Mt. Union Coll., 1931; LL.D., Dickinson Coll., 1933; Litt.D., Grove City Coll., 1937; m. Ruth Marion Canfield, July 3, 1925; ord. dea., 1924; ord. eld., 1926; entered N. Y. East Conf., 1923; alumni secretary, Drew, 1925-27; instructor, Systematic Theology, 1926-27; instruc-tor, Philosophy, 1927-29; assistant to the president, 1927-29; dean, Summer Sch., 1928-29; acting dean and instructor in Philosophy, B r o t h e r s Coll., Drew, 1928-29; associate professor, Philosophy, Drew, 1929-30; associate professor, Philosophy, Brothers Coll., Drew, 1929-30; dean, 1929-31; professor, Philosophy, 1930-31; president, Allegheny Coll., 1931-42; Chancellor, Syracuse University, 1942——; Erie Conf., 1931; chr., exec. comm., Cooperative Study in Gen. Edn. Amer. Council on Edn.; chr., Comm'n. on Academic Freedom and Tenure, Ass'n. of Amer. Colleges; dir., Ass'n. of Amer. Colleges, trustee, Stone Methodist Church, Meadville, Pa.; Pres., Ass'n. of College Presidents of Pa.; University Senate, Methodist Ch.; del., Northeast Jurisdictional Conf., 1920; Phi Beta Kappa; pub., *The Idea of God in the Philosophy of St. Augustine*, 1930; address, Syracuse Univ., Syracuse, N. Y.

The Rev. JOHN KEITH BENTON
AB., B.D., Ph.D.

Assistant Professor of Philosophy, 1931-1934; Associate Professor of Psychology and Philosophy, 1934-1936.

A YOUNG Southerner with a brilliant record in Alabama, Yale, and Edinburgh, with a happy way among students and skill in teaching such as few men can hope to attain, John K. Benton was a marked man from the beginning. His Drew Theological Seminary courses were chiefly in the College of Religious Education and Missions and the bulk of his work at Drew was in Brothers College, where he played a notable part, but the influence of his thought and of his personality was important in the seminary. He asked disconcerting yet constructive questions. His call to head Vanderbilt University's School of Religion in his beloved South was a loss to Drew, but not a surprise.

F. T. J.

JOHN KEITH BENTON: b. Banks, Alabama, May 24, 1896; A.B., Birmingham-Southern Coll., 1923; B.D., Yale Univ., 1926; Ph.D., Univ. of Edinburgh, 1934; m. (1) Mary Edda Cox, June 12, 1928, m. (2) Lois Cooper, Aug. 6, 1934; ord. dea., 1933; ord. eld., 1937; entered North Alabama Conf., 1922; ass't. pastor, Ensley First Ch., Birmingham, Ala., 1921-23; pastor, Clinton, Conn., 1924-26; professor, Philosophy and Religion, Southern Coll., 1926-29; ass't. professor, Philosophy and Psychology, Brothers Coll. of Drew Univ., 1931-34; assoc. professor, 1934-37; professor, 1937-39; visiting professor, Christine Doctrine, Duke Univ., 1938-39; dean, Sch. of Religion, Vanderbilt Univ., 1939——; chairman, Central Comm., National Council on Religion in Higher Edn., 1935-37; fellow, National Council on Religion in Higher Edn.; advisory council, *Religion in Life;* pub., abstracts of lectures on Christianity and Mental Hygiene, in proceedings of the National Conf. on Religion and Mental Hygiene, 1937; contr., relig. journals; address, 205 Walnut Drive, Nashville, Tenn.

The Rev. GEOFFREY WARDLE STAFFORD
A.B., M.A., B.D., Litt.D.

Associate Professor, Church History, 1937-1938; Associate Professor of Christian History, 1938—.

THE TRADITIONS of Methodism in the Old World and in the New are uniquely and happily united in Geoffrey Wardle Stafford. His father Dr. John Thomas Wardle Stafford spent fifty-five years in active ministerial service. He was president of the Wesleyan Conference in 1920. He received the degree Doctor of Civil Law from Durham University. Added to his many years of ecclesiastical activity in England were three years which were spent as pastor of the Metropolitan Church of the United Church of Canada in Toronto. He was fraternal delegate to the General Conference of the Methodist Episcopal Church in the United States in 1902. He received the degree D.D. from Northwestern University and the degree S.T.D. from Syracuse University. In 1926 he was a delegate to the Uniting Conference which marked the organization of the United Church of Canada. With this background of his father's distinguished service in two continents the son of Dr. J. T. Wardle Stafford may well have seemed to be marked for diversified experience and leadership.

Young Stafford attended the University of Durham from 1913 to 1915 receiving the degree B.A. (War degree) from that institution. He attended Oxford University from 1918 to 1921, in the latter year receiving the degree B.A. In 1924 he received the M.A. degree

from Oxford.   He was granted the London University
B.D. in 1924.   During the first World War, he served
as a lieutenant in the Northumberland Fusiliers of the
British Army (1915-1918).   At the age of seventeen he
began his work as a lay preacher at Durham University.
He came to the United States in 1921 and was naturalized in 1928.   From 1921 to 1922 he was a lecturer in
the American University, Washington, D. C.   There
followed a period as associate pastor of the First Methodist Church, Baltimore, Maryland, and then three years
as pastor of Wesley Church of Milwaukee, Wisconsin
and six years as pastor of Court Street Methodist Church,
Rockford, Illinois.   From 1928 to 1932 he was a lecturer
in religion in Rockford College, Rockford, Illinois.
From 1932 to 1937 he was pastor of University Temple,
Seattle, Washington.   Since 1937 he has been associate
professor in charge of the department of Christian
History in Drew ·Theological Seminary.   From 1937 to
1942 he has carried on graduate studies in Columbia
University.   He received the honorary degree Litt.D.
from West Virginia Wesleyan College in 1928.

On December 27, 1923 this son of a distinguished
leader of British Methodism married Helene Hamilton,
the gifted daughter of Bishop John W. Hamilton of the
Methodist Episcopal Church.   Bishop Hamilton was a
member of the first graduating class of Boston University School of Theology in 1871. He was elected bishop
in 1900 and stationed at San Francisco and later in
Boston.   When he retired from active service as a bishop
in 1916 he became Chancellor of the American University which position he held for six years.   Thus in the
Stafford home, British and American Methodism met
and became one in a memorable fashion.

Dr. Geoffrey Stafford published a volume on *The*

Sermon on the Mount (Abingdon Press) in 1927. He has been deeply interested in the Pacific Institute of World Affairs at Riverside, California, and gave the opening address in 1934, 1935, 1938 and 1940. He has often returned to England and was summer preacher at Central Hall, Westminster in 1923, 1930, 1933, 1936, 1937 (eight Sundays) and 1939. He has preached in Lyndhurst Road Congregational Church, Bunyan Meeting, Bedford, and at the Central Mission Hall of Manchester, at Victoria Hall, Sheffield; Oxford Place, Leeds, and the Central Hall of Bristol.

As a preacher Professor Stafford is master of an English style of dignity, force and resonant power. He has brought vitality and energy to every position which he has held. He goes on with his work as a technical scholar with constant fidelity. He makes happy human contacts everywhere and the students who have worked with him at Drew Theological Seminary have learned to think of him not only as a stimulating teacher but as an understanding friend. He is a man of indubitable loyalty to the classical Christian tradition and of eager and responsive interest in that which has promised in the wide world of life and in the wider world of thought.

L. H. H.

GEOFFREY WARDLE STAFFORD: b. Birmingham, England, Jan. 5, 1898; Scarborough Coll., 1907-1913; B.A., Durham Univ., 1916; Wadham Coll. (Oxford Univ.), 1921; M.A., Oxford University, 1924; B.D., London Univ., 1932; Litt.D., West Virginia Wesleyan Coll., 1928; m. Helene Hamilton, December 27, 1923; came to U. S., 1921, naturalized, 1928; assoc. pastor, First M. E. Ch., Baltimore, Md., 1921-23; pastor, Wesley Ch., Milwaukee, Wis., 1923-26; Court St. Ch., Rockford, Ill., 1926-32; Univ. Temple Ch., Seattle, Wash., 1932-37; assoc. prof., Church history, Drew, 1937—; assoc. prof., Christian history, 1938—; lecturer in religion, Rockford Coll., 1928-32; guest preacher, Stanford Univ., 1932-36; Lt., Northumberland Fusiliers, British Army; Opening address at the Pacific Institute of World Affairs, Riverside, Calif., 1934, 1935, 1936, 1938, and 1940 (Political Science Institute); pub., *The Sermon on the Mount*, 1927; address, 52 Hillside Ave., Madison, N. J., Summer home, Marshfield, Mass.

The Rev. STANLEY ROMAINE HOPPER
A.B., S.T.B., Ph.D.

*Instructor of Homiletics, 1935-37; Assistant Professor of
Homiletics and the Christian Criticism of Life, 1937-40;
Associate Professor, 1940—.*

STANLEY R. HOPPER is like a river which draws its waters
from many sources, but brings them down one channel
to the sea. There have been invitations to test his
powers elsewhere than at Drew, notably in the dean-
ships of two other institutions, but so far these have been
like tempting water to run up hill.

Dr. Hopper's intellectual life stems from relationships with Irving Babbitt at Harvard, Emil Brunner at
Zurich, from the University of Southern California,
from Mansfield College, Oxford, and from a host of
American and European poets and philosophers. The
minister's education, as he sees it, needs to cover more
than techniques and to range far beyond formal
theology, although techniques and theology are part of
his own field of teaching. He wants a pulpit which
commands the mind as well as the heart, which has a
sense of values as well as a sense of dramatics, and which
knows it does not need to begin its intellectual life
anew each generation. Books, with him and his students, are living experiences. The criticism and use
of literary materials is his own major interest in the
minister's training, and in seven short years of teaching
at Drew he has made himself an adept at leading young
men toward the kind of literary and philosophical
maturity he covets for them.

In 1942 it is obviously too early to summarize Dr.
Hopper's usefulness at Drew. He has an important and

increasing place in the affections of the students, who
find he understands their speech; he himself filled posts
of student leadership as an undergraduate, and he retains
an easy accessibility to students. Administrative work
is not his specialty, but he handles it ably. His reputation as a teacher is developing steadily. His place as a
scholar and author is just beginning to appear. His
personal qualities, drawing like his intellectual wealth
from east, west, north, and south, blend also to enrich
the one main stream of life which flows through Drew.

F. T. J.

STANLEY ROMAINE HOPPER: b. Fresno,
Cal., March 22, 1907; A.B., Univ. of
Southern Cal., 1928; S.T.B., Boston
Univ. Sch. of Theol., 1931; Harvard
Univ., 1930-31; Univ. of Zurich, 1931-
32; Mansfield Coll., Oxford, 1932;
Ph.D., Drew, 1936; m. Helen Bagby,
March 3, 1928; ord. dea., 1930; ord.
eld., 1931; entered New Hampshire
Conf., 1930; pastor, San Joaquin and
Tranquility, Cal., 1927; First, Dinuba,
Cal., 1928; First Congl., Farmington,
N. H., 1928-31; Southern Cal. Conf.,
1931; Clifford, Pa., 1932-33; Park,
New Haven, Conn., 1933-35; lecturer,
Biblical Lit., Brothers Coll. of Drew
Univ., 1933-34; instructor, Biblical
Lit., 1934-35; instructor, Homiletics,
Drew, 1935-37; ass't. professor, Homi-
letics and the Christian Criticism of
Life, 1937-40; Southern California-
Arizona Conf., 1939; assoc. professor,
Homiletics and the Christian Criticism
of Life, 1940——; assistant to the dean,
Drew, 1935——; Delta Sigma Rho;
Duodecim Society of Historical Theo-
logians; editor, *The Interseminarian*,
1929-30; contr., relig. periodicals; Sec-
retary of the American Assn. of Pro-
fessors of Homiletics, 1942-43; address,
Drew Forest, Madison, N. J.

The Rev. HARRY MILTON TAYLOR
A.B., M.A., B.D., Ph.D.

*Instructor of Systematic Theology, 1937-38; Assistant
Professor, 1938-1942; Associate Professor, 1942——.*

HARRY M. TAYLOR has made himself a secure place at
Drew, but it is not yet time to write his story, for his
main achievements lie ahead. Yet not all of them.
He has won acceptance as a colleague of Edwin Lewis,

which speaks for itself among those who know Drew, he is becoming known as an effective preacher, and he will make a name as an author. Give him twenty-five more years.

A keen sense of the importance of the source documents characterizes his work as a philosophical scholar. This interest is carried over to his teaching and reflects there in precision and fruitfulness of concept and illustration. He has an excellent memory and a ready tongue. He is still inclined to be experimental in the classroom, and probably will be all his life. He writes at least as well as he speaks. His students find his work stimulating, and, as the tradition is in his department, demanding.

Dr. Taylor is not experimental as to his philosophical and theological convictions, or as to his understanding of where his own field of usefulness lies. His philosophical journey has been a long one, carrying him to a position of loyalty to an historic faith which he makes consistent with a clear and wide view of the world of his own day. Theology in his mind becomes queen of the sciences in the sense that a man's view of God and of himself conditions all the rest of his thinking, determines its validity from the beginning.

His particular expression of loyalty to Drew has taken the form of standing firmly by his decision to teach in the face of tempting calls from distinguished pulpits. His reputation as a preacher has to be seen in the light of an eager interest in people and a love of argument which places him at his best in small friendly groups and keeps him up to all hours talking and reading. His home is never closed to his friends or his students, but his study door is scrupulously guarded.

A wholesome, normal sort of man of thirty-four who

is already a competent voice in his own field and who pursues habits of hard, persistent work is a man to watch. He will continue to grow.   And his words will carry.

F. T. J.

HARRY MILTON TAYLOR: b. Tamaqua, Pa., July 7, 1908; A.B., Lafayette Coll., 1930; M.A., Columbia Univ., 1931; B.D., Drew, 1934; Ph.D., 1938; m. Evelyn Frances Freeland, July 3, 1933; ord. dea., 1934; ord. eld., 1936; entered Newark Conf., 1934; pastor, Westtown Circuit, Westtown, N. Y., 1933-36; visiting instructor, System-atic Theology, Drew, 1936-37; pastor, New Providence, N. J., 1937-38; instructor, Systematic Theology, Drew, 1937-38; assistant professor, Systematic Theology, 1938-42; associate professor, Systematic Theology, 1942—; contr., religious periodicals; address, 16 Madison Ave., Madison, N. J.

ASSISTANT PROFESSOR

HARRY WILBUR SIMESTER

B.P.E., A.B.

Assistant Professor, Physical Education, 1935-1941; Director, 1941.

DREW HAS given major attention to health for thirty-two years, leading all its contemporaries.   Ground was broken for a gymnasium in 1909, and from 1910 when it was finished and opened until today Drew has always had a specialist in physical education on the faculty. Harry W. Simester, a notable college coach and counsellor of young men, was chosen to succeed the inimitable "Prof" Wegener as the second full-time occupant of the position.   Stacy B. Betzler of the local Y.M.C.A. had given part-time instruction from the time the gymnasium was opened until 1913, and Byron G. Sherman of the Morristown "Y" during the 1913-1914 year.   Mr. Wegener came in 1914, and by eager persuasion and contagious example made games and gymnastics and swimming popular among the young men of the Seminary, handling the first Brothers College coaching too, when that infant organization began making its demands in 1928. Professor Simester took his place in 1935 and has continued his good tradition. The faculty gave full recognition to the significance of his work in 1936 by making it obligatory for all new men. It is a tribute to "Coach's" powers that the students like the requirement.

Professor Simester, like his predecessor, knows the large and general importance of his work in the life of the minister. Skill in certain games and even personal health are only part of it: under Simester's direction on floor and field men also learn sportsmanship, self control, discipline, the essential nature of teamwork. He has been conspicuously successful in making these the outcome of his training. While he helps men build strong bodies he gives them practice in translating ethics into action.

F. T. J.

HARRY WILBUR SIMESTER: b. Prairie Center, Ill., Aug. 7, 1904; B.P.E., Chicago YMCA College, 1926; A.B., Ohio Wesleyan Univ., 1931; Ohio Wesleyan Univ., 1931-33; m. Helen L. Downing, July 21, 1934; ass't. physical dir., Division St. YMCA, Chicago, Ill., 1925-26; industrial phys. dir., YMCA, Grand Rapids, Mich., 1926-27; dir. of gymnasium work, Ohio Wesleyan Univ., 1927-33; dir. of men's work, Irving Park YMCA, Chicago, Ill., 1933-34; activities dir., YMCA, Summit, N. J., 1934-35; assistant professor, physical education, Drew, 1935-41; director of physical education, Drew, 1941—; address, 45 Highland Avenue, Madison, N. J.

The Rev. JONATHAN KELSEY BURR
A.B., A.M., D.D.

Adjunct Professor of Hebrew and Old Testament Exegesis, 1867-1868.

THE FAILURE of Dr. John W. Lindsay to accept the chair of Exegetical Theology to which he was elected in 1867 necessitated the temporary employment of competent part-time teachers. One of these was Dr. J. K. Burr, a graduate of Wesleyan and of Union Seminary. He served until James Strong was installed the following year.

JONATHAN KELSEY BURR: b. Middletown, Conn., Sept. 21, 1825; A.B., Wesleyan Univ., 1845; A.M., 1848; D.D., 1872; Union Theol. Sem., 1846; m. Pamela C. Brown, Mar. 29, 1858; ord. dea., 1850; ord. eld., 1852; entered New Jersey Conf., 1848; ass't. pastor, Rome and Wantage Circuit, N. J., 1848-49; pastor, Milford, Pa., 1849-51; Orange, N. J., 1851-53; Union and Burlington, N. J., 1853-55; Hoboken, N. J., 1855-57; Union St., Trenton, N. J., 1857-58; Newark Conf., 1858; Clinton St., Newark, N. J., 1858-60; Orange, N. J., 1860-62; Market St., Paterson, N. J., 1862-64; Hoboken, N. J., 1864-67; Central, Newark, N. J., 1867-70; adjunct professor, Hebrew and Old Testament Exegesis, Drew, 1867-68; pastor, Morristown, N. J., 1870-73; Hoboken, N. J., 1873-74; Madison, N. J., 1874-77; Montclair, N. J., 1877-79; supernumerary, 1879-82; del., Gen. Conf., 1872; mem., American New Testament Revision Comm.; pub., Job (*Whedon's Commentary*), 1881; contr., McClintock and Strong's *Cyclopedia;* d. April 24, 1882.

The Rev. JONATHAN TOWNLEY CRANE
A.B.

Adjunct Professor of New Testament Greek and Exegesis, 1867-1868.

DREW opened in 1867 with only two of its four chairs filled. During that first year Dr. McClintock met the

demand for instruction in New Testament by calling
in the Hackettstown, N. J., pastor, a Princeton graduate
of 1843, who served until the young Morristown
preacher, Henry A. Buttz, joined the faculty—for good!
Dr. Crane was an able man in his own right, and his
accomplished wife was the daughter of George Peck,
Advocate editor, and niece of Bishop Peck. The fourteenth child of that union was Stephen Crane, the author
of *The Red Badge of Courage*.

JONATHAN TOWNLEY CRANE: b. near
Elizabeth, N. J., June 19, 1819; A.B.,
Princeton Coll., 1843; m. Mary Helen
Peck, 1848; ord. dea., 1847; ord. eld.,
1849; entered New Jersey Conf., 1845;
pastor, Asbury Circuit, Quarantine and
Port Richmond, N. Y., 1845-46; Hope,
N. J., 1846-47; Belvidere, N. J., 1847-
48; Orange, N. J., 1848-49; principal,
Pennington, Sem., 1849-58; Trinity,
Jersey City, N. J., 1858-60; Haver-
straw, N. Y., 1860-62; Central, Newark, N. J., 1862-64; Morristown, N. J.,
1864-67; Hackettstown, N. J., 1867-68;
adjunct professor, Greek and New
Testament Exegesis, Drew, 1867-68;
sup't., Newark District, 1868-72; sup't.,
Elizabeth District, 1872-76; Cross St.,
Paterson, N. J., 1876-78; Port Jervis,
N. Y., 1878-80; pub., *Essay on Danc-
ing*, 1848; *The Right Way, or Practical Lectures on the Decalogue*, 1853;
Christian Duty in Regard to Slavery,
1860; *Popular Amusements*, 1869; *Arts
of Intoxication*, 1870; *Holiness the
Birthright of all God's Children*, 1874;
Methodism and Its Methods, 1875;
contr., relig. periodicals; d. Feb. 16,
1880.

The Rev. HENRY CLAY WHITING
A.B., A.M., B.D., Ph.D.

*Instructor of Introductory Department and Latin, 1870-
1873. Adjunct Professor of Latin and Greek, 1873-1874.*

BEFORE Drew found itself—indeed a half century before
Brothers College supplied a long-felt want of a feeding
school—various expedients were tried to make up for
the deficiencies in preparatory work of its matriculants.
This accounts for the addition, in 1873, of an adjunct
professor of Latin and Greek, Henry C. Whiting,

graduate of Union College and Drew, and for thirty years the Latin master of Dickinson College.

HENRY CLAY WHITING: b. Speedsville, N. Y., Mar. 27, 1845; A.B., Union Coll., 1867, A.M., 1869; B.D., Drew, 1874; Ph.D., Illinois Wesleyan Univ., 1876; m. Mary Louise Freeman, Nov. 21, 1867; principal, Franklin Acad., 1867-68; principal, Classical Dep't., Union Schs. of Schenectady, N. Y., 1868-70; instructor, Introductory Dep't. and Latin, Drew, 1870-73; entered Troy Conf., 1873; adjunct pro-fessor, Latin and Greek, Drew, 1873-74; Newark Conf., 1875; professor, Ancient Languages, Centenary Collegiate Inst., 1874-78; vice-president, Pennington Sem., 1878-79; Central Pennsylvania Conf., 1879; professor, Latin and German, Dickinson Coll., 1879-84; professor, Latin, 1884-1901; co-author, Seneca's Moral Essays, 1877; contr., McClintock and Strong's Cyclopedia; d. Feb. 1, 1901.

The Rev. WALLACE BRUCE FLEMING
A.B., A.M., B.D., Ph.D., D.D., LL.D.

Instructor in Greek, 1909-1912; Adjunct Professor of Greek and Hebrew, 1912-1915.

IN 1909 a young minister of Newark Conference was called back to his Alma Mater to give instruction in Greek. Three years later he was advanced to an adjunct professorship, to which the registrar's duties were soon added. His character and attainments attracted outside attention and he went on to college presidencies in West Virginia and Kansas.

WALLACE BRUCE FLEMING: b. Cambridge, O., Nov. 22, 1872; A.B., Muskingum Coll., 1894; A.M., 1897; D.D., 1912; B.D., Drew, 1897; Grad. Sch., 1908-09; Ph.D., Columbia, 1914; LL.D., West Virginia Wesleyan Coll., 1922; m. (1) Bertha G. Baldwin, April 8, 1897; m. (2) Helen Wilson, Dec. 16, 1932; ord. dea., 1897; ord. eld., 1899; entered Newark Conf., 1897; pastor, North Paterson, N. J., 1897-99; Bayonne, N. J., 1899-1904; Maple-wood, N. J., 1904-11; instructor, Greek, Drew, 1909-12; registrar, 1911-15; adjunct professor, Greek and Hebrew, 1912-15; West Virginia Conf., 1915; president, West Virginia Wesleyan Coll., 1915-22; Kansas Conf., 1922; president, Baker Univ., 1922-36; vice-president, West Virginia Wesleyan Coll., 1937——; pub., History of the City Tyre, 1915; Guide Posts to Life Work, 1923; address, Buckhannon, W. Va.

The Rev. JOHN GEORGE BENSON
A.B., A.M., D.D.

Adjunct Professor of Applied Christianity, 1920-1921.

SUBJECTS undreamed of in the founders' day have multiplied in the third quarter of Drew's existence. In 1867 there was not a Methodist hospital in America, and there was no compunction of conscience because of the lack. But by 1920 hospital work was accepted as a responsibility of the church, and in that year Dr. Benson was appointed to lecture to the students on this and other practical applications of Christian doctrine. Dr. Benson, the lecturer, has since become one of the leading hospital executives in Methodism.

JOHN GEORGE BENSON: b. near Richmond, Ind., Feb. 1, 1881; A.B, A.M., DePauw, 1906; D.D., 1934; Boston U. Sch. of Theology, 1906-1909; D.D., Ohio Northern U., 1930; m. Henrietta Jordan, Aug. 29, 1906; ord. dea., 1910; ord. eld., 1911; entered N. W. Indiana Conf., 1905; pastor, Morton and Brick Chapel, 1903-1906; Waynetown, Ind., 1909-1911; Montrose, Terre Haute, 1911-1913; Brazil, Ind., 1913-1916; Detroit Conf., 1916; Wesley Ch., Detroit, 1916-1919; New York Conf., 1919; Ed. Sec., Centenary, 1919-1920; Union Church, N. Y., 1920-1923; adjunct professor, Applied Christianity, Drew, 1920-1921; Monte Mario Ass'n. Bd. of F. M., 1923-1925; Ohio Conf., 1925; Supt., White Cross Hospital, Columbus, 1925-1930; gen. supt., Methodist Hospital, Indianapolis, 1931—; N. W. Indiana Conf., 1931; address, 3663 N. Delaware St., Indianapolis, Ind.

INSTRUCTORS

ᵍᵛᵍᵛᵍᵛᵍᵛᵍᵛ ᵍᵛᵍᵛᵍᵛᵍᵛᵍᵛ ᵍᵛᵍᵛᵍᵛᵍᵛᵍᵛ ᵍᵛᵍᵛᵍᵛᵍᵛᵍᵛ ᵍᵛᵍᵛᵍᵛᵍᵛᵍᵛ ᵍᵛᵍᵛᵍᵛᵍᵛᵍᵛ

JAMES HENRY WORMAN

A.M., Ph.D., LL.D.

Instructor in Hebrew and Modern Languages, 1867-1872;
Librarian, 1867-1870; Acting-Librarian, 1871-1872.

IF THERE was ever a general utility man on the Drew campus, it was this brisk little German genius. An accomplished and versatile linguist, an experienced bookman, later to become yoke-fellow with John H. Vincent in the Chautauqua movement, his name appears on the first list of the Drew Faculty. The editorial team of "McClintock & Strong" kept him busy on their various projects, literary, educational and administrative. With him the line of Drew librarians was auspiciously inaugurated.

JAMES HENRY WORMAN: b. Berlin, Germany, Feb. 28, 1845; Univ. of Berlin; Sorbonne, Paris; A.M., Dickinson Coll., 1867; Ph.D., DePauw Univ., 1882; LL.D., Md. Union Coll.; m. (1) Emma Parker Davis, Sept. 10, 1866; m. (2) Mary A. Payne, Apr. 4, 1898. Ass't professor, Knox Coll., 1865-66; librarian, Drew, 1868-70; acting librarian, 1871-72; instructor, Hebrew and Modern Languages, 1867-72; editor, *Chenango Telegraph,* 1877-85; assoc. editor, *National Repository,* 1876-80; head, Southern Chautauqua Sch., 1882-1930; Round Lake Summer Schs., 1885-1930; founded, 1878, and conducted in Chautauqua, N. Y., 1878-80; the corr. system of study; professor, Adelphi Coll., 1877-82; professor, Vanderbilt U., 1882-85; editor *Saratogian,* 1885-87; editor-in-chief, *Outing,* 1887-1900; U. S. consul, Munich, Germany, 1899-1902; consul-general, 1902-04; consul, Three Rivers, Canada, 1904-08; special gov't. work, 1908-30. Prepared commercial courses for French and Spanish instru., Mass. Univ. Extension Bd., 1915; acting professor, Spanish, Univ. of Vt., 1916; head of dep't., 1917; pub., Chautauqua Language Series (French, German and Spanish): also other modern lang. textbooks; contr., McClintock & Strong's *Cyclopedia;* d. Jan. 24, 1930.

204

The Rev. JOHN TALBOT GRACEY

A.M.

Instructor in History, 1870-1871.

HIS DREW year was but an incident in a long and notable career, which had begun as a pastor in the South, continued as a missionary in India, and included important pastorates in western New York, and notable service as author and editor.

JOHN TALBOT GRACEY: b. Haverford, Pa., Sept. 16, 1831; A.M., Dickinson Coll., 1867; studied medicine; m. Annie Ryder, Mar. 10, 1858; ord. dea., 1854; ord. eld., 1856; entered Virginia Conf., 1850; pastor, Caroline Circuit, Va., 1850-52; Philadelphia Conf., 1852; Waynesburg, Pa., 1852-53; Tremont and Pine Grove, Pa., 1853-54; Mount Joy and Bainbridge, Pa., 1854-55; Doylestown, Pa., 1855-56; Second, Pottsville, Pa., 1856-57; Port Richmond, Pa., 1857-58; Georgetown, Pa., 1858-60; Cambridge Circuit, Pa., 1860-61; missionary, Sitapur, India, 1861-65; India Mission Conf., 1865; Bareilly, India, 1865-66; Nynee Tal, India, 1866-68; Philadelphia Conf., 1868; supernumerary, 1868-70; instructor, History, Drew, 1870-71; Media, Pa., 1871-72; Central New York Conf., 1872; University Ave., Syracuse, N. Y., 1872-73; Clifton Springs, N. Y., 1873-76; Penfield, N. Y., 1876-77; ass't. sec'y., Missionary Soc., 1877-78; Genesee Conf., 1878; Dansville, N. Y., 1878-80; sup't., Rochester District, 1880-84; Alexander St., Rochester, N. Y., 1884-86; Grace, Buffalo, N. Y., 1886-89; Conference Tract sec'y., 1889-90; ass't. editor, *Northern Christian Advocate,* 1890-1900; missionary editor, 1900-01; editor, *Missionary Review of the World,* 1901-04; del., Gen. Conf., 1868; pub., *Manual of Modern Missions; India: Its Country, People, and Missions,* 1884; *India: Manners, Customs and Religions; China: Its Country, People, and Missions; China in Outline; Open Doors;* rewrote, Reid's *History of Methodist Missions;* contr., relig. periodicals; d. Jan. 5, 1912.

The Rev. STEPHEN LIVINGSTON BALDWIN

A.M., B.D.

Instructor in Practical Theology, 1870-1871.

DR. BALDWIN, a successful China missionary on furlough, came to the rescue when Dr. McClintock was stricken and the infant faculty crippled almost at birth. It was the only teaching experience in his career. Two facts should be noted regarding him: he had attended the Concord N. H. Biblical Institute, the first Methodist theological school in America; and his daughter, Josephine, became a Drew teacher.

STEPHEN LIVINGSTON BALDWIN: b. Somerville, N. J., Jan. 11, 1835; Newark Wesleyan Inst., 1855; Biblical Inst., Concord, N. H., 1856-58; A.M., Wesleyan Univ., 1867; D.D., 1878; D.D., Rutgers Coll., 1880; m. (1) Nettie M. Graham, Sept. 8, 1858; m. (2) Esther E. Jennan, April 15, 1862; ord. dea., 1858; ord. eld., 1858; entered Newark Conf., 1858; pastor, Foochow, China, 1858-61; Greenville, N. J., 1861-62; Foochow, China, 1862-71; instructor, Practical Theology, Drew, 1870-71; Bloomfield, N. J., 1871-72; Foochow, China, 1872-80; Centenary, Newark, N. J., 1880-82; St. Paul's, Newark, N. J., 1882-84; Nyack, N. Y., 1884-85; New England Conf., 1885; Saratoga St., Boston, Mass., 1885-88; St. John's, Boston, Mass., 1888; rec. sec'y., Missionary Soc., 1888-1902; del., Gen. Conf., 1880, 1896; pub., *The Opium Traffic in China; Foreign Missions of the Protestant Churches*, 1900; translated in Foochow, *Judges, Proverbs, Daniel, and the M. E. Discipline;* translated into English, *Who is Jesus?* by Sia Sek Ong; editor, *Chinese Recorder*, 1867-70; contr., relig. periodicals; d. July 28, 1902.

The Rev. JOHN NEWTON IRVIN

A.B., M.A., B.D.

Assistant in Introductory Department, 1870-1871; Instructor of Greek, 1871-1872.

ONE OF THE young men who taught in the Introductory Department at the outset.

JOHN NEWTON IRVIN: b. Mont Solon, Va., April 20, 1847; A.B., Ohio Wesleyan Univ., 1870; A.M., 1873; B.D., Drew, 1872; Univ. of Leipzig and Univ. of Berlin, 1880-82; m. Mary Humphreys, Oct. 19, 1873; assistant, Introductory Department, Drew, 1870-71; instructor, Greek, 1871-72; ord. dea., 1872; ord. eld., 1874; entered Cincinnati Conf., 1872; pastor, Fairmount, O., 1872-73; Mount Auburn, Cincinnati, O., 1873-75; Lebanon, O., 1875-78; Trinity, Cincinnati, O., 1878-80; supernumerary, 1880-82; Grace, Piqua, O., 1882-83; Roper, Dayton, O., 1883-85; contr., relig. periodicals; d. Mar. 6, 1885.

The Rev. SOLOMON PARSONS
A.B., M.A.

Instructor in Mathematics and Science, 1871-1872.

WHILE PASTOR of the Madison Church, this young graduate of Wesleyan, later influential in Newark Conference affairs, gave instruction to ministerial students who were deficient in their preparation.

SOLOMON PARSONS: b. Millbrook, N. J., Aug. 10, 1832; A.B., Pennington Sem.; A.M., Wesleyan Univ., 1858; m. (1) Mary Martha Peck, Nov. 10, 1859, m. (2) Susan Louise Towt, Sept. 11, 1867; ord. dea., 1860; ord. eld., 1862; entered Newark Conf., 1858; pastor, Chatham, N. J., 1858-59; Basking Ridge, N. J., 1859-60; Perth Amboy, N. J., 1860-61; Spring Valley, N. J., 1861-63; Somerville, N. J., 1863-65; First, Phillipsburg, N. J., 1865-67; Nyack, N. Y., 1867-69; Madison, N. J., 1869-72; instructor, Mathematics and Science, Drew, 1871-72; Hoboken, N. J., 1872-74; Bound Brook, N. J., 1874-76; Trinity, Staten Island, N. Y., 1876-79; Elizabeth Ave., Newark, N. J., 1879-80; St. Paul's, Staten Island, N. Y., 1880-82; Summit, N. J., 1882-84; Belvidere, N. J., 1884-87; Prospect St., Paterson, N. J., 1887-92; conf. temperance agt., 1892-97; del., Gen. Conf., 1880, 1884; d. Nov. 21, 1897.

The Rev. WARREN LANNING HOAGLAND
A.B., M.A., B.D., D.D.

Instructor in Mathematics and Science, 1872-1873.

AT A TIME when public high schools were uncommon and Methodist secondary schools were few, the seminary found it expedient to give instruction in liberal arts courses to students whose preparation was deficient. Mr. Hoagland was one of the young pastors in the vicinity who were employed for this teaching service for brief periods.

WARREN LANNING HOAGLAND: b. Warren Co., N. J., May 11, 1844; A.B., Wesleyan Univ., 1866; A.M., 1869; D.D., 1896; B.D., Drew, 1874; m. (1) Emily C. Cleveland, May 3, 1875, m. (2) Margaret Engel, Mar. 10, 1910; ord. dea., 1872; ord. eld., 1874; entered Newark Conf., 1870; pastor, Lafayette, Jersey City, N. J., 1869-72; instructor, Mathematics and Science, Drew, 1872-73; Bayonne, N. J., 1872-75; Park, Elizabeth, N. J., 1875-78; Bloomfield, N. J., 1878-81; Westfield, N. J., 1881-84; Lafayette, Jersey City, N. J., 1884-87; Centenary, Newark, N. J., 1887-92; Trinity, Paterson, N. J., 1892-94; Passaic, N. J., 1894-97; Emory, Jersey City, N. J., 1897-1900; sup't., Newark District, 1900-06; Park Ave., East Orange, N. J., 1906-08; Simpson, Jersey City, N. J., 1908-09; assoc., Emory, Jersey City, N. J., 1909-10; Nutley, N. J., 1910-13; Wesley, Phillipsburg, N. J., 1913-18; Little Falls, N. J., 1918-19; d. Jan. 9, 1919.

The Rev. RUDOLPH WAHL

A.M.

Instructor in German, 1872-1874.

RUDOLPH WAHL: b. Germany; special student, Drew, 1871-1872; instructor, German, and ass't. librarian, 1872-1874; Protestant Episcopal Missionary in Persia; date of death unknown.

MARK BAILEY

A.B., M.A.

Instructor in Elocution, 1873-1876.

MARK BAILEY: b. Dunbarton, N. H., May 20, 1827; A.B., Dartmouth, 1849; M.A., 1852; professor, Elocution, Yale, 1855-1905; instructor, Elocution, Drew, 1873-1876; d. June 3, 1911.

The Rev. GEORGE J. BROWN

A.B., M.A., B.D.

Instructor in Latin and Greek, 1874-1875.

GEORGE J. BROWN: b. Brainards, N. Y., Nov. 12, 1839; A.B., Wesleyan Univ., 1873; A.M., 1876; B.D., Drew, 1875; ord. dea., 1868; ord. eld., 1876; entered Troy Conf., 1868; pastor, Unionville, South Coventry and East Haven, Mass., 1868-69; Pittsfield, Mass., 1869-70; State St., Troy, N. Y., 1870-71; at sch., 1871-75; instructor, Latin and Greek, Drew, 1874-75; Schenectady, N. Y., 1875-77; State St., Troy, N. Y., 1877-80; d. Dec. 1, 1880.

The Rev. P. T. VALENTI
Ph.D., D.D., LL.D.

Instructor in Italian Language and Literature, 1874-1875.

The Rev. WILLIAM WALLACE MARTIN
A.B., M.A., B.D.

Instructor in Mathematics and Languages, 1874-1876.

DR. MARTIN long ago dropped mathematics and has majored in Semitics, making numerous original and interesting contributions to the literature of the Old Testament.

WILLIAM WALLACE MARTIN: b. Brooklyn, N. Y., June 25, 1851; A.B., Wesleyan U., 1874; A.M., 1877; B.D., Drew, 1877; Leipzig and Bonn, 1878-1880; Union Theol. Sch. 1882; Syria, 1883-1885; m. Elizabeth Hayes, September 4, 1890; ord. dea., 1881; ord. eld., 1882; instructor, Mathematics and Languages, Drew, 1874-1876; ent. N. Y. E. Conf., 1879; pastor, Stepney, Conn., 1879-1880; Mianus, Conn., 1880-1883; professor, Hebrew, DePauw, 1885-1886; professor, Vanderbilt U., 1886-1895; Tenn. Conf. M. E. Ch. South, 1891-1894; N. Y. E. Conf., 1894; ag't. American U., 1898; lecturer, Fine Arts, Syracuse U., 1898-1900; sec., American U., 1900-1902; lecturer, Vanderbilt U., 1902-1905; ass't. ed. S. S. Periodicals, M. E. Church, 1905-1909; Conf. Historian, 1905-1909; pub. *Epworth Catechism of Christian Doctrine*, 1894; *Manual of Ecclesiastical Architecture*, 1897; *The Tora of Moses*, 1900; *The Law and the Covenant*; *The Epistles of Paul*; *The Epistles of Barnabas*, Reconstructed, Retranslated and annotated, 1942; address, 1810 E. Belmont Circle, Nashville, Tenn.

The Rev. JAMES OLIVER WILSON
A.M., B.D., D.D.

Instructor in Elocution, 1876-1878.

JAMES OLIVER WILSON: b. Morgan Co., Ill., April 10, 1849; Northwestern Univ., 1870-71; A.B., Illinois Wesleyan Univ., 1876; A.M., 1878; D.D., 1888; B.D., Drew, 1878; m. (1) Eva E. Kidder, April 16, 1878, m. (2) Minnie L. Welch, May 29, 1884, m. (3) Annie E. Somers, April 8, 1891; ord. dea., 1881, ord. eld., 1882; instructor, Elocution, Drew, 1876-78; entered Philadelphia Conf., 1879; pastor, West Park Ave., Philadelphia, Pa., 1879-81; Tioga,

Pa., 1881-84; Fifth St., Philadelphia, Pa., 1884-87; Tabernacle, Philadelphia, Pa., 1887-91; New York East Conf., 1891; Simpson, Brooklyn, N. Y., 1891-96; New York Conf., 1896; St. Andrews, New York, N. Y., 1896-1903; New York East Conf., 1903; Nostrand Ave., Brooklyn, N. Y., 1903-08; d. June 13, 1908.

The Rev. ROBERT McLEAN CUMNOCK
A.B., A.M., B.D., Ditt.D., LL.D.
Instructor in Elocution, 1878-1884.

IN HIS PRIME Dr. Cumnock was the most popular elocutionary entertainer before the American public. The School of Oratory of Northwestern University bears his name.

ROBERT McLEAN CUMNOCK: b. Johnstown, Scotland, May 31, 1840; A.B., Wesleyan Univ., 1868; A.M., 1871; L.H.D., Dickinson Coll., 1903; Litt.D., Northwestern, 1919; LL.D., Univ. of Southern Cal., 1927; m. (1) Lottie A. Nye, Nov. 25, 1868, m. (2) Annie C. Webster, June 27, 1877; professor, Rhetoric and Elocution, Northwestern Univ., 1868-1929; instructor, Elocution, Drew, 1878-84; professor, Elocution and Oratory, Garrett Biblical Inst.; director and instructor, School of Oratory, Northwestern Univ.; Phi Beta Kappa; pub., *Cumnock's Choice Readings,* 1887; *Cumnock's School Speaker,* 1893; d. Nov. 27, 1929.

JOHN PHILIP SILVERNAIL
A.B., M.A., B.O.
Instructor in Elocution, 1884-1891.

JOHN PHILIP SILVERNAIL: b. Prattsville, N. Y., June 5, 1851; A.B., Hamilton, 1874; A.M., 1877; m. Ella M. Dales, July 24, 1876; professor, elocution, Brooklyn Poly., 1874-1884; instructor, elocution, Drew, 1884-1891; professor, elocution, Rochester Theol. Sem., 1891-1923; d. March 8, 1930.

HENRY WILSON SMITH
A.B., M.A., B.O.
Instructor in Elocution, 1891-1896.

HENRY WILSON SMITH: b. Williamstown, Mass., Feb. 25, 1849; A.B., Williams Coll., 1869; M.A., 1872; B.O., Boston Univ., 1874; Princeton

Theological Sem., 1883-85; m. Isabel Davidson Hubbard, Dec. 23, 1896; instructor, Williams Coll., 1869-73; instructor, Elocution and Rhetoric, Boston Univ., 1875-77; professor, Adelphi Academy, 1877-78; instructor, Elocution, Princeton Theological Sem., 1878-1926; instructor, Elocution, Drew, 1891-96; d. March 9, 1926.

The Rev. MICAH* JOHN CRAMER
A.B., D.D., LL.D.

Instructor in Historical Theology, 1895-1896.

DR. CRAMER performed this service somewhat late in life. A native of Switzerland, thoroughly educated, experienced in the Methodist ministry, and having enjoyed long periods of residence abroad as U. S. Consul and as American Minister in Denmark and Switzerland, he was an interesting personality, as was his wife, the sister of General Ulysses S. Grant.

MICAH JOHN CRAMER: b. Schaffhausen, Switzerland, Feb. 6, 1835; A.B., Ohio Wesleyan Univ., 1859; LL.D., D.D., Syracuse Univ., 1873; LL.D., Taylor Univ., 1895; m. Mary F. Grant, Oct. 27, 1863; ord. dea., 1862; ord. eld., 1864; entered Cincinnati Conf., 1860; pastor, Pearl St., Cincinnati, O., 1863; English and German churches, Nashville, Tenn., 1864; post chaplain, Newport Barracks; U. S. Consul, Leipzig, 1867-71; U. S. minister, Denmark, 1871-81; minister and consul gen., Berne, Switzerland, 1881-86; Newark Conf., 1895; professor of Systematic Theology, Boston Univ. Sch. of Theol., 1885-86; lecturer, 1886-87; instructor, Historical Theology, Drew, 1895-96; professor, Philosophy, Dickinson Coll., 1896-98; pub., *Conversations and Unpublished Letters of Ulysses Grant,* 1897; ass't. editor, *Zeitschrift für Theologie und Kirche;* d. Jan. 23, 1898.

*The name is given as "Michael" in Cincinnati Conference Minutes, 1860.

The Rev. SHADRACH LAYCOCK BOWMAN
A.B., M.A., S.T.D., D.D.

Instructor in Historical Theology, 1895-1897; Instructor of Systematic Theology, 1903-1904.

ON TWO OCCASIONS the scholarly brother of Bishop Thomas Bowman was called upon to teach in emergencies.

SHADRACH LAYCOCK BOWMAN: b. Columbia Co., Pa., May 2, 1829; Wyoming Sem., 1846-47; dip., Concord (N.H.) Bib. Inst., 1851; Williamsport Dickinson Sem., 1852-53; A.B., Dickinson Coll., 1855; A.M., 1864; D.D., Rutgers Coll., 1870; S.T.D., Indiana Asbury Univ.; m. Margaret Elizabeth Aber, Nov. 25, 1856; ord. dea., 1855; ord. eld., 1857; entered Baltimore Conf., 1855; pastor, Carlisle Circuit, Pa., 1855-56; East London, Pa., 1856-57; Newark Conf., 1857; Passaic, N. J., 1857-58; located, 1858-60; Central Pennsylvania Conf., 1860; Berwick, Pa., 1860-62; Bellefonte, Pa., 1862-64; Emory, Carlisle, Pa., 1864-65; professor, Greek, Hebrew and Biblical Literature, Dickinson Coll., 1865-72; Lock Haven, Pa., 1872-73; Bedford, Pa., 1873-74; Lock Haven, Pa., 1874-76; York, Pa., 1876-79; Newark Conf., 1879; Morristown, N. J., 1879-82; St. Paul's, Jersey City, N. J., 1882-83; dean, Theol. Sch., and professor, Systematic Theol., De Pauw Theol. Sem., 1883-90; North Indiana Conf., 1888; New York Conf., 1890; Katonah, N. Y., 1890-93; Highland-on-Hudson, N. Y., 1893-94; instructor, Historical Theology, Drew, 1895-97; Newark Conf., 1899; instructor, Systematic Theology, Drew, 1903-04; pub., *Silence of Women in the Churches; The Bowman Family,* 1886; *Revised Version of the New Testament,* 1903; *Historical Evidence of the New Testament,* 1903; contr., relig. periodicals; d. Sept. 16, 1906.

Colonel HOMER BAXTER SPRAGUE
A.B., M.A., Ph.D., LL.D.
Instructor in Elocution, 1896-1899.

A PICTURESQUE figure and gracious personality: teacher, lawyer, soldier, publicist, author, Shakespearean scholar and orator.

HOMER BAXTER SPRAGUE: b. Sutton, Mass., Oct. 19, 1829; A.B., Yale Univ., 1852; A.M., 1855; Yale Law Sch., 1853-54; Ph.D., Univ. of New York, 1873; LL.D., Temple Univ., 1916; m. Antionette E. Pardee, Dec. 28, 1854; editor, *Yale Literary Magazine,* 1852; lawyer, Worcester, Mass., 1855-56; principal, High Sch., Worcester, Mass., 1856-59; lawyer, New Haven Conn., 1859-61; mem., New Haven Bd. of Edn., 1860-61; lt. colonel, 13th Conn. Vols., 1861-66; principal, Connecticut Normal Sch., 1866-67; mem., House of Representatives, Conn., 1868; professor, Rhetoric and English Literature, Cornell Univ., 1868-70; principal, Adelphi Acad., Brooklyn, N. Y., 1870-75; headmaster, Girls High Sch., Boston, Mass., 1876-85; president, Mills Coll., Cal., 1885-86; president, Univ. of North Dakota, 1887-91; univ. ext. lecturer, 1892-96; instructor, Elocution, Drew, 1896-99; president, Martha's Vineyard Summer Inst., 1879-82; editor, Dep't. Rhetoric, *Students' Journal,* 1898-1903; president, American Inst. of Instruction, 1883-85; dir. and mem., exec. comm., American Peace Ass'n.; dir., Mass. Peace Soc.; pub., *Fellowship of Slaveholders,* 1857; *History of the 13th Connecticut Infantry,* 1867; *Free Text Books for Public Schools,* 1879;

Anthony Comstock and Societies for the Suppression of Vice, 1882; *Money and Manhood*, 1882; *High School and Citizenship*, 1883; *Beecher's Metaphors and Similes*, 1883; *Educational Party Needed*, 1886; *Voice and Gesture*, 1874-1903; *American Liberty*, 1900; *The Two Parties*, 1900; *The Assassination*, 1901; *Alleged Law Blunders in Shakespeare*, 1902; *The Nation's Honor Roll*, 1902; *Right and Wrong in Our Civil War*, 1903; *The People's Party*, 1904; *Recollections of Henry Ward Beecher*, 1905; *The True Mac-Beth*, 1909; *Appreciation of Daniel C. Gilman*, 1910; *War Pensions and Promises*, 1910; *Caesar and Brutus*, 1911; *The Elevation of His Satanic Majesty*, 1912; *Metrical Version of the Book of Job*, 1913; *The European War,—Its Cause and Cure*, 1914; *Lights and Shadows in Confederate Prisons*, 1915; d. Mar. 23, 1918.

The Rev. MERLE NEGLEY SMITH

A.B., B.D., D.D., LL.D.

Instructor in Elocution and Registrar, 1899-1902.

FOR THREE YEARS after graduation Merle Smith remained in the service of the seminary before entering upon a pastoral career of great distinction.

MERLE NEGLEY SMITH: b. Lake City, Ia., Dec. 11, 1872; Epworth (Ia.) Sem., 1888; A.B., Cornell Coll., 1894; D.D., 1906; LL.D., 1924; B.D., Drew, 1898; LL.D., Univ. of Southern Calif., 1929; m. Mae Wolfe, July 19, 1898; instructor and registrar, Drew, 1898-1902; ord. eld., 1900; pastor, Ackley, Ia., 1902-05; Marshalltown, 1905-09; Colorado Springs, Colo., 1909-16; Pasadena, Calif., 1916-37; Y. M. C. A., in France and Italy, 1917-18; trustee, Univ. of Southern Calif.; mem. Bd. Foreign Missions M. E. Ch.; del. to five Gen. Confs.; Phi Beta Kappa; address, 1680 E. California St., Pasadena, Calif.

LIVINGSTON BARBOUR

B.O., M.El.

Instructor in Elocution, 1902-1903.

LIVINGSTON BARBOUR: b. Philadelphia, Pa., July 31, 1865; M.El., Nat. Sch. of Elocution, 1898; m. Lola Diehl; Instructor, Elocution, Virginia Military Inst., 1889-91; Instructor, Rutgers Coll., 1891-1911; Professor, public speaking, 1911-1930; Instructor, Drew, 1902-1903; d. April 15, 1930.

WALTER VINCENT HOLT

Instructor in Elocution, 1903-1912.

WALTER VINCENT HOLT: b. Brooklyn, N. Y., Feb. 26, 1857; educated in Paris and London; m. (1) Maria Dolores Trayer, Jan. 17, 1884; m. (2) Georgia Anderson, Nov. 26, 1902; director, Dep't. Oratory, Adelphi Coll.; master, Operatic and Ballad Diction, National Conservatory of Music, New York, N. Y.; conducted American Sch. of Elocution, Brooklyn, N. Y., 1891-1911; instructor, Oratory, Pratt Inst.; instructor, Elocution, Drew, 1903-12; co-principal, New York Sch. of Expression; professor, Biblical Expression, Bible Teachers' Sch., New York, N. Y.; professor, Bible and Hymn Reading, Diocesan Theol. Coll., Presbyterian Theol. Coll., Methodist Theol. Coll. and Congregational Theol. Coll., Montreal, Canada; professor, Public Reading and Speaking, Loyola Coll., and Montreal High Sch.; instructor, Public Speaking, Montreal Y. M. C. A., and Women's Club; pub., *We Should All Talk Alike.* Address.

The Rev. CHARLES AUGUSTUS GILBERT

A.B., M.A., B.D.

Instructor in Music and Hymnology and Registrar, 1903-1907.

CHARLES AUGUSTUS GILBERT: b. Marshfield, Mo., Nov. 5, 1872; Marionville Collegiate Inst., 1897; A.B., Ohio Wesleyan Univ., 1900; A.M., 1903; B.D., Drew, 1903; Grad. Sch., 1906-07; Columbia Univ., 1902-06; m. Elizabeth C. Long, Sept. 4, 1902; ord. dea., 1902; ord. eld., 1904; entered New York Conf., 1903; registrar and instructor, Music and Hymnology, Drew, 1903-07; dean, West Virginia Coll. of Fine Arts, 1907-10; pastor, Marshalltown, Ia., First, 1910-11; Upper Iowa Conf., 1911; Union, Ia., 1911-14; Epworth, Ia., 1914-17; captain, American Red Cross, U. S. Navy British Comm'n, 1917-19; St. Louis Conf., 1919; Marionville, Mo., First, 1919-21; president, Ozark Wesleyan Coll., 1921-23; Kansas City, Mo., St. Paul's, 1923-24; Clinton, Mo., First, 1924-27; St. Louis, Mo., Elmbark, 1927-1928; Kansas City, Mo., Quayle, 1928-1930; Oak Grove, Mo., 1930-1933; Centerview, Mo., 1933-1935; Wheaton-Muncey Chapel, Mo., 1935-1936; Iberia, Mo., 1936; d. Dec. 29, 1936.

LEONARD BEECHER McWHOOD

A.B., M.A.

Instructor, Music and Hymnology, 1907-1916.

LEONARD BEECHER McWHOOD: b. Brooklyn, N. Y., Dec. 5, 1870; A.B., Columbia, 1893; M.A., Dartmouth, 1918; m. Leita Janet Rogers, Apr. 29,

1909; teacher, Newark Seminary, 1891-92; pupil of MacDowell, 1896-97; assoc. with MacDowell, 1897-1904; adjunct professor, Psychology, Columbia Univ., 1904-10; instructor, Music, Vassar Coll., 1902-07; instructor, Music and Hymnology, Drew, 1907-16; National Park Seminary, 1910-13; teacher, Newark High School, 1913-18; professor, music, Dartmouth Coll., 1918-39; Univ. of Cal., 1926-28, on leave from Dartmouth; composed for organ, voices and instrumental combinations; cantata, *The Village Blacksmith;* d. Dec. 4, 1939.

STACY BEEKS BETZLER

B.P.E.

Instructor in Physical Culture and Hygiene, 1910-1913.

STACY BEEKS BETZLER: Springfield College, 1913-1916, B.P.E.; m. Winifred———, 1903; Instructor, Physical Culture and Hygiene, Drew, 1910-1913; instructor, Physical Culture, Int. Y. M. C. A. Coll., Springfield, Mass., 1916-1942; address, Springfield, Mass., R.F.D. 1.

BYRON G. SHERMAN

Instructor in Physical Training and Hygiene, 1913-1914.

The Rev. ISAAC J. LANSING

A.B., A.M., D.D.

Instructor in Expression, 1912-1913.

ISAAC J. LANSING: b. Watervliet, N. Y., Oct. 3, 1846; A.B., Wesleyan, 1872; A.M., 1875; D.D., Lafayette, 1909; m. Ella Theresa Griswold, Oct. 21, 1873; ent. N. Y. E. Conf. 1873; pastor, Embury, Brooklyn, N. Y., 1873-1874; Georgia Conf. 1874; President, Clark Univ., Atlanta, Ga., 1874-1876; Savannah Conf., 1876; pastor, Lloyd St., Atlanta, 1876-1877; Freedmen's Aid Soc., 1876-1878; N. Y. E. Conf., 1878; pastor, Meriden, Conn., 1880-1881; Stamford, Conn., 1881-1884; Summerfield, Brooklyn, N. Y., 1884-1887; Salem St., Cong., Worcester, Mass., 1892-1893; Park St. Cong., Boston, Mass., 1893-1897; Green Ridge Presbyterian, Scranton, Pa., 1897-1911; sec., Int. Reform Bureau, 1911; Men & Religion Forward Movement, 1911-1912; instructor, Expression, Drew, 1912-1913; pastor, West Side Pres., Ridgewood, N. J., 1912-1913; pub., *Romanism and the Republic,* 1889; *Romanism and the Nation,* 1892; *Why Christianity Did not Prevent the War,* 1918; d. 1923.

ALBERT BEN WEGENER
B.P.E., B.S.

Physical Director and Instructor in Physical Training and Recreation, 1914-1935.

THERE ARE MEN all over the world who go about the business of life with a springier step and a straighter back because "Prof" Wegener taught them the value of play and gave them an example of moderation in all things except courage and laughter.   As classrooms hold forever, for the alumni, the figures of loved teachers who spoke there, so the Drew gymnasium is, in the minds of a host of men, a frame for "Prof."

Mr. Wegener was, as far as it is known at Drew, the first full-time physical education director in any theo-olgical seminary.   He had seen fine minds and needed voices stifled by insufficient strength of body, and he worked at Drew for twenty-one years to correct that kind of human wastage.   Furthermore, he knew that directed play could be a social and religious tool, a skilled technique in a minister's resources.   He was an adept at creating that skill.   By his work he made generation after generation of Drew students stronger men and more effective ministers.

"Retirement" with him, as with some other Drew people, was a kind of figurative term, a word to be used only with quotes.   When at last tennis, "Drewball" and gymnastics began to be out of the question (for twenty years he could lick any Drew undergraduate at his chosen sport), he plunged avidly into oil painting, seeking instruction for which earlier life had not allowed the time.   Soon his work was on display here and there, and increasingly it did him credit.   Every ounce a teacher, before long he was organizing art clubs to help people see God's world more clearly through trying to catch its lines and colors on canvas and paper.

"Prof" is an eager lover of life. He took up watercolors last winter, and his mind still leaps ahead. His chapter has not yet reached its end.

F. T. J.

ALBERT BEN WEGENER: b. Waldenburg, Mich., Sept. 3, 1869; B. P. E., Y. M. C. A. Institute and Training Sch. (now George Williams Coll.), 1892 (awarded 1911); B.S., Univ. of Tennessee, 1896; San Diego Art Academy, 1936; Northwestern Medical Sch., 1897-1900; Art Institute, Chicago, 1896-97; Ringling Art Sch., 1941; Norton Sch. of Art, 1942; m. Helen T. DuBois, May 21, 1902; physical dir., Y. M. C. A., Kalamazoo, Mich., 1889-90; Chicago Dep'ts., Y. M. C. A., Chicago, Ill., 1890-92; Univ. of Tennessee, 1892-96; Central Y. M. C. A., Chicago, Ill., 1896-1900; Y. M. C. A., Rochester, N. Y., 1900-06; Y. M. C. A., St. Louis, Mo., 1906-09; Y. M. C. A., Duluth, Minn., 1909-13; Y. M. C. A., Camden, N. J., 1913-14; Director of Physical Education and Health, Drew, 1914-35; pub., *Graded Calisthenics and Dumb-bell Drills,* 1904; *Track and Field Athletics,* 1924; *Church and Community Recreation,* 1924; *Play Games,* 1930; co-author, *Graded Exercises on Horse, Parallel and Horizontal Bar,* 1890; *Gymnastic Nomenclature,* 1905; contr., newspapers and periodicals; address, 9 Glendale Rd., Madison, N. J.

The Rev. HOMER KINGSLEY EBRIGHT

A.B., M.A., B.D., Th.D.

Instructor, Greek, 1915-1916.

HOMER KINGSLEY EBRIGHT: b. Hartford, Ky., Aug. 30, 1878; A.B., Baker Univ., 1900; B.D., Drew, 1904; Th.D., 1916; A.M., New York Univ., 1904; Columbia Univ., summer, 1914; Univ. of Chicago, summer, 1909, 1915; D.D., Southwestern Coll., 1923; m. Marie Moorhead, June 6, 1905; ord. dea., 1905; ord. eld., 1907; entered Kansas Conf., 1905; pastor, Lakin, Kans., 1898-99; Linwood, Kan., 1899; Rockaway Valley, N. J., 1902-03; Weehawken and Grantwood, N. J., 1903-04; Argentine Ch., Kansas City, Kan., 1904-05; prof., Greek, Baker Univ., 1905-17; instructor, Greek, Drew, 1915-16; prof., Biblical Literature, Baker Univ., 1917——; dean, Baker Univ., 1924-35; mem., American ass'n. of Univ. Professors; mem., National Ass'n. Biblical Instructors; pub., *The Petrine Epistles,* 1917; *Two Letters for you,* 1919; *Recreation for Old and Young,* 1920; *Three Voices,* 1934; address, Baldwin, Kansas.

The Rev. PHILIP SIDNEY WATTERS
A.B., A.M., B.D.
Instructor, Hymnology, 1921-1927.

DURING HIS PASTORATE in Madison, Drew students and
other lovers of the ministry of music had the privilege
of association with and instruction by this accomplished
musician and hymnologist.

PHILIP SIDNEY WATTERS: b. Dobbs
Ferry, N. Y., Feb. 4, 1890; A.B.,
Princeton Univ., 1910; B.D., Drew,
1913; Grad. Sch., 1923-25; A.M., New
York Univ., 1918; m. Grace Catherine
Briggs, Sept. 3, 1914; ord. dea., 1914;
ord. eld., 1916; entered Newark Conf.,
1914; pastor, Tenafly and Demarest,
N. J., 1914-18; Port Jervis, N. Y.,
1918-21; Madison, N. J., 1921-27;
instructor, Hymnology, Drew, 1921-
27; First, Plainfield, N. J., 1927-30;
New York Conf., 1930; Memorial Ch.,
White Plains, N. Y., 1930——; sec.,
Com. on Worship, Federal Council of
Churches of Christ in Am.; mem.,
Hymn Soc. of Am. (pres., 1935-37,
1939-41); mem., Com. on Worship
and Music, M. E. Ch. (chrn. 1932-40);
trustee, Drew; mem., Phi Beta Kappa;
address, 34 Gedney Park Drive, White
Plains, N. Y.

The Rev. HALFORD EDWARD LUCCOCK
A.B., A.M., B.D., Litt.D., D.D.
Instructor in New Testament, and Registrar, 1916-1918.

ON HIS UPWARD way to his high place as a religious
teacher with voice and pen, this more brilliant son of a
gifted father tarried two years at Drew.

HALFORD EDWARD LUCCOCK: b. Pittsburgh, Pa., Mar. 11, 1885; A.B.,
Northwestern Univ., 1906; B.D.,
Union Theol. Sem., 1909; A.M.,
Columbia, 1909; D.D., Syracuse Univ.,
1924; Litt.D., Allegheny Coll., 1927;
D.D., Wesleyan Univ., 1928; D.D.,
Univ. of Vermont, 1933; m. Mary
Whitehead, of Simsbury, Conn., June
17, 1914; ord. M. E. Ministry, 1910;
pastor, Windsor, Conn., 1910-12;
instructor, Hartford Theol. Sem., 1912-
14; pastor, St. Andrew's, New Haven,
Conn., 1914-16; registrar and instruc-
tor, New Testament, Drew, 1916-18;
editorial Sec. Meth. Bd. Foreign
Missions, 1918-24; contbg. editor The
Christian Advocate, 1924-28; professor, Homiletics, Yale Univ. Div. Sch.,
1928——; author, Fares, Please, 1916;
The Mid-Week Service, 1916; Five-
Minute Shop-Talks, 1916; Studies in
the Parables of Jesus, 1917; The
Christian Crusade for World Democ-

racy, 1918; *The New Map of the World*, 1919; *Skylines, The Haunted House and Other Sermons*, 1923; *The Story of Methodism* (with Paul Hutchinson), 1926; *Preaching Values in New Translations of the New Testament*, 1928; *Jesus and the American Mind*, 1930; *Contemporary American Literature and Religion*, 1934; *Christian Faith and Economic Change*, 1936; *Christianity and the Individual*, 1937; *The Acts of the Apostles in Present Day Preaching*, 1938; address, 300 Ridgewood Ave., New Haven, Conn.

WALTER O. ROBINSON

Litt.D.

Instructor in Public Speaking, 1916-1929.

WALTER O. ROBINSON: b. Hamilton, Canada, May 12, 1883; Upper Canada Coll., Toronto; Trinity Coll., Toronto; Litt.D.; m. Minnie Hessin, Sept. 27, 1906; Tenor soloist, Cathedral St. John the Divine, N. Y., Church of the Heavenly Rest, N. Y., St. James Episcopal Church, N. Y.; instructor, Public Speaking, Jewish Theological Seminary, New York, N. Y., 1915-1930; instructor, Public Speaking, West Side Y. M. C. A., New York, N. Y., 1915-1932; instructor, Public Speaking and Voice Culture, Drew, 1916-29; instructor, Public Speaking, General Theological Seminary, New York, N. Y., 1921-28; instructor, Public Speaking, St. John's Coll., Brooklyn, N. Y., 1924——; mem., Canadian Soc. of New York; Advertising Club of New York, address, Carnegie Hall, New York, N. Y.

The Rev. THOMAS FULTON CUMMINGS

A.B., D.D.

Instructor in Phonetics and the Science of Language, 1916-1923.

THOMAS FULTON CUMMINGS: b. New Wilmington, Pa., Sept. 3, 1863; A.B., Westminster Coll., 1884; D.D., 1912; dip., Pittsburgh-Xenia Theological Seminary, 1889; m. Anna Wallace, July 11, 1889; ord., United Presbyterian Ch., 1889; missionary, India, 1889-1909; itinerant evangelistic missionary, United Presbyterian Mission, Punjab, India, 1890-98; professor, Old Testament and Hebrew, United Presbyterian Theological Seminary, Punjab, India, 1904-07; professor, Phonetics and Missionary Languages, Biblical Seminary, New York, N. Y., 1912——; instructor, Phonetics and the Science of Language, Drew, 1916-23; pub., *Children's Catechism* in Punjabi, 1907; *Beginner's Catechism* (Hindustani), 1904; *Urdu by the Direct Method*, 1916; *How to Learn a Language*, 1916; co-author, *Punjabi Manual and Grammar*, 1912; *Suwal and Jawáb; Fonetik Qaida; Parli Dusri Kitáb; The Oral-Pattern Method* (ready for posthumous publication); d. Feb. 11, 1942.

The Rev. CHARLES STEWART DAVISON
A.B., B.D., D.D.
Instructor in New Testament Exegesis, 1918-1919.

FOR PERHAPS the first time the son of a Drew alumnus, himself an alumnus, who, like his distinguished father, pursued a brilliant career as a missionary in Japan, was called to Drew for a brief period of teaching service.

CHARLES STEWART DAVISON: b. Nagasaki, Japan, Feb. 14, 1877; Centenary Collegiate Inst.; Univ. of Calif., 1894-95; A.B., Dickinson Coll., 1898; D.D., 1918; B.D., Drew, 1901; m. Florence May Bower, June 1, 1905; ord. dea., 1902; ord. eld., 1903; entered Newark Conf., 1901; pastor, South Market St., Newark, N. J., 1901-03; Japan Conf., 1903; sup't., Sendai District, 1903-05; principal, Philander Smith Biblical Inst., Tokyo, Japan, 1905-10; professor, Aoyama Gakuin, Japan; dean, Chinzei Gakuin, Nagasaki, Japan; instructor, New Testament Exegesis, Drew, 1918-19; d. May 10, 1920.

The Rev. CHARLES BURGESS KETCHAM
A.B., M.A., B.D., D.D.
Librarian, and Instructor in English Bible, 1919-1923.

OF METHODIST preacher lineage on both sides of the house, Charles Ketcham gave a good account of himself as student and teacher in Drew, and later in his native state as preacher and educator.

CHARLES BURGESS KETCHAM: b. Mechanicsburg, O., Dec. 4, 1889; A.B., Ohio Wesleyan, 1913; D.D., 1932; M.A., Columbia Univ., 1916; B.D., Drew, 1916; m. Lucile Brown, Apr. 8, 1918; ord. dea., 1914; ord. eld., 1916; entered West Ohio Conf., 1913; pastor, Goshen, O., 1916; director of religious edu., Trinity Ch., Youngstown, O., 1916-17; professor, English Bible, Mt. Union Coll., 1917-18; Chaplain, A.E.F., 1918-19; librarian and instructor, English Bible, Drew, 1919-20; Ohio Conf., 1920; pastor, Grandview Ch., Columbus, O., 1920-22, Northeast Ohio, 1922; Parkwood-Asbury Ch., Cleveland, O., 1922-23; Oberlin, O., 1923-30; First Ch., Warren, O., 1930-37; dist. sup't., Cleveland Dist., 1937-38; president, Mt. Union Coll., 1938——; chmn., bd. of trustees, Elyria Home for Aged, 1929-40; alternate, General Conferences 1932, 1936; delegate Uniting Conference 1939; General Conference 1940; North Central Jurisdictional Conference 1940; trustee, Ohio Wesleyan Univ., 1932-38; president, Ohio Meth. Coll., Ass'n., 1939-41; chmn., Stark

County Bd. of Public Assistance, 1941-42; treasurer, Association of Schools and Colleges of the Methodist Church, 1941—; Phi Beta Kappa; contr. religious articles; address, 1304 S. Union Ave., Alliance, O.

The Rev. EDWARD EDGERTON BEAUCHAMP

A.B., B.D.

Director and Instructor in Rural Extension, 1919-1923.

EDWARD EDGERTON BEAUCHAMP: b. Atchison, Kan., May 29, 1883; A.B., Baker Univ., 1908; B.D., Drew, 1917, graduate study, 1920-24; m. Lona Butler, Dec. 1, 1908; ord. dea., 1909; ord. eld., 1913; entered Kansas Conf., 1909; pastor, Edwardsville, Kan., 1906-08; Corning, Kan., 1908-10; Valley Falls, Kan., 1910-12; Powhattan, Kan., 1912-14; Epworth Ch., Whitestone, N. Y., 1914-17; Mt. Zion and Irvin Chapel, White Cloud, Kan., 1917-18; High-land, Kan., 1919; dir. and instructor, Rural Extension Work, Drew, 1919-23; pastor, Council Grove, Kan., 1924-26; Sabetha, Kan., 1927-30; Burlington, Kan., 1931-32; Columbus, Kan., 1933-35; Euclid Ave. Ch., Topeka, Kan., 1936-39; Osawatomie, Kan., 1939-40; sec., South Central Jurisdictional Bd. of Missions and Ch. Extension, 1940—; Shawnee, Kan., 1941—; writer on religious matters; address, Shawnee, Kansas.

The Rev. STALEY FRANKLIN DAVIS

B.S., B.D., M.A.

Instructor in Pedagogy, 1920-1922.

A PROMISING young minister of Newark Conference, who had proven his attainments and his teaching gifts when his health failed.

STALEY FRANKLIN DAVIS: b. Pataskala, O., April 8, 1877; B.S., Ohio Wesleyan Univ., 1902, M.A., 1904; B.D., Drew, 1904, fellow, Drew, 1904-05, Grad. Sch., 1905-06; m. Helen Larter Fredericks, Nov. 4, 1907; ord. dea., 1905; ord. eld., 1907; entered Newark Conf., 1907; pastor, Grace, Kearny, N. J., 1905-06; Epworth, Elizabeth, N. J., 1906-11; Hackensack, N. J., 1911-18; West Side Ave., Jersey City, N. J., 1918-20; instructor, Pedagogy, Drew, 1920-22; Eastern Division, Bd. of Sunday Schs., M. E. Ch., 1920-26; d. Feb. 18, 1926.

ESTHER TURNER WELLMAN
A.B., B.D., Ph.D.

Instructor in Spanish, 1920-1922.

ESTHER TURNER WELLMAN: b. Lynn. Indiana, Nov. 1, 1893; A.B., Univ. of Southern California, 1919; B.D., Drew, 1921; Ph.D., Columbia Univ., 1936; m. Coe Rushford Wellman, June 10, 1919; missionary, Latin American Mission, Los Angeles, Cal., 1909-19; Spanish American Institute, Gardena, Cal., 1909-19; Frances De Pauw Industrial Sch., Hollywood, Cal., 1909-19; Univ. of Southern California. 1915-17; instructor, Spanish, Drew, 1920-22; missionary, Mexico Annual Conf., Mexico City, 1923-28; missionary, Puerto Rico Mission Conf., Rio Piedras, 1930——; Univ. of Puerto Rico, 1937-38; George O. Robinson Sch., San Juan, P. R., 1940-41; Phi Beta Kappa; pub., *Amado Nervo, Mexico's Religious Poet,* 1936; *Democracy and Other Verse; A Rosary of Madrigals;* editor, *Mexico,* 1923-28; contr., Spanish and American periodicals; address, Evangelical Seminary, Rio Piedras, Puerto Rico.

HENRY WESTON SMITH

Organist and Instructor in Church Music, 1920——.

FOR MORE than 20 years Mr. Smith has been the leader of the musical activities of the seminary, and has stimulated musical taste in Madison and neighboring towns.

HENRY WESTON SMITH: b. Lynn, Mass., Nov. 6, 1880; student under Alexander Guilmant, 1900-01; Edward MacDowell, 1901-02; J. Warren Andrews, 1902-03; m. Louise Augusta Kuhnbaum, Oct. 12, 1905; ass't. organist, Ch. of the Divine Paternity, New York, N. Y., 1902-03; organist, Presbyterian Ch., Madison, N. J., 1903-17; organist, Methodist Ch., Summit, N. J., 1917-24; organist and instructor, Church Music, Drew, 1920——; accompanist, Marcella Sembrich Studios, New York, N. Y. and Lake George, N. Y., 1921-25; contr., *Survey of Ch. Music,* 1924-32; organist and choirmaster, St. Stephen's P. E. Ch., Millburn, N. J., 1932-41; choir director, Methodist Ch., Madison, N. J., 1934——; organist, Presbyterian Ch., Madison, N. J., 1941——; at times accompanist to Evan Williams, Florence Mulford, Geraldine Farrar, Milo Picco, Cecil Arden, and other Metropolitan stars; private teacher of organ and voice; pub., compositions for piano, voice and organ; contr., musical magazines on church music; address, 75 Prospect St., Madison, N. J.

ELIZABETH LOUISA FOOTE
A.B., M.A., B.L.S.

Librarian and Instructor in Library Science, 1920-1922.

MISS FOOTE's professional training in library science was of especial value in organizing the overwhelming accessions of the preceding period, when the library had repeatedly doubled at seven year intervals and had overgrown and outgrown the shelf-capacity of the Cornell Building.

ELIZABETH LOUISA FOOTE: b. Rome, N. Y., Aug. 23, 1866; Wellesley Coll., 1884-86; A.B., Syracuse Univ., 1888; M.A., 1924; B.L.S., New York State Library Sch., 1892; teacher, Canandaigua, N. Y., 1888-89; examiner, New York State Regents' office, 1889-90; New York State Library staff, 1892-95; organizer of libraries, 1895-97; ass't., New York Public Library, 1897-1920; librarian, Drew, 1920-22; instructor, Introduction in Library Science, Drew, 1920-22; pub., *The Librarian of the Sunday School,* 1897; *Strengthening the Sunday School Library,* 1903; d. Nov. 30, 1936.

CLARA FRANCES CHASSELL COOPER
A.B., M.A., M.D., Ph.D.

Instructor in Psychology, 1920-1923.

MRS. COOPER was one of the specialists who were added to the Drew Faculty during the brief period when Centenary funds supported several special training ventures.

CLARA FRANCES CHASSELL (Mrs. Homer E.) COOPER: b. Sundance, Wyo., Mar. 24, 1893; A.B., Cornell Coll., 1912; M. Di., Iowa State Teacher's Coll., 1913; M.A., Northwestern Univ., 1914; Univ. of Chicago, summer, 1915; fellow, American Univ., 1916-17; scholar, Teachers Coll., Columbia Univ., 1917; Ph.D., 1920; m. Homer Eber Cooper, Dec. 31, 1922; teacher, public sch., Ida Grove, Iowa, 1913; head of dept., Philosophy and Edu., William Woods Coll., 1914-15; ass't. professor, English Literature, Simpson Coll., 1915-16, summer sessions, 1915, 1916; sch. psychologist, Horace Mann Sch., and instructor, Experimental Educ., Teachers College, Columbia Univ., 1917-22; assistant and instructor, Educational Psychology, Columbia Univ., summer sessions, 1920-22; research ass't., Institute of Educational Research, Teachers Coll., Columbia Univ., 1922; instructor, Psychology, Drew, 1920-

23; Phi-Beta Kappa, Pi Gamma Mu, lecturer on psychological, educational and religious subjects; author, *The Relation Between Morality and Intellect,* 1935; joint-author *The Indiana Survey of Religious Education,* vol. II; *Measurements and Standards in Religious Education,* 1924; contr., religious, psychological and educational periodicals and journals; address, New Windsor, Maryland.

The Rev. HARRISON SACKETT ELLIOTT
A.B., M.A., B.D., Ph.D.
Instructor in Religious Psychology, 1921-1923.

DR. ELLIOTT here entered on the teaching career which has brought him distinction as author and instructor.

HARRISON SACKETT ELLIOTT: b. St. Clairsville, O., Dec. 13, 1882; Antioch Coll., 1898-1900; Valparaiso Univ., 1900-01; A.B., Ohio Wesleyan, 1905; B.D., Drew, 1911; M.A., Teacher's Coll., Columbia; Oxford, 1931; Ph.D., Yale Univ., 1940; m. Grace Hunsberger Loucks, June 24, 1927; sec., Bishop J. W. Bashford, China, 1905-08; corr., Ass'n. Press, Shanghai, China, 1906-08; Ass't. sec., Africa Diamond Jubilee, M. E. Ch., 1908-10; sec., International Comm. Y. M. C. A., 1910-22; personnel and training sec., National War Work Council, Y.M.C.A., 1917-18; editorial sec., Ass'n. Press, Y. M. C. A., 1918-22; teacher, National Training Sch., Y. W. C. A., 1920-25; instructor, Religious Psychology, Drew, 1921-23; Religious Work Dept., International Comm., Y. M. C. A., 1922; faculty, Teachers Coll., Columbia Univ., summers, 1923-29; ass't. professor, Religious Edu. and Psychology, Union Theological Seminary, 1922-23; assoc. professor, 1923-25; professor, Practical Theology, and head, dept. Religious Edu. and Psychology, 1925——; dir., summer courses, Union Theological Sem., 1937——; mem., National Council, and chairman, National Boys' Work Com. of Y. M. C. A.; v. p., Religious Edn. Ass'n., 1937-1938; pres., 1939-1942; pub., *How Jesus Met Life Questions,* 1920; *Why and How of Group Discussions,* 1923; *The Bearing of Psychology upon Religion,* 1927; *The Process of Group Training,* 1928; *Group Discussion in Religious Education,* 1930; *Can Religious Education Be Christian?,* 1940; co-author, *Student Standards of Action,* 1914; *Solving Personal Problems,* 1936; contr., religious and edu. journals; address, 99 Claremont Ave., New York, N. Y.

CHARLES WILLIAM TURNER
A.B., B.D., M.A., Ph.D.
Instructor in Spanish, 1923-1924.

CHARLES WILLIAM TURNER: b. Buenos Aires, Argentina, S. A., Oct. 12, 1899; A.B., Ohio Wesleyan Univ., 1923; B. D., Drew, 1930; M.A., 1931; Ph.D.,

1932; instructor, Spanish, Drew, 1923-24; ass't. sec., Am. Bible Society for Brazil, 1933-34; acting sec., 1935; sec., 1936——; address, Avenida Erasmo Braga, 12, Rio de Janeiro, Brazil, S. A.

ELIZABETH COLSON

Instructor in Religious Education, 1922-24; 1925-26;
Assistant in Religious Education, 1926-1927.

ELISABETH EDLAND

Instructor in Religious Education, 1922-1926.

ELISABETH EDLAND: b. Brooklyn, N. Y.; Columbia Univ.; New York Univ.; various dramatic schs.; Thomas A. Edison Co., West Orange, N. J., 1912-14; Editorial staff, Methodist Episcopal Board of Sunday Schs., 1914-24; Westchester Co. S. S. Ass'n., Westchester, N. Y., 1924-32; dir. of dramatics, Second Presbyterian Ch., Newark, N. J., 1932-39; director of Camp Edwald, Putney, Vt., 1937——; instructor, Religious Education, Drew, 1922-36; pub., *Spring in the Brown Meadow,* 1923; *The Children's King and other plays for children,* 1928; *Principles and Technique in Religious Dramatics,* 1926; *Plum Blossoms, and other plays,* 1925; *Children's Dramatizations,* 1926; *Children of Galilee,* 1935; co-author, *Exploring the Trail with the Master Guide,* 1934; *various pageants;* contr., current periodicals; address, Putney, Vermont.

HEBERTO MARRIAGA SEIN
A.B.

Instructor in Spanish, 1922-1923.

HEBERTO MARRIAGA SEIN: b. Mexico, Dec. 7, 1898; A.B., Univ. Cal., 1922; Drew, 1922-1923; instructor, Spanish, Drew, 1922-1923; Mexican Consulate, New York, 1924-1925; address, Colegio Juarez, Malahuala, S.L.P., Mexico.

SARAH ANNE DAVIES
A.B.

Instructor in English Literature, 1923-1938.

AN HONORS graduate of the University of Wales, with successful teaching experience in Britain, Mrs. Davies' courses in Shakespeare and other English classics long filled a definite need among the students, and at the same time attracted many intellectual women of the local community.

SARAH ANNE DAVIES: b. Barmouth, North Wales, Great Britain, Aug. 12, 1882; A.B., University of Wales, 1903; (First Class Honors in English Literature), Teacher's Diploma, 1904; m. John Newton Davies, Aug. 24, 1909; Senior Mistress, Hengoed County Sch., Glamorgan, England, 1904-09; instructor, English Literature, Drew, 1923-38; address, 41 Pomeroy Rd., Madison, N. J.

The Rev. EDMUND DE SCHWEINITZ BRUNNER
A.B., B.D., M.A., Ph.D., L.H.D.

Lecturer and Instructor in Rural Work, 1923-1929.

EDMUND DE SCHWEINITZ BRUNNER: b. Bethlehem, Pa., Nov. 4, 1889; A.B., Moravian Coll., 1909; M.A., 1912; Ph.D., 1914; L.H.D., 1935; B.D., Moravian Theological Seminary, 1911; m. Mary W. Vogler, Dec. 16, 1912; ord., Moravian Ch., 1911; pastor, Coopersburg, Pa., 1911-14; First Ch., Easton, Pa., 1914-17; rural sec., Com. on War Industrial Communities, 1917-19; dir., Town and Country Survey Dept., Interchurch World Movement, 1919-20; dir., Town and Country Surveys, Institute of Social and Religious Research, 1921-33; lecturer and instructor, Rural Work, Drew, 1923-29; associate in rural edu., Teachers Coll., Columbia Univ., 1926-31; professor, Rural Edu., Teachers Coll., Columbia Univ., 1931——; lectured in Japan, Korea, China, India, and Egypt to universities and missions, 1927, and in New Zealand and Australia state univs., 1937; collaborator, Bur. of Agricultural Economics, U. S. Dept. of Agriculture, 1926-38; Pres. Roosevelt's advisory com. on edu.; dir., American Ass'n. Adult Edu.; pub., *History of Moravian Missions to the* *Indians of So. Cal.*, 1915; *Cooperation in Coopersburg,* 1916; *The New Country Church Building,* 1917; *The Country Church in the New World Order,* 1919; *A Church and Community Survey of Salem County, N. J.,* 1922; *Church Life in the Rural South,* 1923; *Tested Methods in Farm and Country Churches,* 1923; *Churches of Distinction in Town and Country,* 1923; *Surveying your Community,* 1925; *Village Communities,* 1927; *Rural Korea,* 1928; *Immigrant Farmers and Their Children,* 1929; *Industrial Village Churches,* 1930; *The Larger Parish— A Sociological Analysis,* 1934; *Rural Australia and New Zealand,* 1938; *Working with Rural Youth,* 1942; *Community Organization and Adult Education,* 1942; co-author, *Irrigation and Religion,* 1922; *A Church and Community Survey of Pend Oreille County, Wash.,* 1922; *The Town and Country Church in the United States,* 1923; *American Agricultural Villages,* 1927; *Rural Social Trends,* 1933; *The Protestant Church as a Social Institution,* 1934; *A Study of Rural Society,* 1935; *The School in American Society,*

1936; *Rural Trends in Depression Years,* 1937; editor and part author, National Crisis Series; editor, *Town and Country Studies* (22 vols.); ad-dress, Waquoit, Mass., and Teachers Coll., Columbia Univ., New York, N. Y.

JESSIE ELEANOR MOORE
B.S., M.A.

Instructor in Religious Education, 1923-1926; Assistant, 1926-1929.

JESSIE ELEANOR MOORE: b. Newark, N. J., Dec. 1, 1886; B. S., Teachers Coll., Columbia Univ., 1919; M.A., 1922; Union Theological Seminary, 1929-30; kindergartener, Public Schs., Newark, N. J., 1907-18; 1919-20; supervisor, Field Work, Dept. of Religious Edn., Teachers Coll., Columbia Univ., 1921-23; instructor, Religious Edn., Drew, 1923-26; ass't. editor, Sunday Sch. Lit., M. E. Ch., 1924-29; assoc. ed., Pilgrim Press, 1930——; International Lesson Comms., Children's Work Professional Advisory Section; Editor's Professional Advisory Section, Comm. on Religious Edn. of Children, all of the International Council of Religious Edn.; Children's Comm., Missionary Edn. Movement; Educ. Comm., N. J. Council of Religious Edn.; pub., *The Cradle Roll Manual,* 1921; *The Little Child and His Crayon,* 1922; *Missionary Education of Beginners,* 1927; *First Bible Stories,* 1929; *Bible Stories to Read,* 1929; *Three Years Old,* 1933; *Experiences in the Church School Kindergarten,* 1935; *Welcome House,* 1939; *Vacation Church School Manual,* 1924; *Beginners' Closely Graded Lessons,* 1928 ed., 1937 ed.; *Little Pilgrim Lesson Pictures,* 1937; *Pilgrim Bible Stories for Children,* 1938; editor, *First Steps in Christian Nurture,* 1924-29; *Pilgrim Elementary Teacher,* 1930-38; *Children's Religion,* 1940; address, 119 Essex Ave., Bloomfield, N. J.

The Rev. DAVID KEEFER SLOATMAN
A.B., B.D.

Instructor in Spanish, 1923-1926.

DAVID KEEFER SLOATMAN: b. Williamsport, Pa., Nov. 8, 1901; Williamsport Dickinson Sem., 1919; A.B., Ohio Wesleyan Univ., 1923; B.D., Drew, 1926; Columbia Univ., 1925, 1926; Cambridge Univ., 1926-27; Yale Univ., 1927-32; Hartford Seminary Foundation, 1934-35; m. Esther Hughes, June 19, 1926; ord. dea., 1925; ord. eld., 1926; entered Cent. Penn. Conf., 1922; ass't. pastor, Emory Ch., Jersey City, N. J., 1924-25; instructor, Spanish, Drew, 1923-26; pastor, Cutchogue, L. I., N. Y., 1926; New York East Conf., 1926; Rowayton, Conn., 1927-30; Howard Ave., New Haven, Conn., 1930-32; Plainville, Conn., 1932-35; Lake Ronkonkoma, Commack, Coram,

L. I., N. Y., 1935-38; Greenport, L. I., N. Y., 1938-40; Westville Ch., New Haven, Conn., 1940——; Phi Beta Kappa; contr., relig. periodicals and newspaper; address, 980 Whalley Ave., New Haven, Conn.

EDNA M. WESTON

Instructor in Religious Education, 1924-1925.

EDNA M. WESTON: instructor, Relig. Education, Drew, 1924-25; with New Jersey Council of Relig. Educ., Children's Division; address, 45 Bleeker Street, Newark, N. J.

FRANCES MATILDA HEDDEN
A.B., M.A.

Instructor in Religious Education, 1924-1925.

FRANCES MATILDA HEDDEN: b. Newark, N. J., Sept. 2, 1880; B.A., Vassar College, 1904; M.A., Columbia Univ., 1920; sup't., Jr. Dep't. of Ch. Sch., 6th Presbyterian Ch., Newark, N. J., 1904-06; sup't. Intermed. Dep't., 1906-21; Winter Course, Auburn Sch. of Rel., 1925; Sup't. Nursery Dept., 1922-28; N. J., Council of Rel. Ed., dir. of children's work, Sept. 1920——; dir. of vacation ch. schools, 1928——; Presbyterian Bd. of Christian Ed., field dir. Synod of N. J., 1930——; address, 157 Halsted Street, East Orange, N. J.

The Rev. FRANK LAUREL PIZZUTO
A.B., M.A., Th.B.

Instructor in Italian Language and Literature, 1925-1927.

FRANK LAUREL PIZZUTO: b. Campobasso, Italy, October 7, 1896; Scuola Technica, Italy, 1910; Came to America in 1913; Naturalized in 1921; E. Greenwich Academy, 1919; A.B., Boston Univ., 1923; Drew Theological Seminary, 1926-27; M.A., Webster Univ., 1929; Th.B., Milton Coll., 1938; A.M., Harvard Univ., 1940; m. Santina Mazzarino, Sept. 11, 1926; ord. dea., 1924; ord. eld., 1925; entered New England Conf., 1924; past, Italian Ch., Methuen, Mass., 1921-24; Italian Mission, First Ch., Lynn, Mass., 1924-25; instructor, Italian Language and Literature, Drew, 1925-27; pastor, St. Paul's Italian Ch., East Boston, Mass., 1928——; instructor, Italian, Suffolk Univ., Boston, Mass., 1938-40; ass't. professor, Italian, 1940-41; chrn., Foreign Language Dept., 1941——; Phi Beta Kappa; pub., *La Religione di Dante; Catechismo Cristiano;* contr., Italian and American magazines; address, 105 Lexington St., East Boston, Mass.

The Rev. JOHN AUBONE BOOTHROYD HOYLE
B.Pd., M.A.

Instructor in Religious Education, 1926-1928.

JOHN A. B. HOYLE: b. Marin, Spain, Dec. 13, 1894; Dulwich Coll., London; B.Pd., Hartford, 1924; M.A., Drew, 1928; m. (1) Olive Alice Owen, Feb. 6, 1918; m. (2) Marguerite Ina McDonald, June 18, 1932; Newark Conf., 1925; director Rel. Ed., 1st Pres. Ch., Victoria, B. C., 1919-22; Canadian Army, (C.E.F.) 1916-19; director Rel. Ed. Prospect M. E. Ch., Bristol, Conn., 1922-24; director Rel. Ed. Roseville Ch., Newark, N. J., 1924-27; instructor, Rel. Ed., Drew, 1926-28; gen. sec. Intern. Convention, Rel. Ed. Toronto, 1930; sec. Rel. Ed. Council Toronto, 1930-39; ed. minister, Yorkminster Baptist Ch. Toronto, 1939——; pub., *Toward the Understanding of Youth;* address, "Hoylands," Wexford, Ontario, Canada.

The Rev. FRITZ HONG KEW PYEN
A.B., B.D., Th.M., Th.D.

Teaching Fellow in German, 1927-1928; *Instructor,* 1928-1930.

A SAINTLY, scholarly, happy-spirited Korean who came to America over great obstacles to fit himself to be a Christian teacher. He learned German and acquired his surprising first name when he was interned with a German Lutheran missionary in Japan during the first World War. It was his habit at Drew to spend the first moments of each hour in prayer, almost to disregard the clock otherwise, and to carry a Testament in one of the many languages at his command, adding a new one every year, reading the Testament while he walked about or waited for classes to begin. He suffered deeply for his faith in later years, and his fate is not known.

FRITZ HONG KEW PYEN: b. Korea, July 1, 1900; Kongju Mission School, 1906-1913; A.B., Hamline U., 1926; B.D., Drew, 1928; Th.M., 1929; Th.D., 1931; teaching fellow, Drew, 1927-1928; instructor, 1928-1930; Korean M. E. Ch., Honolulu, Hawaii, 1930-1933; Korean M. E. Ch., Harbin,

Manchuria, 1933-1934; professor, New Testament and Theology, Union Methodist Theological Seminary, Seoul, Korea, 1934——; president, 1939——; political prisoner later; present address unknown.

The Rev. ERNEST ARTHUR WALL
B.S., M.A., B.D., Ph.D.

Teaching Fellow in French, 1927-1928; Instructor, 1928-1930.

ERNEST ARTHUR WALL: b. Coalbrookdale, Shropshire, Eng., Feb. 24, 1894; Gripton Coll., Birmingham, Eng.; Westgrove Missionary Training Sch., London; Higher Literary and Commercial French Diploma, Royal Soc. of Arts; Livingstone Coll., London, 1919-20; dip. in Theology, Crozer Theol. Seminary, 1926; B.S. in Edn., New York Univ., 1928; M.A., 1930; Ph.D., 1932; B.D., Drew, 1929; Univ. of Berlin, 1929; Fordham Univ., 1933; m. Doris Gladys Young, Mar. 26, 1919; ord. dea., 1929; ord. eld., 1931; entered N. Y. East Conf., 1929; missionary, Algeria, North Africa, 1920-27; teaching fellow, French, Drew, 1927-28; instructor, French and Psychology, 1928-30; pastor, Simpson, Brooklyn, N. Y., 1930-33; Huntington, N. Y., 1933-38; First, West Haven, Conn., 1938-42; Trinity Church, Richmond Hill, New York City, 1942——; contr., relig. and current periodicals; address, 8508 108th Street, Richmond Hill, New York City.

The Rev. SAMUEL LOWRIE HAMILTON
A.B., B.D.

Instructor in Religious Education, 1928-1929

SAMUEL LOWRIE HAMILTON: b. Wilmington, Del., Nov. 1, 1885; A.B., Princeton Univ., 1910; B.D., Drew, 1913; m. Jeanette Eckart, June 12, 1912; ord. dea., 1915; ord. eld., 1917; entered N. Y. East Conf., 1913; pastor, Stony Brook, N. Y., 1913-14; ass't. gen. sec., World's S. S. Ass'n., 1914-16; sup't., Metropolitan Dist., Anti-Saloon League, 1916-18, 1919-24; 1st lieut., U. S. Army, France, 1918-19; gen. sec., N. J. Council of Religious Edn., 1924-29; ass't. professor, Education, New York Univ., 1929-30; assoc. professor, 1930-32; professor, 1932——; instructor, Religious Edn., Drew, 1928-1929; lecturer, Extension Div., Columbia Univ., 1929; exec. comm., Internatl. Council of Religious Edn., 1934——; president, Bd. of Edn., N. Y. East Conf., 1936-39; Comm. on Worship, Federal Council of Churches of Christ in Amer., 1938——; Comm. on Evangelism, Federal Council of Churches of Christ in Amer.; trustee, Newark Free Public Library; Comm. on Program and Study, World's S. S. Ass'n.; contr., various publications; address; 240 Montclair Ave., Newark, N. J.

The Rev. HARRY JASON SMITH
B.S., B.D., Th.M., Th.D., Ph.D.

Teaching Fellow in Systematic Theology and Church History, 1926-1927; Instructor in Church History and Librarian, 1928-1930.

A STUDENT who met the demands and won the affection of both Professor Faulkner and Professor Lewis, under each of whom he took doctorates (only one other man, Paul T. Fuhrmann, '29, has taken two doctor's degrees at Drew), and who proved himself an effective teacher and library administrator as well. Among many other services to Drew he began "The Gateway" and edited its first number before Baldwin-Wallace called him to his present position.

HARRY JASON SMITH: b. Hornell, N.Y., May 29, 1891; B.S., Alfred Univ., 1920; B.D., Drew, 1923; Th.M., 1927; Th.D., 1929; Ph.D., 1941; m. Ruth Williams, Nov. 15, 1923; ent. Genesee Conf., 1915; ord. dea., 1917; ord. eld., 1919; pastor, Lindley, N. Y., 1915-1917; So. Dansville, N. Y., 1917-1920; ent., Troy Conf., 1923; E. Main Street, Amsterdam, N. Y., 1923-1924; Fonda, N. Y., 1924-1926; teaching fellow, systematic theology and ch. history, Drew, 1926-1927; teaching fellow and acting assistant librarian, 1927-1928; instructor in ch. history and librarian, 1928-1930; ass't. professor, ch. hist., Nast Theological Sem., 1930-1933; professor, English, Baldwin-Wallace Coll., 1933—; address, 141 Fifth Ave., Berea, O.

PIERSON PENROSE HARRIS
Instructor in Public Speaking, 1929-1937.

PIERSON PENROSE HARRIS: b. Philadelphia, Pa., Dec. 3, 1898; B.A., Haverford College, 1920; B.D., Union Theological Seminary, 1923; S.T.M., 1925; Columbia University, 1920-23; m. Ella Margaret Freas, April 12, 1928; ord., May 16, 1923; N. Y. C. Presbytery, 1923-24; Ass't., Fifth Ave. Presbyterian, N. Y. C., 1923-24; Presbyterian Ch. in the U. S. A., 1923-28; pastor, Ft. Hamilton Presbyterian, Brooklyn, 1924-26; instructor, Public Speaking and Oral Interpretation, Union Theological Seminary, 1924-27; Brooklyn Presbytery, 1924-28; instructor, Public Speaking, Jewish Inst. of Rel., 1925-26; Assoc., Overbrook Presbyterian, Philadelphia, Pa., 1926-28; instructor, Public Speaking, New Brunswick Theological Seminary, 1926-29; Haverford College, 1927-29; Congregational, 1928——; N. J. Ass'n of Congregational Chs., 1928-37; pastor, Stanley Congregational, Chatham, N. J., 1928-37; Instructor, Public Speaking, Drew University, 1929-37; del., General Council of Congregational Chs., 1931, 1936, 1938, 1942; exchange preacher to Great Britain, summer, 1933; Moderator, Middle Atlantic Conference of Congregational Churches, 1935-39; Worcester Centr. Ass'n Congregational Chs., 1937——; pastor, Central Congregational, Worcester, Mass., 1937——; address, 8 Institute Road, Worcester, Mass.

MILDRED OLIVIA MOODY EAKIN
A.B., M.A.

Teaching Fellow in Religious Education, 1932-1934; Instructor, 1934——.

MILDRED OLIVIA MOODY EAKIN. b. Wilson, N. Y., Mar. 28, 1890; grad., Wilson Acad., 1906; A.B., Syracuse Univ., 1910; grad. work, 1913; Chicago Univ., 1929-30; M.A., New York Univ., 1934; Drew; m. Frank Eakin, Mar. 28, 1931; teacher, high sch., Wilson, N. Y., 1910-16; dir., children's activities, W.C.T.U., 1916-19; assoc. nat. dir., 1919; dir., elementary edn., divisional office, Bd. of Edn., M. E. Ch., Kansas City, Mo., 1919-21; supt., dep't. of elementary edn., central office, Bd. of Edn., M. E. Ch., Chicago, 1921-32; teaching fellow, Relig. Edn., Drew, 1932-34; instructor, 1934——; dir., demonstration sch. in relig. edn. dept. since 1937; dir. of relig. edn., Wyoming Presbyterian Ch., Millburn, N. J., 1932-36; dir. of relig. edn., Hillside Ave. Presbyterian Ch., Orange, N. J., 1937-41; chrn., Children's Advisory Section, Internat. Council of Relig. Edn., 1926; dir. of leadership training, Com. on Relig. Edn. of Children, Internat. Council of Relig. Edn., 1927-32; pub., *Tales of Golden Deeds,* 1923; *Kindergarten Course for the Daily Vacation Church School,* 1925; *Teaching Junior Boys and Girls,* 1934; *Exploring Our Neighborhood, Under the Church Flag,* 1936; co-author, *Junior Teacher's Guide on Negro Americans,* 1936; co-author, *Your Child's Religion,* 1942; contr., relig. and ednl. publications; address, 39 Green Village Rd., Madison, N. J.

HARRY ARTHUR WANN
A.B., M.A., Ed.D.

Teaching Fellow in Education, 1933-1934; Instructor, 1934-1935.

HARRY ARTHUR WANN: b. Arcadia, Ind., June 24, 1892; A.B., DePauw Univ., 1917; M.A., Columbia Univ., 1926; Ed.D., 1935; m. Clara Herr, 1914; teacher, elem. schools, Jackson Twp., Arcadia. Ill., 1910-14; U.S. Army YMCA, 1917-18; sec., Lake County, O., YMCA, 1918-19; principal, consolidated school, Ind., 1919-26; principal, Madison, N. J., high school, 1926-30; supervising principal, Madison public schools, 1930-40; teaching fellow, Edn., Drew, 1933-34; instructor, 1934-35; superintendent of schools, Morris City, N. J., 1940-41; director, dept. community organization, nat'l hdqrs. U.S.O., 1941-42; ass't admin., service to the armed forces, Amer. Nat'l. Red Cross, 1942——.

HELENE KATHERINE MOSIER

Teaching Fellow in Education, 1930-1934; Instructor, 1934-1939.

The Rev. MURRAY ALEXANDER CAYLEY

A.B., M.A., B.D.

Instructor in Public Speaking, 1937-1940.

MURRAY ALEXANDER CAYLEY: b. Stratford, Ont., Canada, Aug. 27, 1899; A.B., Toronto Univ., 1922; Victoria Seminary, Toronto, 1922-23; B.D., Union Theological Seminary, 1926; graduate study, 1926-29; M.A., Columbia Univ., 1926; clinical training, Morris Plains Mental Hospital, 1938; m. (1) Agnes E. Donegan, May 20, 1926; m. (2) Arline F. Herting, July 16, 1931; entered London Conf., Canada, 1921; home missionary, Ritchie, Saskatchewan, 1923; dir., Religious Edn., Mt. Washington Presbyterian Ch., New York, N. Y., 1923-26; ord., United Ch. of Canada, 1926; assoc. pastor, North Ave. Presbyterian Ch., New Rochelle, N. Y., 1926-31; instructor, Public Speaking, Union Theologi-cal Seminary, 1926-28; entered Presbyterian Ch. U. S. A., 1928; pastor, Greystone Presbyterian Ch., Elizabeth, N. J., 1931-40; instructor, Public Speaking, Drew, 1937-40; pastor, First Presbyterian Ch., Rochester, N. Y., 1940——; lecturer, Psychology and Economics, Rochester Athenaeum and Mechanics Institute, Rochester, N. Y., 1941——; Lieut. R.A.F., 1918-19; sup't., National Missions, Elizabeth Presbytery, 1937-40; del., General Assembly of the Presbyterian Ch., U. S. A., 1939 and 1942; pub., *Are We Spiritually Dead?*, 1932; co-author, *Drama and Pageantry*, 1940; contr., poetry, religious periodicals; address, 101 South Plymouth Avenue., Rochester, N. Y.

The Rev. CHARLES LAREW MEAD, Jr.

A.B., M.A., B.D.

Instructor in Public Speaking, 1940——.

CHARLES LAREW MEAD, JR.: b. New York, N. Y., Nov. 24, 1913; A.B., Univ. of Denver, 1935; M.A., 1939; Univ. of Southern Cal., 1935; B.D., Drew, 1940; graduate study, 1940——; m. Martha Lee Moore, Aug. 4, 1937;

ord. dea., 1940; ord. eld., 1942; entered Newark Conf., 1940; instructor, Speech and Dramatic Art, Kansas Wesleyan Univ., 1935-36; ass't. minister, Christ Ch., New York, N. Y., 1937; pastor, Barnum Ch., Denver, Col., 1937; teaching fellow, Speech, Brothers Coll., 1937-39; ass't. minister, First Ch., Montclair, N. J., 1938; pastor, Grace Ch., Dover, N. J., 1940—; instructor, Public Speaking, Drew, 1940—; address, 96 North Sussex St., Dover, N. J.

VISITING INSTRUCTORS

The Rev. DONALD STEWART TRAILL
M.A., S.T.M.

Visiting Instructor in Church History, 1931-1932.

INSTRUCTION in Church History was given by several visiting instructors in the interim between Professor Faulkner's death and the appointment of Professor Stafford.

DONALD STEWART TRAILL: b. Edinburgh, Scotland, May 4, 1904; M.A., Univ. of Edinburgh, 1925; Coll. dip., New College, Edinburgh, 1928; S.T.M., Union Theological Seminary, New York, N. Y., 1929; Harvard Theological Sch., 1930-31; m. Lorraine Lillian Tanner, Nov. 29, 1933; ord., Presbyterian Ch. in Canada, 1930; ass't. pastor, Ch. of St. Andrew and St. Paul, Montreal, P. Q., 1929-30; pastor, First Congregational Ch., New Bedford, Mass., 1931-32; visiting instructor, Church History, Drew, 1931-32; pastor, First, Pembroke, Ont., 1933-34; St. Andrew's, Levis, P. Q., 1935-42; professor of history, Brandon College, Brandon, Manitoba, Canada, 1942—; contr., relig. journals; address, Brandon College, Brandon, Manitoba, Canada.

The Rev. CYRIL CHARLES RICHARDSON
B.A., Th.L., S.T.M., Th.D.

Visiting Instructor in Church History, 1934-1935.

DR. RICHARDSON was another man who carried this work before Dr. Faulkner's successor was appointed.

CYRIL CHARLES RICHARDSON: b. London, Eng., June 13, 1909; B.A.. Univ. of Saskatchewan, 1930; Th.L., Emmanuel Coll., Saskatoon, 1931; S.T.M., Union Theol. Sem., 1932; Th.D., 1934; Univ. of Göttingen, 1933; ord. dea., 1934; ord. priest, 1934; instructor, Church History, Union Theol. Sem., 1934-35; visiting instructor, Church History, Drew, 1934-35; ass't. professor, Church History, Union Theol. Sem., 1935-39; assoc. professor, 1939——; pub., *The Christianity of Ignatius of Antioch,* 1935; *The Church Thru the Centuries,* 1938; *The Sacrament of Reunion,* 1940; address, Union Theol. Sem., New York, N. Y.

The Rev. MELVIN MACYE CAMMACK
A.B., B.D., M.A.

Visiting Instructor in New Testament Greek Exegesis,
1937-1938.

MELVIN MACYE CAMMACK: b. Liberty, Kansas, June 29, 1908; Junior Coll., Independence, Kan., 1926-27, 1928-29; Georgia Sch. of Technology, 1927-28; A.B., Baker Univ., 1931; B.D., Drew, 1935; M.A., 1936, graduate study, 1936-37; Cambridge Univ., Eng., 1938-39; m. Irene E. Penland, Dec. 25, 1930; ord. dea., 1934; ord. eld., 1936; entered Kansas Conf., 1930; pastor, White Post Ch., near Independence, Kan., 1929, 1933; Lone Elm, Kan., 1929-32; teacher, Walnut Grove Rural Sch., near Lone Elm, Kan., 1931-32; pastor, Community Ch., Brookside, N. J., 1935-37; visiting instructor, New Testament Greek Exegesis, Drew, 1937-38; pastor, Virgil, Kan., 1939——; Quincy, Kan., 1939——; Neal, Kan., 1941——; pres., County Council of Chs.; pub., *John Wyclif and the English Bible,* 1938; contr., religious periodicals; address, Virgil, Kan.

TEACHING FELLOWS

The Rev. JOSE L. VALENCIA
A.B., D.D.

Assistant in Spanish, 1926-1927; *Teaching Fellow,* 1927-1928.

JOSE L. VALENCIA: b. Tagudin, Ilocos Sur. P. I., Aug. 25, 1898; A.B., Cornell Coll., 1925; Garrett Biblical Institute, 1925, 1928; B.D., Drew, 1929; ord. dea., 1928; ord. eld., 1930; ass't. in Spanish, Drew, 1926-27; teaching fellow, Drew, 1927-28; entered Upper Iowa Conf., 1928; pastor, Vigan Ch., Nandan-Cavayan, Ilocos Sur., P. I., 1929-31; Philippine Island Conf.,

1930; dean, Wesley Hall, Vigan, Ilocos Sur., P. I., 1930-31; withdrawn from Philippines Island Conf., 1931; Tagu-din, Ilocos Sur., P. I., 1931-32; address, Tuguegarao, Cagayan, P. I.

The Rev. MARK WEBER BROWN
A.B., B.D., Th.M., Th.D., Ph.D., D.D.

Teaching Fellow in Psychology and Systematic Theology, 1927-1930.

A BRILLIANT and fine-spirited missionary who taught theology in the College of Missions while he was completing his own graduate work at Drew. He received the first Ph.D. degree granted by Drew Theological Seminary. His early death was a great loss to China and to America.

MARK WEBER BROWN: b. Weldbank, Pa., Sept. 4, 1887; A.B., Scio Coll., 1911; B.D., Drew, 1914, Th.M., 1928, Ph.D., 1930; D.D., Mount Union Coll., 1926; m. Ocie Rentsch, June 11, 1913; ord. dea., 1913; ord. eld., 1915; entered Northeast Ohio Conf., 1913; pastor, Chelsea-on-Hudson, N. Y., 1911-12; Middle Village Ch., Brooklyn, N. Y., 1912-13; Kingsland Ch., Lyndhurst, N. J., 1913-14; North China Conf., 1914; missionary, Peking, 1914-15; supt., Taianfu Dist., 1915-16; supt., Tientsin Dist., 1916-17; missionary in charge, Lanhsien District, 1917-20; missionary-in-charge, Shanhaikuan Dist., 1920-21; missionary-in-charge Shanhaikuan and Lanhsien Dists., 1921-24; professor, Systematic Theology, Peking Theological Seminary, 1924-34; teaching fellow, Psychology and Systematic Theology, Drew, 1927-30; an editor, *China Christian Advocate,* 1921-25; mem., bd. of examiners in Chinese lang., North China Conf., lecturer, Coll. of Chinese Studies; pub., *Chinese Translation of Basic Beliefs* by H. Maldwyn Hughes (completed by Prof. Y. L. Yang), 1937; contr., *The Chinese Recorder;* d. April 14, 1934.

The Rev. JOHN DOW HERR
B.Arch., B.D., Th.M., Th.D.

Teaching Fellow in English Bible, 1928-1929.

JOHN DOW HERR: b. Poughkeepsie, N. Y., Feb. 8, 1901; B. of Arch., Univ. of Penna., 1922; B.D., Drew, 1926; Th.M., 1927; Th.D., 1929; m. Esther Morton, Sept. 8, 1925; ord. dea., 1926; ord. eld., 1928; entered Philadelphia Conf., 1925; pastor, Analomink, Pa., 1925-26; Mount Pocono, 1926-29; teaching fellow, English Bible, Drew, 1928-29; ass't. pastor, St. James, Philadelphia, Pa., 1929-30; pastor, Summerfield, Philadelphia, Pa., 1930-33; Chelten Ave., Germantown, Philadelphia, Pa., 1933-35; Asbury Univ. Ch., Philadelphia, Pa., 1935-42; dir., Wesley Foundation, Philadelphia, Pa., 1935-42; Mt. Airy, Philadelphia, Pa., 1942—; professor, Systematic Theology, Temple Univ., 1929—; address, 111 W. Mt. Pleasant Ave., Philadelphia, Pa.

The Rev. ELLIS ERNEST PIERCE

A.B., M.A., S.T.B., Th.D.

Teaching Fellow in English Bible, 1925-1931.

ELLIS ERNEST PIERCE: b. East Palmyra, N. Y., Aug. 27, 1903; A.B., Syracuse Univ., 1924; M.A., 1925; Auburn Theological Seminary, 1925-26; S.T.B., Boston Univ., 1928; Th.D., Drew, 1931; m. Alma Blodget, Sept. 3, 1930; ord. eld., 1925; entered Central New York Conf., 1921; Syracuse Univ., 1924-25; assistant, English Bible, Drew, 1928-29; teaching fellow, English Bible, Drew, 1929-31; Genesee Wesleyan Junior Coll., 1931-32; pastor, Fleming Hill Ch., Auburn, N. Y., 1932-34; New Hope Ch., Moravia, N. Y., 1934-36; First Ch., Cazenovia, N. Y., 1936-39; Cazenovia Junior Coll., 1936-39; First Ch., Truxton, N. Y., 1939-40; Enfield Larger Parish, 1940-41; Woodbury Memorial Ch. (Universalist-Unitarian), Hornell, N. Y., 1941—; contr., relig. periodicals and journals; contr., original poems and metrical translation from the Hebrew in magazines and anthologies; address, 23 Genesee St., Hornell, N. Y.

The Rev. CALVIN CLYDE HOGGARD

B.A., B.D.

Teaching Fellow in Religious Education, 1930-1933.

CALVIN CLYDE HOGGARD: b. Purcell, Okla., Jan. 4, 1906; Southern Methodist Univ., 1924-27; B.A., Oklahoma City Univ., 1930; B.D., Drew, 1932; graduate study, 1937-39; m. Mary Helen Gibbs, Dec. 2, 1926; ord. dea., 1933; ord. eld., 1935; entered West Oklahoma Conf. on trial, 1929, in full membership, 1934; pastor, Bellport, N. Y., 1930-33; teaching fellow, Religious Education, Drew, 1930-33; Oklahoma Conf., 1933; Glenwood Ch., Tulsa, Okla., 1933-35; First Ch., Chelsea, Okla., 1935-37; Orient, N. Y., 1937-39; Westbury, N. Y., 1939-41; New York East Conf., 1940; St. Paul's Ch., Northport, N. Y., 1941—; pub., Attitudes of Christians Toward Jews, 1933; address, 283 Main St., Northport, N. Y.

The Rev. CHARLES ABNER WHITEMARSH
A.B., M.A., B.D., D.D.
Teaching Fellow in Systematic Theology, 1928-1931.

CHARLES ABNER WHITEMARSH: b. Greenspond, Newfoundland, Oct. 20, 1878; A.B., Mt. Allison Univ., 1906; M.A., 1908; D.D., 1930; B.D., Drew, 1908; m. Drue Frost, Sept. 11, 1906; ord. eld., 1906; entered Newfoundland Conf., 1899; pastor, Central Ch., Bay Roberts, N. F., 1908-12; Cochrane St. Ch., St. John's, N. F., 1912-16; First Ch., Brigus, N. F., 1916-17; sec., Newfoundland Meth. Conf., 1916-17; New York East Conf., 1920; Trinity Ch., City Island, N. Y., 1920-23; Diamond Hill, Greenwich, Conn., 1923-28; Rye, N. Y., 1928-31; Ocean Parkway Ch., Brooklyn, N. Y., 1931-34; First Ch., Islip, L. I., N. Y., 1934-40; Trinity Ch., City Island, N. Y., 1940—; address, 113 Bay St., City Island, New York, N. Y.

The Rev. RALPH REDDINGTON JOHNSON
A.B., M.A., B.D.
Teaching Fellow, Homiletics, 1931-1935.

RALPH REDDINGTON JOHNSON: b. Grand Rapids, Mich., Nov. 9, 1899; A.B., Univ. of Mich., 1923, M.A., 1928; B.D., Drew, 1935; Oxford, 1939-40; m. Ruth Katherine Busso, June 26, 1922; ord. dea., 1938; ord eld., 1941; entered Newark Conf., 1941; teacher, English and Public Speaking, Highland Park Junior Coll., 1923-25; instructor, English, Univ. of Mich., 1925-31; assistant dir. of Wesley Foundation, 1927-29; director of Wesley Foundation, Ann Arbor, Mich., 1929-31; teaching fellow, Homiletics, Drew, 1931-35; ass't. to the president, 1931-32; instructor, English, Brothers Coll., 1931-37; ass't. prof., English and Dramatics, 1937—; dir., student employment, 1937-39; part-time pastor, Presbyterian Ch., Parsippany, N. J., 1941—; address, 223 Central Ave., Madison, N. J.

The Rev. EVERETT ROSS CLINCHY
B.S., M.A., Ph.D.
Teaching Fellow in Religious Education, 1934—.

EVERETT ROSS CLINCHY: b. New York, N. Y., Dec. 16, 1896; Wesleyan Univ., 1916-18; B.S., Lafayette Coll., 1920; M.A., Columbia Univ., 1921; Union Theological Seminary, 1920-21; Yale Divinity Sch., 1922-23; Ph.D., Drew, 1934; m. Winifred Marcena Mead, Sept. 21, 1918; ord., Presbyterian Ch., 1921; pastor, Fairmount, N. J., 1921-23; Ch. of Christ, Wesleyan Univ., Middletown, Conn., 1923-28; sec., Federal Council of the Chs. of Christ in America, 1928-33; dir. and pres., The National Conf. of Christians and Jews, 1928——; teaching fellow, Religious Edu., Drew, 1934——; originated "seminar" confs. for study Catholic— Protestant-Jewish relations; directed Williamstown Inst. of Human Relations, 1935, 1937, 1939, 1941; second lieut., F. A., U. S. A., first World War; pub., *All in the Name of God,* 1934; *The World We Want to Live In,* 1942; contr., religious and ednl. publications; address, 381 Fourth Ave., New York City.

The Rev. ALFRED BURTON HAAS
A.B., B.D.

Teaching Fellow in Hymnology, 1941——.

ALFRED BURTON HAAS: b. Shamokin, Pa., July 21, 1911; A.B., Bucknell Univ., 1933; B.D., Drew, 1936, graduate study, 1941——; ord. dea., 1935; ord. eld., 1938; entered Cent. Penn. Conf., 1936; pastor, Holy Trinity, Hazleton, Pa., 1936; ass't. minister and dir. of Christian Ed., Grace, Harrisburg, Pa., 1936-1941; teaching fellow, Hymnology, Drew, 1941——; address, Drew Forest, Madison, N. J.

LECTURERS

The Rev. JAMES MONROE BUCKLEY
A.M., D.D., LL.D., L.H.D.

Lecturer on Ecclesiastical Law and Philosophy of Christianity, 1912-1920.

DR. BUCKLEY, the distinguished editor of *The Christian Advocate* for thirty years and during the same period a dominant personality in American Methodism, had appeared many times before the student body at Drew, speaking on a great variety of subjects in which he had the rank of specialist. But not until his retirement as editor in 1912 was he formally elected to the faculty. His immense and diversified learning, his ready wit, and his reputation as a kind of Methodist Pope commanded for him an audience which usually included members of the faculty. At his decease the seminary received the choicest volumes from his extensive library.

JAMES MONROE BUCKLEY: b. Rahway, N. J., Dec. 16, 1836; Pennington Sem.; A.M., Wesleyan Univ., 1869; D.D., 1872; LL.D., Emory and Henry Coll., 1882; L.H.D., Syracuse Univ., 1906; m. (1) Eliza A. Burns, m. (2) Sarah I. Staples, m. (3) Adelaide S. Hill; ord. dea., 1861; ord. eld., 1863; entered New Hampshire Conf., 1859; pastor, St. John's, Dover, N. H., 1859-61; St. Paul's, Manchester, N. H., 1861-63; abroad, 1863-64; Michigan Conf., 1864; Central, Detroit, Mich., 1864-66; New York East Conf., 1866; Summerfield, Brooklyn, N. Y., 1866-69; Stamford, Conn., 1869-72; Summerfield, Brooklyn, N. Y., 1872-75; Stamford, Conn., 1875-78; Hanson Place, Brooklyn, N. Y., 1878-80; editor, *The Christian Advocate*, N. Y., 1880-1912; lecturer, Ecclesiastical Law and Philosophy of Christianity, Drew, 1912-20; president, Methodist Episcopal Hospital, Brooklyn, N. Y., 1882-1916; del., Gen. Conf., 1872, 1876, 1880, 1884, 1888, 1892, 1896, 1900, 1904, 1908, 1912, 1916; mem., Ecumenical Confs., 1881, 1891, 1911; pub., *Oats or Wild Oats*, 1885; *Faith Healing, Christian Science and Kindred Phe-*

240

nomena, 1892; *Christians and the Theater; The Land of the Czar and the Nihilist; Travels in Three Continents—Europe, Asia, Africa*, 1895; *History of Methodism in the United States*, 1897; *Extemporaneous Oratory for Professional and Amateur Speakers*, 1898; *Supposed Miracles; The Funda-* *mentals and Their Contrasts*, 1906; *The Wrong and Peril of Woman Suffrage*, 1909; *Theory and Practice of Foreign Missions*, 1911; *Constitutional and Parliamentary History of the Methodist Episcopal Church*, 1912; d. Feb. 8, 1920.

The Rev. WILBERT FRANCIS HOWARD

M.A., B.D., D.D.

Lecturer on Greek New Testament, 1918-1919.

ONE OF PRESIDENT TIPPLE'S innovations was the introduction of distinguished scholars from Britain to supplement the faculty instruction. Mr. Howard was one of the earliest, as well as one of the ablest and most charming of these transient lecturers. He already ranked high among the younger New Testament scholars of Wesleyan Methodism, and was a favorite pupil and collaborator of Dr. James H. Moulton. The condensed record of his career, which is given below, proves that the last twenty years have amply fulfilled the promise of his year at Drew.

WILBERT FRANCIS HOWARD: b. England, Dec. 30, 1880; King Edward VI. School, Birmingham; M.A., Manchester U.; D.D., London U., Didsbury Coll.; D.D., St. Andrews U.; m. Winifred Worsley; B.D., Bedale, 1909; tutor, N. T. Language and Literature, 1919——; entered Wes. Meth. ministry 1906; pastor, Glasgow; Bowes Park, London; Manchester, Handsworth, Wallasey; lecturer, Greek N. T. 1918-1919; lecturer Hellenistic Greek, Univ. of Birmingham; examiner Biblical Languages, London Univ. 1923-1926, 1935-1938; in Theology, 1929-1931, 1938-1941; Examiner Hellenistic Greek and N. T., Manchester Univ. 1926-1928, 1941——; examiner Leeds Univ., 1938-1940; examiner Hellenistic Greek, Glasgow U., 1928, 1934; examiner, Theology, Oxford, 1939; Dale Lecturer, Mansfield College, Oxford, 1940; fraternal delegate to M. E. Gen. Conf., 1932; editor vol. 2, J. H. Moulton's *Grammar of N. T. Greek*, contrib. to *Abingdon Commentary*, Study Bible, etc.; address, Oakfield, Priory Road, Handsworth Wood, Birmingham, England.

The Rev. CHARLES LE ROY GOODELL
A.B., A.M., D.D.
Lecturer on Evangelism, 1918-1930.

DR. GOODELL came before the student audiences at Drew with an enviable reputation as a successful pastor of leading churches in Boston, Providence, Brooklyn and New York City. The evangelistic note was always dominant in his preaching, and his long experience and kindling personality qualified him for exceptional service as a counselor of young ministers on this department of their pastoral activity.

CHARLES LE ROY GOODELL: b. Dudley, Mass., July 31, 1854; A.B., Boston Univ., 1877; A.M., New York Univ., 1900; D.D., Wesleyan Univ., 1906; m. Mary F. Blair, June 3, 1896; ord. dea., 1881; ord. eld., 1883; entered New England Southern Conf., 1879; pastor, Acushnet, Mass., 1879-80; Broadway Ch., Province, R. I., 1880-83; Chestnut St., Providence, R. I., 1883-86; Trinity, Providence, R. I., 1886-88; New England Conf., 1885; Winthrop St., Boston, Mass., 1885-94; First (formerly Temple St.), Boston, Mass., 1894-97; New York East Conf., 1897; Hanson Pl., Brooklyn, N. Y., 1897-1904; New York Conf., 1904; Calvary, New York, N. Y., 1904-13; St. Paul's, New York, N. Y., 1913-18; lecturer, Evangelism, Drew, 1918-30; in charge religious work, Camp Meade, Md., 1918; exec. sec., Comm'n. on Evangelism of Federal Council of Churches, 1918-30; pub., *My Mother's Bible*, 1891; *The Drill Master of Methodism*, 1902; *The Price of Winning Souls*, 1906; *Pathways to the Best*, 1907; *Pastoral and Personal Evangelism*, 1907; *The Old Darnman*, 1911; *Followers of the Gleam*, 1911; *Heralds of a Passion*, 1921; *Pastor and Evangelist*, 1922; *What Are You Worth?*, 1923; *Tales of Old New England*, 1924; *Motives and Methods of Modern Evangelism*, 1925; *The Book We Love*, 1929; *Twilight Reveries*, 1929; *Life Reveries*, 1930; *Soul Reveries*, 1931; *Prayers for Sabbath Reveries*, 1931; *Black Tavern Tales*, 1932; *Radiant Reveries*, 1932; mag. writer, radio preacher; d. Apr. 27, 1937.

The Rev. BRENTON THOBURN BADLEY
A.B., A.M., D.D., LL.D.
Lecturer on Applied Christianity in India, 1918-1919.

THE SON of an India missionary, born in a mission bungalow, accustomed from childhood to the life and thought of the Indian people, Dr. Badley brought to his own missionary service a deep and strong evangelical conviction. This year of his residence in Madison came when he was serving as an associate secretary of the Board of Foreign Missions in a brief interval in his long missionary life. Five years later he was elected bishop.

BRENTON THOBURN BADLEY: b. Gonda, U. P. India, May 29, 1876; Simpson Coll., Ia.; A.B., Ohio Wesleyan U., 1897; A.M., Columbia, 1899; D.D., 1922; LL.D., Simpson, 1926; m. Mary Putnam Stearns, Apr. 29, 1903; ent. N. India Conf., 1901; ord. dea., 1903; ord. eld., 1905; professor, Eng. Lit., Lucknow Christian Coll., 1900-1910; gen. sec., Epworth League for India-Burma, 1910-1917; assoc. sec., Bd. of F. M., 1917-1919; lecturer, Applied Christianity in India, Drew, 1918-1919; exec. sec., Centenary Movement for India, 1919-1923; editor, *Indian Witness,* 1924; bishop, M. E. Church, 1924——; Phi Beta Kappa; pub., *The New American Indian,* 1904; *The Making of a Christian College in India,* 1906; *David Livingstone—The Man of Sacrifice,* 1914; *God's Heroes our examples,* 1914; *New Etchings of Old India,* 1918; *Hindostan's Horizons,* 1923; *Indian Church Problems,* 1929; *India Making and Forsaken Gods—The Solitary Three, and Some Beliefs of Mahatma Ghandhi,* 1931; *Visions and Victories in Hindostan,* 1931; *Warne of India,* 1932; *Faith,* 1933; co-author *India Beloved of Heaven.* 1918; address, 12 Boulevard Road, Delhi, India.

Dr. H. KARL W. KUMM
M.A., Ph.D.

Lecturer on Missions and the Exploration of Africa, Ph.D., 1918-1920.

DR. KUMM, native of Germany, educated in England, resident of America, was for two years the mouthpiece of Africa as a mission field. He had traveled and worked in many parts of the Dark Continent, and written extensively on its geography, ethnology and missions.

H. KARL W. KUMM: b. Markoldendorf, Germany, Oct. 19, 1874; studied, London, Heidelberg, Jena, Paris, Freiburg, Cambridge; M.A., Ph.D.; m. F. Gertrude Cato, Jan. 23, 1912; lecturer, Missions and Exploration in Africa, Drew, 1918-1920; founder, Sudan Missions and Board for Medical Research and Education in Africa; pub., *Political Economy of Nubia,* 1903; *Tribes of the Nile Valley,* 1903; *The Sudan,* 1906; *From Hausseland to Egypt,* 1910; *The Lands of Ethiopia,* 1910; *African Missionary Heroes and*

Heroines, 1919; *Raymond Lull,* 1920; *African Wealth and Health,* 1925; *Greek and Roman Geographers and* *Africa,* 1925; *Arab Geographers and Africa,* 1925.

AGNES CRAWFORD LEAYCRAFT DONOHUGH
B.A., M.A.
Lecturer on Village Life in Africa, 1918-1919.

MRS. DONOHUGH's missionary interest, which came naturally enough to her, as daughter and wife of mission-minded Christians, was heightened by close study of the anthropology of the peoples of mission lands, specifically Africans. When Dr. Tipple visualized a College of Missions at Drew, she was a first choice as lecturer upon this phase. Subsequently she became an authority upon the subject and has held a full professorship in the Kennedy School of Missions in Hartford Seminary.

AGNES CRAWFORD LEAYCRAFT (Mrs. Thomas Smith) DONOHUGH: b. New York, N. Y., Apr. 25, 1876; B.A., Barnard Coll., 1901; M.A., Columbia Univ., 1916; m. Thomas S. Donohugh, June 14, 1906; lecturer, Village Life in Africa, Drew, 1918-19; visiting lecturer, Kennedy Sch. of Missions, 1918, 1919; instructor, 1919-21; ass't. professor, 1921-24; assoc. professor, 1924-35; professor, 1935——; address, 23 Midland Ave., White Plains, N. Y.

Dr. HERMAN HARRELL HORNE
A.B., A.M., Ph.D., LL.D.
Lecturer on Religious Pedagogy, 1919-1920.

DR. HORNE, a recognized authority in this branch of education, gave two years of effective service at Drew as a lecturer in the early years of President Tipple's administration.

HERMAN HARRELL HORNE: b. Clayton, N. C., Nov. 22, 1874; A.B., Univ. N. C., 1905; LL.D., 1934; A.M., Harvard, 1897; Ph.D., 1899; Univ. Berlin, 1906-1907; LL.D., Wake Forest Coll.; m. Alice Elizabeth Herbert

Worthington, Aug. 29, 1901; instructor, Mod. Lang., Univ. N. C., 1894-1896; instructor, Philosophy, Dartmouth, 1899-1900; ass't. professor, Philosophy and Pedagogy, 1900-1905; professor, Philosophy, 1905-1909; professor, Hist. of Education and Hist. of Philosophy, N. Y. U., 1909——; lecturer, Religious Pedagogy, Drew, 1919-1920; lecturer, summer sessions, Harvard, Univ. N. C., N. Y. U., etc.; Norton Lecturer, So. Bapt. Theol. Sem., 1923; Carew Lecturer, Hartford Sem., 1935; Sprunt Lecturer, Union Sem., 1937; pub., *The Philosophy of Education*, 1904; *The Psychological Principles of Education*, 1906; *Idealism in Education*, 1910; *Free Will and Human Responsibility*, 1912; *Leadership of Bible Study Groups*, 1912; *Story-telling, Questioning and Studying*, 1916; *The Teacher as Artist*, 1917; *Jesus— Our Standard*, 1918; *Modern Problems as Jesus Saw Them*, 1918; *Jesus, the Master Teacher*, 1920; *Christ in Man-Making*. 1925; *Jesus as a Philosopher*, 1927; *This New Education*, 1931; *The Essentials of Leadership*, 1931; *John Dewey's Philosophy*, 1931; *The Democratic Philosophy of Education*, 1932; *Syllabus in the Philosophy of Education*, 1934; *The Philosophy of Christian Education*, 1937; co-author *Quintilian on Education*, 1936; with others, *Introduction to Modern Education*, 1937; *Tomorrow in the Making*, 1939; *Southern Songs*, 1916; *Songs of Sentiment*, 1917; *Romantic Rambles*, 1925; contrib. Monroe's *Cyclopedia of Education* and Nelson's *Encyclopedia of Sunday Schools;* address, 341 Summit Ave., Leonia, N. J.

The Rev. JOHN RUSSELL DENYES
A.B., S.T.B., D.D.
Lecturer on Missions, 1919-1920.

DR. DENYES had performed notable service in the Methodist missions in Southeastern Asia, and had shown exceptional ability in presenting the motives, difficulties and results of missionary effort among the mixed peoples of Straits Settlements and the Dutch East Indies, before he was called upon by Dr. Tipple to represent that field in the College of Missions at Drew.

JOHN RUSSELL DENYES: b. Brookfield, Mo., Jan. 24, 1869; Coll. of the Pacific; A.B., Northwestern U., 1895; S.T.B., Garrett, 1897; D.D., 1912; entered Malaysia Conf., 1898; ord. dea., 1900; ord. eld., 1902; teacher, Anglo-Chinese School, Singapore, 1898-1899; city-evangelist, 1899-1903; Supt. missions in Dutch E. I., 1905-1912; sec., education Malaysia and supt., Penang Dist., 1914-1917; lecturer for Bd. F. M., 1917-1919; lecturer, Missions, Drew, 1919-1920; lecturer on Missions, Garrett B. I., 1920-1921; fin. agt., Wesley Foundation, Madison, Wis., 1921-1923; professor, Religion and Missions, Lawrence College, 1925-1936; del., Gen. Conf., 1912, 1928; Phi Beta Kappa, etc.; d. Jan. 22, 1936.

The Rev. ERIC McCOY NORTH
B.A., M.A., B.D., Ph.D., D.D.

Lecturer on Religious Education and Foreign Missionary Problems, 1919-1924.

DR. NORTH, who in 1928 became General Secretary of the American Bible Society, was a member of the staff of the Methodist Board of Foreign Missions when Dr. Tipple drafted him as a lecturer. His familiarity with the subject was exceptional, and his analytical mind and gift of lucid and forceful statement qualified him for his task. Exceptional also was the fact that at one time or another both his parents, Dr. Frank Mason North and Mrs. Louise McCoy North, were among the teachers of Drew.

ERIC McCOY NORTH: b. Middletown, Conn., June 22, 1888; B.A., Wesleyan U., 1909; M.A., 1910; D.D., 1931; M.A., Columbia, 1910; Ph.D., 1914; graduate, Union T. S., 1913; m. Gladys Haven, Apr. 17, 1920; ass't. in Systematic Theol., Union T. Sem., 1913-1914; ass't. professor, Hist. of Christianity, O. W. U., 1915-1917; ass't. ed. S. S. pubs., M. E. Church, 1917-1926; ord. ministry M. E. Church, 1918; dept. sec., Bd. of F. M., 1919-1926; lecturer, Drew, 1919-1924; sec., China Union Univs., 1924-1927; assoc. sec., Am. Bible Soc., 1927-1928; gen. sec., 1928——; Phi Beta Kappa; pub., *Early Methodist Philanthropy*, 1915; *Organization and Administration of the S. S.* (with J. L. Cunningim), 1917; *The Kingdom and the Nations*, 1921; *The Worker and His Church*, (with Louise M. North), 1921; editor, *The Book of a Thousand Tongues*, 1938; address, 32 Badeau Ave., Summit, N. J.

The Rev. THOMAS SMITH DONOHUGH
LL.B., M.A., D.D.

Lecturer on Missionary Efficiency and Missions in India, 1919-1927; Lecturer on Personal Efficiency, 1927-1930.

DR. DONOHUGH had seen mission work from the inside and from the outside. He had been a missionary in

India, and he had served in the Board Rooms in New York. As head of the candidate department he has studied the personal problem at the grass-roots. Moreover, having been trained for the law as well as the Gospel, he had the type of mentality required for the analysis of the efficiency problem.

THOMAS SMITH DONOHUGH: b. Philadelphia, Pa., Sept. 13, 1875; Swarthmore Coll., 1888-92; LL.B., Univ. of Pennsylvania, 1895; Union Theol. Sem., 1912-13; M.A., Columbia, 1913; D.D., Univ. of So. Dak., 1942; m. Agnes Crawford Leaycraft, June 14, 1906; practiced law, 1895-1904; ord. dea., 1905; ord. eld., 1905; entered Northwest India Conf., 1905; missionary, Meerut, India, 1904-12; sec., Candidates Dep't., Bd. of Foreign Missions, M. E. Church, 1912-18; staff sec., Bd. of Foreign Missions, 1917-18; assoc. sec. for Bd. of Foreign Missions, in charge of work in Africa, India, Burma, Europe, and Latin America, 1918——; New York Conf., 1924; lecturer, Missionary Efficiency and Missions in India, Drew, 1919-27; lecturer, Personal Efficiency, Missions in India and Africa, 1927-30; del., Gen. Conf., 1912; mem., Bd. of Directors, Isabella Thoburn Coll., Lucknow, India; Santiago Coll., Santiago, Chile; Ward Coll., Buenos Aires, Argentina; address, 23 Midland Ave., White Plains, N. Y.

The Rev. VERNON MONROE McCOMBS

A.B., A.M., B.D., D.D.

Lecturer on Missions in Latin America, 1919-1927.

VERNON McCOMBS knows his Latins. He became acquainted with them during the period when he worked in South America—a model "Good Neighbor"—as superintendent of the North Andes Mission, and what he learned there he turned to good account in Southern California, where he has given many years of able and understanding service to the swarms of good Americans of Spanish blood who have come north of the border to help with our housekeeping and to be a part of the American nation. It was a clever move to bring this graduate of Drew back to the Forest to lecture on this highly important phase of home missions.

VERNON MONORE McCOMBS: b. Parkers Prairie, Minn., July 7, 1875; Minn. Teachers Coll.; A.B., Hamline U., 1903; A.M., 1906; D.D., 1917; B.D., Drew, 1906; A.M., New York U., 1906; m. Eva M. White, Jan. 2, 1906; ord. Meth. ministry, 1906; pastor, Eden Prairie and Bloomington, Minn.; Knickerbocker Ave., Brooklyn, N. Y.; supt., N. Andes Mission, Peru, 1906-10; dist. supt., So. Cal. Conf., 1913-19; supt., Lat. Amer. Mission, 1919-40; supt., Lat. Amer. Provisional Annual Conf., 1940——; president, Interdenominal Council on Spanish-speaking Work; pub., *From Over the Border;* address, 5202 Townsend Ave., Los Angeles, Cal.

LOUISE McCOY NORTH

A.B., A.M.,

Lecturer on Missions, 1920-1921; Instructor in New Testament Greek, 1926-1929.

MRS. NORTH, whether on the platform of the lecturer on Missions, where she had a right to speak because of her long and distinguished service in the New York Branch of the Woman's Foreign Missionary of the Methodist Episcopal Church, or in the more intimate associations of the class-room, where she taught Greek to young men with the same skill which had marked her service as one of the classical faculty of Wellesley College, was the same gracious personality, reigning over the Drew young men as she had reigned over the young women of Wellesley.

LOUISE McCOY NORTH: b. Lowell, Mass., Oct. 31, 1859; A.B., Wellesley Coll., 1879; A.M., 1882; m. Frank Mason North, Dec. 23, 1885; instructor, Greek and Biblical Lit., Wellesley Coll., 1880-85; lecturer, Missions, Drew, 1920-21; instructor, New Testament Greek, 1926-29; trustee, Wellesley Coll., 1894-1927; trustee emeritus, 1927-39; president, Board of Mgrs., St. Christopher's Home for Children; mem., Central Comm. on United Study of Foreign Missions; Phi Beta Kappa; pub., *The Story of the New York Branch of the Woman's Foreign Missionary Society,* 1926; co-author, *The Worker and His Church,* 1921; d. Oct. 15, 1939.

The Rev. GEORGE GIVEN HOLLINGSHEAD

Ph.B., Ph.M., B.D., D.D.

Lecturer on The Church and Social Problems, 1920-1921.

AFTER SERVING several pastorates in rural, suburban and urban charges, this young man found his life work in the social service of the Goodwill Industries, where he has had ample opportunities to observe how the other half live and to devise measures for improving their condition. He could tell his hearers at Drew many things which would help them in the social aspects of their pastoral work.

GEORGE GIVEN HOLLINGSHEAD; b. Young Hickory, O., Nov. 1, 1886; Ph.B., Franklin Coll., 1907; Ph.M., 1910; B.D., Drew, 1911; Columbia Univ., 1911-1914; D.D., Syracuse Univ., 1922; m. Ethelwyn Alward Pell, Apr. 15, 1915; entered East Ohio Conf., 1908; ord. dea., 1910; ord. eld., 1912; pastor, Boyce chapel, E. Liverpool, O., 1907-1908; Scotch Plains, N. J., 1909-1911; ass't.-pastor, Roseville, Newark, N. J., 1911-1913; Ft. Lee, N. J., 1914-1915; St. Paul's, Jersey City, N. J., 1915-1937; Centenary, Jersey City, N. J., 1919-1933; supt., City Surveys, Inter-Church World Movement, 1919-1920; supt., Goodwill Industries of N. J., 1919——; supt., Goodwill Community Center, Jersey City, 1917——; lecturer, Church and Social Problems, Drew, 1920-1921; Centenary Campaign, Washington Area, 1918-1919; pub., *Songs of a Teakettle,* 1932; address, 47 Afterglow Way, Montclair, N. J.

The Rev. MILLARD LYMAN ROBINSON

A.B., S.T.B., Ph.D., D.D.

Lecturer on The Church in The City, 1920-1930.

DR. ROBINSON'S 16 years as executive of the New York City Society, which is essentially the Methodist agency for taking care of churches that can not yet—or can no longer—take care of themselves, gave him plenty of material for these lectures. For he was in the position of a physican whose practice deals with all or almost all

the ills which ecclesiastical flesh is heir to. He knew
the sick churches, and he had to know the sound ones
also. No city pastor, not even the resident bishop, sits
by so many bedsides and counts so many pulse-beats.
As a business man, moreover, he had to solve problems
of church finance, which the young pastor soon learns
are matters with which the seminary concerns itself very
little.

MILLARD LYMAN ROBINSON: b. West-field, Mass., July 28, 1880; A.B., Boston Univ., 1905; S.T.B., 1906; Ph.D., 1915; m. Edna W. Stitt, Feb. 5, 1914; ord. dea., 1906; ord. eld., 1908; entered N. H. Conf., 1906; pastor, First, Manchester, N. H., 1906-08; Philadelphia Y. M. C. A., 1908-09; N. Y. East Conf., 1909; associate pastor, Hanson Place, Brooklyn, N. Y., 1909-11; pastor, 17th St., New York, N. Y., 1911-13; 17th St. and 11th St., 1913-14; exec. sec., N. Y. City Society, 1914-30; lecturer, the Church in the City, Drew, 1920-30; ex. sec., New York Bible Society, 1930——; address, 316 West 79th St., New York, N. Y.

The Rev. HARRY FARMER

B.S., B.D., D.D.

*Lecturer on Missions in Roman Catholic Countries,
1920-1925.*

HARRY FARMER was a middle Westerner of unusually
attractive personality, who joined the missionary forces
in the Philippine Islands in the early days, and helped
mightily in laying the foundations of the strong Methodism of those islands. He had all the equipment necessary for such a lectureship. He had seen the Catholic
Church where it was most strongly entrenched, and he
had seen Protestantism make healthy progress on its
merits.

HARRY FARMER: b. West Bend, Wis., Apr. 18, 1872; B.S., Geo. Washing-ton Univ., 1908; B.D., Garrett, 1902; D.D., 1917; m. Olive Osborn, Oct. 6, 1902; entered Upper Ia. Conf., 1901; ord. dea., 1902; ord. eld., 1905; pastor, Center Point, Ia., 1902-1904; Dagupan, Pangasinan, P. I., 1904-1907; P. I.

Mission Conf., 1905; Manila, 1907-1916; assoc. sec., Bd. of F. M., 1916-1924; Upper Ia. Conf., 1920; lecturer,

Missions in R. C. Countries, Drew, 1920-1925; gen. sec., Am. Mission to Lepers, 1924-32; d. Sept. 27, 1932.

Dr. JOHN GEORGE VAUGHAN
B.S., M.D.

Lecturer on Health and Hygiene in Mission Lands, 1920-1929.

DR. VAUGHAN early won a reputation as a medical missionary in China. Returning to America he specialized in the care of the health of mission personnel, as the appended record shows. Young men and women looking forward to missionary service were fortunate to have the advice which these courses brought to them.

JOHN GEORGE VAUGHAN: b. Titusville, Pa., May 31, 1878; B.S., Northwestern Univ., 1903; M.D., 1907; house physician, Wesley Hospital, Chicago, 1907-09; London Sch. of Tropical Medicine, 1909; m. (1) Daisy Mathis, Apr. 9, 1909; m. (2) Golda Faye Sherwood, Sept. 19, 1921; conducted medical work, Bd. of For. Missions, M. E. Ch., Nanchang, China, 1909-16; medical adviser, City of Nanchang and Provincial Court of Kiangsi, 1913-16; on staff of chief surgeon, Chicago, Rock Island and Pacific Railway, 1917-18; med. adviser, Internat. Comm. of Y. M. C. A., 1918——; assoc. sec., medical work, M. E. Bd. of For. Missions, 1919-23; medical adviser, 1924——; med. adviser, Dep't. of Missions, Nat'l. Council, P. E. Ch., 1924——; med. adviser, Friends B. of For. Missions; Christian and Missionary Alliance; sup't., Attleboro Springs Sanitarium, 1922-23; lecturer, Health and Hygiene in Mission Lands, Drew, 1920-29; acting sup't., Wuhu (China) Gen. Hosp., 1929-30; ass't. physician, N. Y. Hosp., N. Y. City, 1933-39; dir., American Mission to Lepers, since 1933; American Advisory Comm., China Council on Health Educ., 1925; trustee, Internat. Med. Missionary Soc. since 1922; dir., Asso. Mission Med. Office since 1933; Vice-Chairman Christian Med. Council for Overseas Work, 1941——; mem., American Med. Ass'n., the China Med. Ass'n., the American Society of Tropical Medicine; address, 8 Lee Ave., White Plains, N. Y.

PAUL LEROY VOGT
A.B., Ph.D.

Lecturer on The Church and Industrial Problems, 1921-1922.

DR. VOGT at the time of his lectureship was superintendent of rural work on the staff of the Methodist Episcopal Board of Home Missions and Church Extension. He had previously taught rural economics in Ohio State University and had considerable experience in social work under the Federal Government and with the N. Y. City Charity Organization Society.

PAUL LEROY VOGT: b. Upper Sandusky, O., May 28, 1878; A.B., Ohio Northern Univ., 1901; A.B., Butler College, 1903; A.B., Univ. Chicago, 1903; Columbia Univ., 1904-1906; Ph.D., U. of Penn., 1907; m. Caroline Ada Pennell, 1905; N. Y. Charity Org. Soc., 1907-1908; spcl. agt., U. S. Bureau of Labor and Corporations, 1908-1909; professor, economics, State Coll. of Washington, 1909-1911; professor, Sociology, Miami Univ., 1911-1915; professor, Rural economics, Ohio State U., 1915-1917; supt., Rural Work, M. E. Bd. Home Missions and Church Extension, 1917-1925; lecturer, the Church and Industrial Problems, Drew, 1921-1922; pub., *Sugar Refining Industry in the U. S.,* 1908; *Introduction to Rural Sociology,* 1918; *The Church Co-operating in Community Life,* 1921; *Introduction to Rural Economics,* 1925; address, U. S. Dept. of Agriculture, 3754 South Bldg., Washington, D. C.

The Rev. MORTIMER POWELL GIFFIN
B.D., D.D.

Lecturer on Homiletics, 1922-1935.

DR. GIFFIN, a preacher and son of a preacher, has helped the young men of Drew to understand the fine art of preaching, and to appreciate aesthetics through his lectures on the fine arts in Brothers College. He has an usual fund of information touching the history of Methodism and the present-day currents of thought in the church. His lectures are characterized by

common sense, humor, optimism and sound judgment.
No wonder young men like him.

MORTIMER POWELL GIFFIN: b. Cairo,
N. Y., Aug. 15, 1869; dip., Drew,
1898; Union Theol. Sem., 1898-1900;
New York Univ., 1898-99; D.D., Syracuse Univ., 1919; B.D., Drew, 1929;
m. Anna Marsh Baker, Jan. 8, 1907;
ord. dea., 1899; ord. eld., 1906; entered
New York East Conf., 1898; pastor,
Bayside Ch., New York, N. Y., 1898-
99; Goodsell Ch., Brooklyn, N. Y.,
1899-1900; Borough Park Ch., Brooklyn, N. Y., 1900-01; supernumerary,
1901-04; Westchester Ch., New York,
N. Y., 1904-05; South Ch., Middle-
town, Conn., 1905-07; Shelton, Conn.,
1907-10; Torrington, Conn., 1910-13;
St. Paul's, Northport, N. Y., 1913-15;
Indiana Conf., 1915; Trinity Ch.,
Evansville, Ind., 1915-17; Genesee
Conf., 1918; Richmond Ave., Buffalo,
N. Y., 1917-20; leave of absence, 1920-
21; West Ohio Conf., 1921; Clifton
Ch., Cincinnati, O., 1921-22; super-
numerary, 1922-23; New York East
Conf., 1925; lecturer, Homiletics,
Drew, 1922-35; lecturer, History and
Appreciation of Fine Arts, Brothers
Coll., 1929-35; address, 48 Hill St.,
Morristown, N. J.

The Rev. ARTHUR BRUCE MOSS
A.B., M.A., B.D., D.D.

Lecturer on Missions, 1923-1927.

AFTER SEVERAL years' experience in India missions,
Dr. Moss became a member of the Centenary staff, and
then for seven years was an associate secretary of the
Board of Foreign Missions. Thus he secured material
for his lectures to the Drew students who were preparing
for missionary work or for pastoral activity which can
not be complete without acquaintance with many aspects
of one of the main interests of the Church.

ARTHUR BRUCE MOSS: b. New York,
N. Y., July, 24, 1888; A.B., Columbia
U., 1909; B.D., Drew, 1912; M.A.,
1935; United Free Ch. Coll., Glasgow,
1912-1913; m. (1) Anna Laura Taylor,
Sept. 20, 1914; (2) Mary E. Tuthill,
Aug. 24, 1926; ent. N. Y. Conf., 1913;
ord. dea., 1913; ord. eld., 1915; pastor,
Woodycrest, N. Y. City, 1914-1916;
Bengal Conf., 1916; Darjeeling, India,
1916-1918; N. Y. Conf., 1918; Cen-
tenary Staff, 1918-1919; asso. sec., Bd.
of For. Miss., 1919-1926; N. Y. East
Conf., 1926; pastor, First Ch., Jamaica,
N. Y. C., 1926-1930; lecturer, Foreign
Missions, Drew, 1923-1927; New York
Ave. Ch., Brooklyn, N. Y., 1930-1941;
Bay Shore, N. Y., 1941——; chaplain
8th Div. British Army in India, 1916-
1918; chaplain 13th Reg. N. Y. Guard,
1941——; address, Bay Shore, L. I.,
N. Y.

The Rev. FRANK MASON NORTH
A.B., A.M., D.D., LL.D.

Lecturer on The Missionary Idea in Origin, Principle and Action, 1925-1936.

THREE NORTH generations have been intimately related to Drew and have made large contributions to its efficiency. Charles C. North, New York merchant, was influential with Mr. Drew, the founder, and was a trustee from 1868 to 1876. His son, Frank Mason North, preacher, missionary secretary, promoter of Protestant Church federation, and hymn-writer, was one of the most cultured Methodists of his time, and one of the most useful. His scholarly wife, Louise McCoy North, was a teacher at Wellesley and at Drew, and their son, Dr. Eric McCoy North, now secretary of the American Bible Society, has been a lecturer here and has succeeded to a place on the board of trustees honorably filled by his father and grandfather. Dr. Frank Mason North's conception of the "missionary idea" was of the broadest. He had found it equally applicable to the American city, "where cross the crowded ways of life," and to those who sit in darkness in the African jungle. In his later years he established his home in Madison on the edge of The Forest and not too remote from the hospitable mansion of "Squier" and Edna Tipple, whose door always stood ajar for "the Norths." His frequent presence on the campus and his participation in numerous academic functions, and perhaps most valuable of all, his intimate contacts with individual students, were assets which could never show on the seminary balance sheet, but which were of incalculable value to the institution.

FRANK MASON NORTH: b. New York, N. Y., Dec. 3, 1850; A.B., Wesleyan Univ., 1872; A.M., 1875; D.D., 1894; LL.D., 1918; m. (1) Fannie Laws Stewart, May 27, 1874, m. (2) Louise Josephine McCoy, Dec. 23, 1885; ord. dea., 1875; ord. eld., 1877; entered New York Conf., 1873; in business, 1872-73; pastor, Florida, N. Y., 1873-74; Amenia, N. Y., 1874-76; Cold Spring-on-Hudson, N. Y., 1876-78; 109th St. Ch. (now Ch. of the Saviour), New York, N. Y., 1879-81; White Plains, N. Y., 1882-84; Calvary, New York, N. Y., 1884-87; New York East Conf., 1887; Middletown, Conn., 1887-92; corr. sec., New York City Church Extension and Missionary Soc., 1892-1912; corr. sec., National City Evangelization Union, 1897-1912; corr. sec., Bd. of Foreign Missions, 1912-24; sec.-counsel, 1924-27; corr. sec., emeri-tus, 1928-36; lecturer, The Missionary Idea in Origin, Principle, and Action, Drew, 1925-36; chief sec., Inter-Church Conf. on Federation, 1905; chairman, Comm. on the Church and Modern Industry, Federal Council of the Churches of Christ in America, 1908; chairman, executive comm., Federal Council of Churches of Christ in America, 1912-16; president, 1916-20; del., Gen. Conf., 1908, 1912, 1916, 1920, 1924, 1928; del., Methodist Ecumenical Conf., 1901, 1911, 1921, 1931; trustee, Wesleyan Univ., 1899-1935; trustee, Drew, 1907-35; chevalier, Legion of Honor, France, 1919; Officier de l'Instruction Publique, France, 1920; officer, Royal Order of George I, Greece, 1920; Phi Beta Kappa; editor, *The Christian City*, New York, 1892-1912; writer of hymns, and contr., relig. periodicals; d. Dec. 17, 1935.

CARL FOWLER PRICE
A.B., A.M.
Lecturer on Hymnology, 1927-1941.

IT WAS A Baltimore layman, David Creamer, who first made a study of American Methodist hymnology and published at his own expense the first book on the subject, a century ago. His extraordinary collection of hymnals, numbering several hundred volumes, including some of the rarest, is among the most prized special collections in the Drew Library. Mr. Price, also a layman, who has been the lecturer on this subject at Drew for the past fifteen years, is the son of a Newark Conference preacher, the late Dr. Jacob Embury Price, and a graduate of Wesleyan University and its historian. His interest in hymns began very early; his first book on the subject was written thirty years ago; and 20 years ago he was president of the Hymn Society of America. His dramatic talks on the hymns of the Wesleys are unique in Methodism. No lecturer could present this important department of ministerial training more effectively than Carl Price.

CARL FOWLER PRICE: b. New Brunswick, N. J., May 16, 1881; grad., Centenary Collegiate Inst., 1898; B.A., Wesleyan Univ., 1902; M.A., 1932; m. (1) Leila A. Field, Apr. 24, 1905; m. (2) Flor Draper Treat, June 19, 1913; insurance brokerage business, N. Y. City, 1909—; rec. sec., N. Y. City Soc. M. E. Ch., 1910—; sec., Nat. Bd., Epworth League, 1912-24; president, Meth. Soc. Union, 1919-21; president, The Hymn Soc., 1922-26; lecturer, Hymnology, Drew, 1927-41; president, Meth. Hist. Soc., 1937-1940; trustee, John Street Endowment Fund; Methodist Ecumenical Conf., 1931; Gen. Conf., 1932; pub., *The* *Music and Hymnody of the Methodist Hymnal,* 1911; *A Year of Hymn Stories,* 1914; *Who's Who in American Methodism,* 1916; *One Hundred and One Hymn Stories,* 1923; *Curiosities of the Hymnal,* 1926; *More Hymn Stories,* 1929; *Wesleyan's First Century,* 1932; *The Mystical Seven,* 1937; *Yankee Township,* 1941; editor, *Wesleyan Song Book,* 1901; *A Year of Song,* 1910; *Wesleyan Verse,* 1914; *Songs of Life,* 1921; *Intercollegiate Song Book,* 1931; *Sing, Brothers, Sing,* 1940; also 7 hymnals, etc.; composer of more than 200 hymn tunes and various cantatas; address, 1868 Amsterdam Ave., New York, N. Y.

The Rev. HERMANN NELSON MORSE

A.B., D.D.

Lecturer on Rural Work, 1927-1930.

THE LECTURER has specialized in the study of country life from the standpoint of religion, and is a recognized authority in his field. It is significant of the breadth of outlook of Drew administrations that Drew, though a denominational school, draws upon the best men of other denominations for its instructors and lecturers when such men have a valuable contribution to make.

HERMANN NELSON MORSE: b. Ludington, Mich., Sept. 29, 1887; A.B., Alma Coll., 1908; D.D., 1927; dip., Union Theol. Sem., 1911; Columbia Univ., 1908-12; m. Florence Vorpe, 1913; ord. Presbyn. ministry, 1911; Presbyn. Bd. Home Missions, spl. investigator, 1912-13; sec., Bennington Co. (Vt.) Improvement Ass'n., 1913-14; Presbyn. Bd. Home Missions, assoc. dir., country ch. work, 1914-18; dir., research and publicity, 1918-23; recording sec. and dir. of budget and research, Presbyn. Bd. of Nat. Missions, 1923—; administrative sec., Presbyn. Bd. of Nat Missions, 1930—; dir., surveys, Home Missions Council (Interdenom.), 1928-30; lecturer, Rural Work, Drew, 1927-30; chmn., staff Interseminary Comm'n. for Training for the Rural Ministry, 1931—; lecturer on Rural Sociology and Ch. Work; pub., *The Country Church in Industrial Zones*, 1922; *The Town and Country Church in the United States* (with E. de S. Brunner); *The Social Survey in Town and Country Areas; The Every Community Survey of New Hampshire; The Every Community Survey of Maine; Toward a Christian America*, 1935; editor, *Home Lands*, 1918-24; *Home Missions Today and Tomorrow;* address, 229 W. 105 St., New York, New York.

The Rev. HENRY LYLE LAMBDIN

A.B., A.M., B.D., Ph.D.

Lecturer on Homiletics, 1928-1930.

A LIFE-LONG scholar who is markedly successful in making his pulpit work interesting and effective, Dr. Lambdin responded generously to an emergency call to help with the homiletics teaching in the year and a half after Professor Hannan's untimely death. He also found time to complete his doctoral work at Drew in the midst of a seventeen-year pastorate in a busy and important church, and he has served actively for the past seven years as a Drew trustee.

HENRY LYLE LAMBDIN: b. Grainger Co., Tenn., Nov. 18, 1892; A.B., Carson-Newman Coll., 1911; A.M., 1914; B.D., Drew, 1914; Ph.D., 1935; A.M., New York Univ., 1915; m. Cornelia Vivian Morrow, Oct. 9, 1917; ord. dea., 1915; ord. eld., 1917; entered Newark Conf., 1915; ass't. pastor, Centenary, Newark, N. J., 1914-19; pastor, First, Arlington, N. J., 1919-21; Port Jervis, N. Y., 1921-23; First, Summit, N. J., 1923-40; lecturer, Homiletics, Drew, 1928-30; dist. sup't., Newark Dist., 1940—; trustee, Drew, 1935—; alt. del., Northeastern Jurisdictional Conf., 1940; address, 280 Prospect St., East Orange, N. J.

The Rev. KARL KLINE QUIMBY

A.B., A.M., B.D., D.D.

Lecturer on Religious Education, 1927-1930.

DR. QUIMBY'S success in the pastorate has been characterized by his intelligent effort to impress young life with the truths of religion. In these lectures his purpose has been to awaken young men to the necessity of such educational processes and to indicate some of the ways in which the end can be achieved.

KARL KLINE QUIMBY: b. Pottersville, N. J., Nov. 26, 1887; A.B., Dickinson Coll., 1911; A.M., 1914; D.D., 1923; B.D., Drew, 1914; m. M. Lilian Marten, Oct. 4, 1916; ord. dea., 1911; ord. eld., 1914; entered Newark Conf., 1914; pastor, Greencastle, Pa., 1909-11; Carteret, N. J., 1911-12; assoc. pastor, Calvary, East Orange, N. J., 1912-13; pastor, West Orange, 1913-1916; Irvington, N. J., 1916-20; Roseville, N. J., 1920-26; Ridgewood, N. J., 1926-36; lecturer, Religious Edn., Drew, 1927-30; district superintendent, Jersey City Dist., 1936-41; Exchange preacher with Great Britain summer 1935; delegate Oxford Conference, 1937; cultivation sec., Bd. of Missions, 1941——; del., Gen. Conf., 1936, 1940, alter. del., 1939; President of the New Jersey Council of Christian Education 1941-42; pub., *How to Conduct a Church Membership Class for Boys and Girls*, 1938; contr., religious periodicals; address, 300 Orchard Place, Ridgewood, N. J.

The Rev. CHARLES WHEELER IGLEHART

A.B., B.D., S.T.M., Ph.D., D.D.

Lecturer on Missions, 1942——.

CHARLES WHEELER IGLEHART: b. Evansville, Ind., April 17, 1882; A.B., Columbia Univ., 1902; N. Y. Law Sch., 1902-1903; B.D., Drew, 1906; United Free Church College, Glasgow, 1906-1907; D.D., Syracuse, 1925; Union Theol. Sem., 1933; Ph.D., Drew, 1934; m. Florence Stratton Allchin, April 6, 1911; ord. dea., 1906; ord. eld., 1909; New York Conf., 1904——; missionary in Japan, 1909-1941; Gen. Conf., Japan Meth. Ch., 1926, 1930, 1934, 1938, 1941; Far Eastern Consultant, Int. Miss. Council, 1940——; Associate Sec. Bd. Missions and Ch. Extension, 1942——; lecturer, Missions, Drew, 1942——; pub., *To-Hoku: A Corner of Japan*, 1818; *Shinto and the Christian Approach*, 1933; *The Japanese Spirit*, 1934; editor, *Japan Christian Year Book*, 1938, 1939, 1940; contrib., periodicals; address, Board of Missions, 150 Fifth Ave., New York, N. Y.

The Rev. FLOYD SHACKLOCK
A.B., M.A., S.T.B., Ph.D.

Lecturer on Missions, 1942—.

FLOYD SHACKLOCK: b. Archer, Neb., Jan. 16, 1899; A. B., Nebraska Wesleyan U., 1920; M.A., Boston U., 1927; S.T.B., Boston U., 1927; Ph.D., Hartford Seminary Foundation, 1937; m. Louise H. Dunlop, 1923; ord., 1920; ent. Neb. Conf., 1920; private secretary to Bishop Herbert Welch, Seoul, Korea, 1919-20; mgr., Meth. Publishing House, Tokyo, 1920-1922; educational, rural and literature work, Hirosaki, Japan, 1922-1925, 1929-1940; lecturer, Missions, Drew, 1942—; candidate sec., Student Vol. Movement, 1927-1929; Meth. Com. for Overseas Relief, 1941—; pub., *Selected Essays of Manshi Kiyozawa* (Tr.); address, 150 Fifth Ave., New York, N. Y.

SPECIAL LECTURERS ON PREACHING
Four Bishops of the Methodist Episcopal Church

The Rev. Bishop FRANCIS JOHN McCONNELL
A.B., S.T.B., Ph.D., D.D., LL.D.

FRANCIS JOHN McCONNELL: b. Trinway, O., Aug. 18, 1871; A.B., Ohio Wesleyan Univ., 1894; D.D., 1905; S.T.B., Boston Univ., 1897; Ph.D., 1899; D.D., Yale Univ., 1930; LL.D., Wesleyan Uni., 1909; Boston Univ.. 1929; m. Eva H. Thomas, Mar. 11, 1897; ord. dea., 1898; ord. eld., 1900; entered New England Conf., 1896; pastor, W. Chelmsford, Mass., 1894-97; Newton Upper Falls, Mass., 1897-99; Ipswich, Mass., 1899-1902; Harvard St., Cambridge, Mass., 1902-03; New York Ave., Brooklyn, N. Y., 1903-09; president, De Pauw Univ., 1909-12; bishop, M. E. Ch., 1912; president, Religious Edn. Ass'n., 1916; president, Federal Council of Churches of Christ in America, 1929; special lecturer, Preaching, Drew, 1929-30; Lyman Beecher lecturer, Yale Univ., 1930; Barrows lecturer, India, 1931; president, Amer. Ass'n. Social Security; pub., *The Diviner Immanence,* 1906; *Edward Gayer Andrews,* 1909; *Religious Certainty,* 1910; *Christian Focus,* 1911; *The Increase of Faith,* 1912; *Personal Christianity,* 1914; *Understanding the Scriptures,* 1917; *Democratic Christianity,* 1919; *Public Opinion and Theology,* 1920; *The Preacher and the People,* 1922; *Is God Limited?,* 1924; *The Christlike God,* 1927; *Borden Parker Bowne,* 1929; *The Prophetic Ministry,* 1930; *The Christian Ideal and Social Control,* 1933; *Christianity and Coercion,* 1933; *John Wesley,* 1939; *Evangelicals, Revolutionaries and Idealists,* 1942;* address, 460 Riverside Drive, New York, N. Y.

The Rev. Bishop WILLIAM FRASER McDOWELL
A.B., A.M., S.T.B., D.D., LL.D.

WILLIAM FRASER McDOWELL: b. Millersburg, O., Feb. 4, 1858; A.B., Ohio Wesleyan Univ., 1879; Ph.D., 1893; D.D., 1894; S.T.B., Boston Univ., 1882; D.D., Wesleyan Univ., 1903; LL.D., Univ. of Denver, 1904; Northwestern Univ., 1904; American Univ., 1934; L.H.D., Univ. of Vermont, 1914; m. Clotilda Lyon, Sept. 20, 1882; ordained M. E. ministry, 1882; pastor, Lodi, O., 1882-83; Oberlin, O., 1883-85; Tiffin, O., 1885-90; chancellor, Univ. of Denver, 1890-99; corr. sec., Bd. Edn., M. E. Ch., 1899-1904; bishop, M. E. Ch., 1904; Cole lecturer, Yale Univ., 1917; Mendenhall lecturer, De Pauw Univ., 1922; Merrick lecturer, Ohio Wesleyan Univ., 1924; Earl lecturer, Pacific School of Religion, 1926; alumni lecturer, Gammon School of Theology, 1927; Wilkin lecturer, Wesley Foundation Univ. of Ill., 1928; Tipple lecturer, Drew, 1933; pub., *In the School of Christ*, 1910; *A Man's Religion*, 1913; *Good Ministers of Jesus Christ*, 1917; *This Mind*, 1922; *Making a Personal Faith*, 1924; *That I May Save Some*, 1927; *Them He Also Called*, 1929; *Fathers and Brethren (Drew Lectures on Christian Biography)*, 1933; d. April 26, 1937.

The Rev. Bishop HARRY LESTER SMITH
A.B., A.M., B.D., D.D., LL.D.

HARRY LESTER SMITH: b. Indiana, Pa., Apr. 15, 1876; A.B., Allegheny Coll., 1904; A.M., 1906; D.D., 1913; LL.D., 1921; Columbia Univ., B.D., Drew, 1905; LL.D., Albion Coll., 1920; m. Ida L. Martin, June 29, 1899; ord. eld., 1907; entered Pittsburgh Conf., 1900; pastor, Pitcairn, Pa., 1897-1900; ass't. pastor, Meadville, Pa., 1900-01; pastor, Corry, Pa. (Congl.), 1901-03; Leonia, N. J., 1903-05; Bellevue, Allegheny, Pa., 1905-09; Genesee Conf., 1909; Delaware Ave., Buffalo, N. Y., 1909-12; Detroit Conf., 1912; Central, Detroit, Mich., 1912-20; elected bishop, 1920; appointed to Bangalore, India, in supervision of missionary work, 1920-24; resident bishop, Helena area, 1924-28; Chattanooga area, 1928-32; Cincinnati area, 1932——; del., Gen. Conf., 1916, 1920; Phi Beta Kappa; address, 1002 Crest Circle, Cincinnati, Ohio.

The Rev. Bishop WILBUR PATERSON THIRKIELD
A.B., A.M., S.T.B., D.D., LL.D.

WILBUR PATERSON THIRKIELD: b. Franklin, O., Sept. 25, 1854; A.B., Ohio Wesleyan, 1876; A.M., 1879; D.D., 1889; LL.D., 1906; S.T.B., Boston Univ., 1881; D.D., Emory Univ., 1889; m. Mary Haven, Oct 27, 1881; ord. dea., 1881; ord. eld., 1883; entered Cincinnati Conf., 1878; Savannah

Conf., 1883; first president, Gammon Theol. Sem., 1883-1900; gen. sec., Epworth League, 1899; gen. sec., Freedmen's Aid and Southern Edn. Soc., M. E. Ch., 1900-06; president, Howard Univ., 1906-12; elected bishop, 1912; ret., 1928; chairman, Comm'n. on Worship and Music, M. E. Ch.; president, Bd. of Trustees, Gammon Theol. Sem. and Bennett Coll. for Women; trustee, Meharry Med. Coll., Clark Univ., Howard Univ.; Phi Beta Kappa; pub., *The Personality and Message of the Preacher; The Higher Education of the Negro; Service and Prayers for Church and Home; The Negro and Organic Union of Methodism; The English Speaking Peoples— Will They Fail in Their Mission to the World; Book of Common Worship for the Several Communions of the Church of Christ;* editor and compiler, *Hymns of Faith and Life;* d. Nov. 7, 1936.

ASSISTANT

The Rev. CHARLES RANDALL BARNES
A.B., M.A., D.D.

Assistant in Introductory Department, 1869-1870.

ONE OF James Strong's favorite pupils in Troy University, and one of his Cyclopedia staff, he was employed in the formative years of Drew to assist young men whose preparation for the theological work was not up to the standards. Later he was pastor of leading churches in Newark Conference.

CHARLES RANDALL BARNES: b. New York, N. Y., Feb. 2, 1836; Columbia Coll. Grammar Sch.; Fort Edward Inst.; Troy Univ.; A.B., N. Y. U., 1863; M.A., 1866; D.D., 1890; m. Caroline Darrow, July 6, 1864; entered Newark Conf., 1865; pastor, Franklin, N. J., 1865-66; Otisville, N. Y., 1866-69; Andover, N. J., 1869-71; assistant Introductory Dept., Drew, 1869-70; West End, Jersey City, N. J., 1871-73; Linden Ave., Jersey City, N. J., 1873-75; Centenary, Newark, N. J., 1875-78; Madison, N. J., 1875-1881; Centenary, Jersey City, N. J., 1881-84; superintendent, Paterson Dist., 1884-88; Hoboken, N. J., 1888-93; Plainfield, N. J., 1893-97; Lafayette, Jersey City, N. J., 1897-98; Washington, N. J., 1898-1901; Centenary, Jersey City, N. J., 1901-1903; field agt., Evangelism Union of Jersey City, Hoboken, and Bayonne, 1903-04; supernumerary, 1904-09; retired, 1909-23; pub., *The Official Member of the Methodist Episcopal Church; Handbook of Bible Biography,* 1884; contrib., *People's Cyclopedia; Bible Encyclopedia;* relig., periodicals, d. Apr. 27, 1923.

JOSEPHINE LOUISE BALDWIN

Instructor in Religious Education, 1922-1926; Assistant in Religious Education, 1926-1930.

Miss Baldwin's gift for imparting life and action to everything which she wrote or spoke on the subject of the religious education of children fitted her admirably for her work in Drew. It may be noted that her father, Dr. Stephen L. Baldwin, had been one of the earliest members of the Drew faculty.

Josephine Louise Baldwin: b. Foochow, China, Dec. 22, 1859; Centenary Collegiate Inst.; state Sunday Sch. worker, Pittsburgh, Pa., 1900-01; writer, Primary Lesson Helps, Presbyterian Ch., 1900-05; elementary supt., New Jersey S. S. Ass'n., 1901-05; writer, Junior Lesson Helps, Methodist and Presbyterian Chs., 1905-09; writer, Junior Graded Lessons, M. E., M. E. South, Congl., and Presbyterian Chs., 1909-13; ass't. ed., children's publications, M. E. Ch., 1913-30; instructor, Religious Edu., Drew, 1922-26; ass't., Religious Edu., 1926-30; sec., Graded Lessons Conf., sec.-treas., Hymn Soc. of America; sec., N. J. Summer Sch. Com.; pub., *Shepherd Psalm for Children,* 1899; *Junior Graded Lessons,* 1916-20; *The Junior Worker and Work,* 1919; *Services and Songs for Junior Department,* 1923; *Worship Training for Juniors,* 1927; co-author, *Primary and Junior Songs* for the S. S.; d. Sept. 16, 1931.

FINIS

INDEX